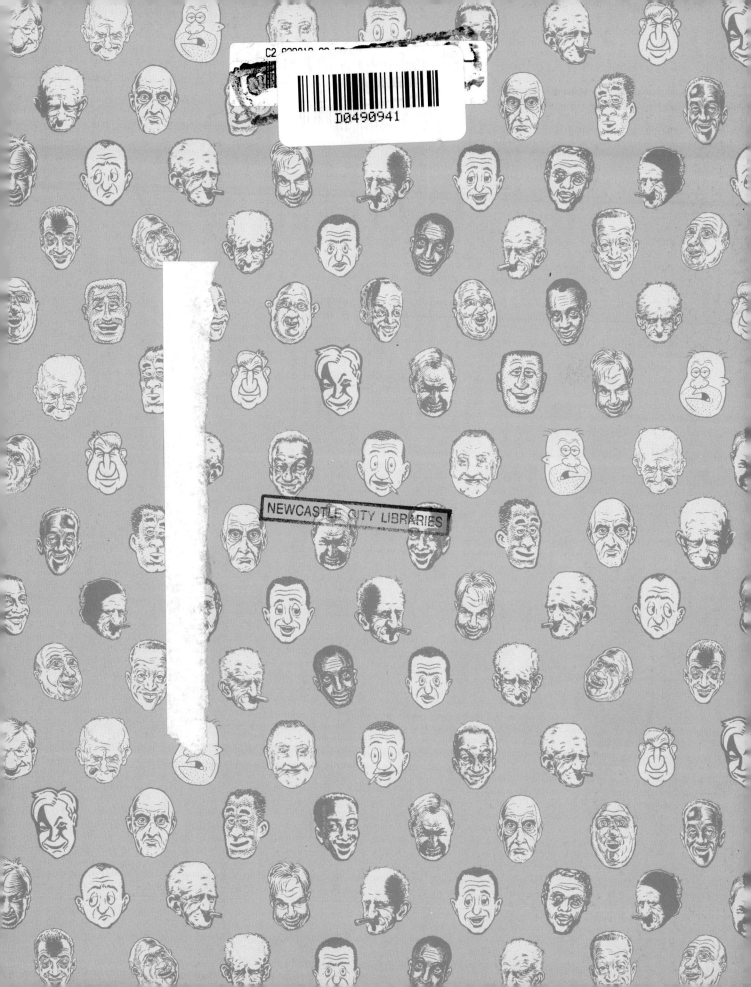

NO MORE SHAVES

DAVID GREENBERGER

FANTAGRAPHICS BOOKS

SEATTLE, WASHINGTON

FANTAGRAPHICS BOOKS

7563 Lake City Way NE
Seattle, WA 98115

Design and Art Direction by Pat Moriarity
Production by Peppy White, Carrie Whitney and Paul Baresh
Gary Groth and Kim Thompson, publishers

Much of the material in this collection originally appeared in *Duplex Planet Illustrated*.

To receive a free catalog of further Fantagraphics comics and graphic novels, call 1-800-657-1100
or write us at Fantagraphics Books, 7563 Lake City Way NE, Seattle, WA 98115;
you can also visit the Fantagraphics website at www.fantagraphics.com!

First Fantagraphics Books edition: January 2003

ISBN: 0-56097-257-2

Printed in Canada

Table of Contents

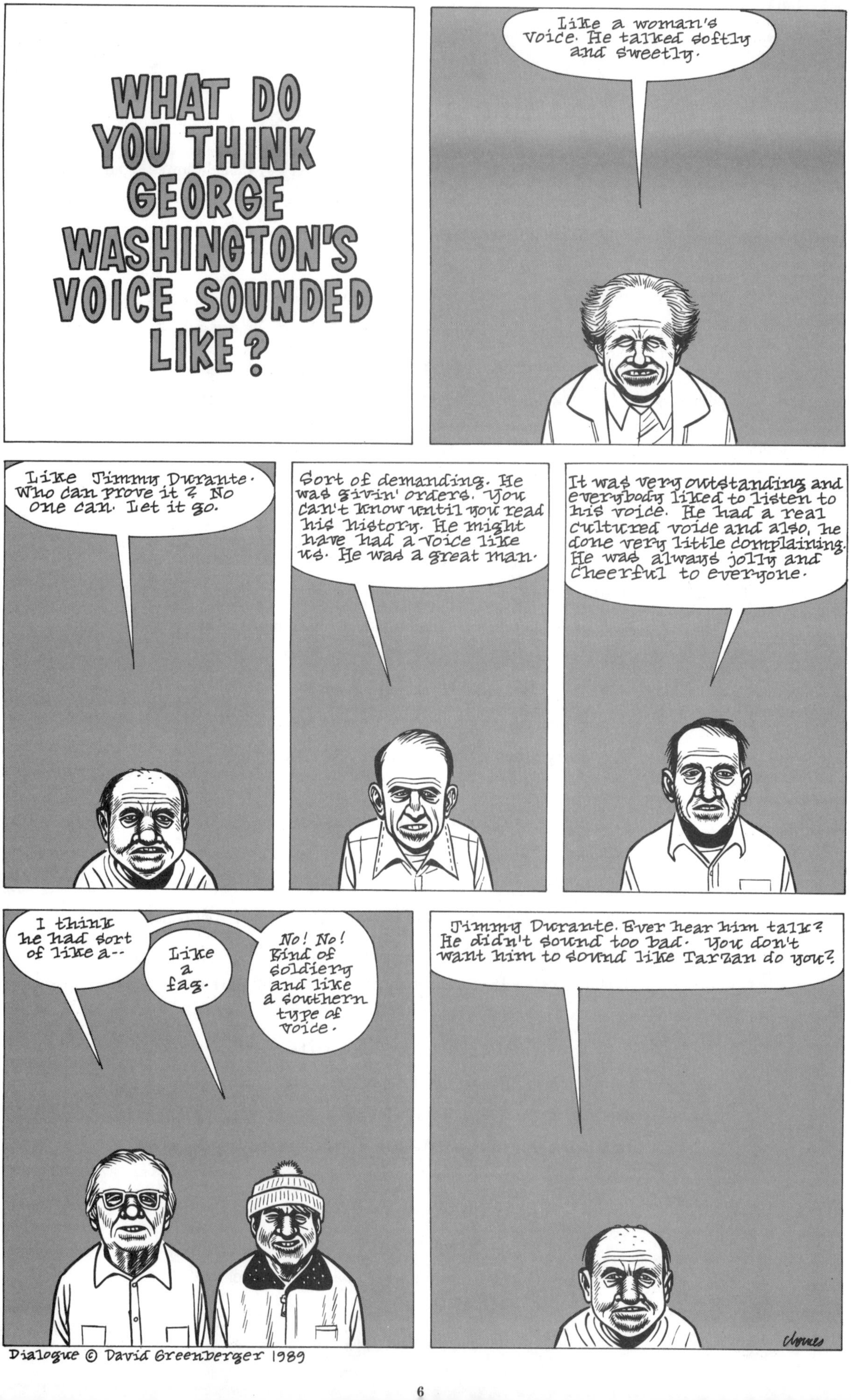
WHAT DO YOU THINK GEORGE WASHINGTON'S VOICE SOUNDED LIKE?
Like a woman's voice. He talked softly and sweetly.
Like Jimmy Durante. Who can prove it? No one can. Let it go.
Sort of demanding. He was givin' orders. You can't know until you read his history. He might have had a voice like us. He was a great man.
It was very outstanding and everybody liked to listen to his voice. He had a real cultured voide and also, he done very little complaining. He was always jolly and cheerful to everyone.
I think he had sort of like a--
Like a fag.
No! No! Kind of soldiery and like a southern type of voice.
Jimmy Durante. Ever hear him talk? He didn't sound too bad. You don't want him to sound like Tarzan do you?
Clowes

Dialogue © David Greenberger 1989

When I began *The Duplex Planet* in 1979 my goals were much the same as what they remain today: to sketch a range of individuals residing in elderly nursing homes. We're used to thinking of them by what they have in common, that they're all old and in varying stages of decline. I sought to discover the particular and singular qualities of these people and our conversations informed the direction of my work.

Humor has always played a key role in my work, and this is for a most simple reason: humor is a step by which we get to know another person. Humor is the first socially acceptable level of emotional exchange. Assessing someone else's sense of humor is a determining factor in whether or not a friendship is built. A great deal of information is being evaluated in those early stages of relating to another. Since my quest has been to show a sweeping spectrum of people in their waning, I also needed to include those who have lost the ability to maintain linear thought and orderly discourse. They're not going to return to reality, so I needed to follow wherever they may go.

It became my aim to reveal these characters as individuals. By giving a name and a unique individual character to these faces of decline — by seeing them all for their differences — we begin to see what we have in common with them. Every one of us is yet another bundle of foibles, ticks, passions and sorrows, and somewhere in those differences, we can begin to see how we fit in between them.

Another way we, as a society, avoid looking too closely at people living near the ends of their lives, is to put them on a pedestal, which cuts off avenues of real one-on-one communication and closeness. Meaningful friendship is reached through knowing a person well enough to recognize their characteristic take on the world. It arises through the rich and intimate language of private poetics, accidental utterances, and exuberant expressions that are the result of the brain working faster than the mouth.

With most every important transition in our lives we draw on our observations of others who have made similar changes. In the universal experience of aging we are desperately short of relevant guidance. *The Duplex Planet* offers some lessons and examples.

Duplex Planet Illustrated came to life at around the ten year mark, when, with about a hundred issues behind me, Dan Clowes asked if he could adapt some of the material into a full page presentation in the new comic book he was just starting, *Eightball*. Those original, elegant question and answer pages brought forth the idea that a full comic book adaptation of this material would be worthy new avenue. This book is organized around six of the men I originally met at the Duplex Nursing Home in Boston in 1979, when I worked at the small all-male facility as the activities director. What conveys a greater contrast to public perceptions of aging more than populating a comic book with the elderly? In some instances, artists used actual photos to base the characters on, but in most cases, I wanted to let nature take its course. Even its literary form, I have not tried to create a documentary about these people. Rather, the focus has been on how all of *us* fit in with *them*. If what the elderly have in common — that they're all old — is taken out of the equation, then what we gain are encounters with a remarkable array of individual beings. And isn't that exactly what we are?

— David Greenberger

WHAT CAN ROBOTS DO?
Make things. Drugs.
Change identity.
I don't know what a robot is -- never heard of it before. I don't even know what you mean.
A robot can make a hole in the ground.
Shoots up in the air and explodes up in the air.
Can he swim?
Clowes

Dialogue © David Greenberger 1990

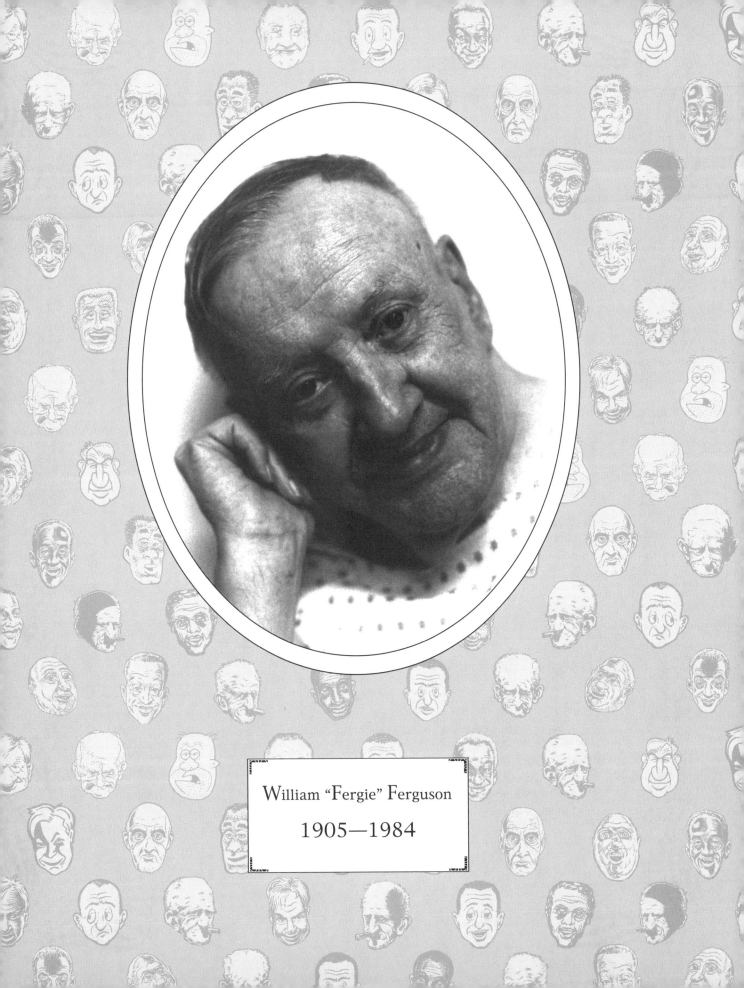

William "Fergie" Ferguson

1905—1984

I am William Gunn Ferguson. G-u-n-n, that's a family name. It's one of the very first names in the dictionary.

◆

We are all sweethearts — some of us are fresh sweethearts, and some of us are stale.

◆

Goldfish grow to the size of horses. They're bit trained in Brazil.

◆

You're a swell guy when your wife is with you. But when she's not with you — oh! — you're a Rip van Winkle!

◆

Everything is wonderful! Wonderful: w-o-n-d-e-r-f-u-l, wonderful!

◆

Some days you can eat your dinner, table and all, and other days you just don't feel like seeing the table.

◆

Squeegee, that means "take it all" in French.

◆

My feet are like your head — empty.

◆

Corn is pretty good. You've got to chew it a lot, but what the hell.

◆

You're looking like a million bucks, without the million. How close are you to the million? Forty thousand?

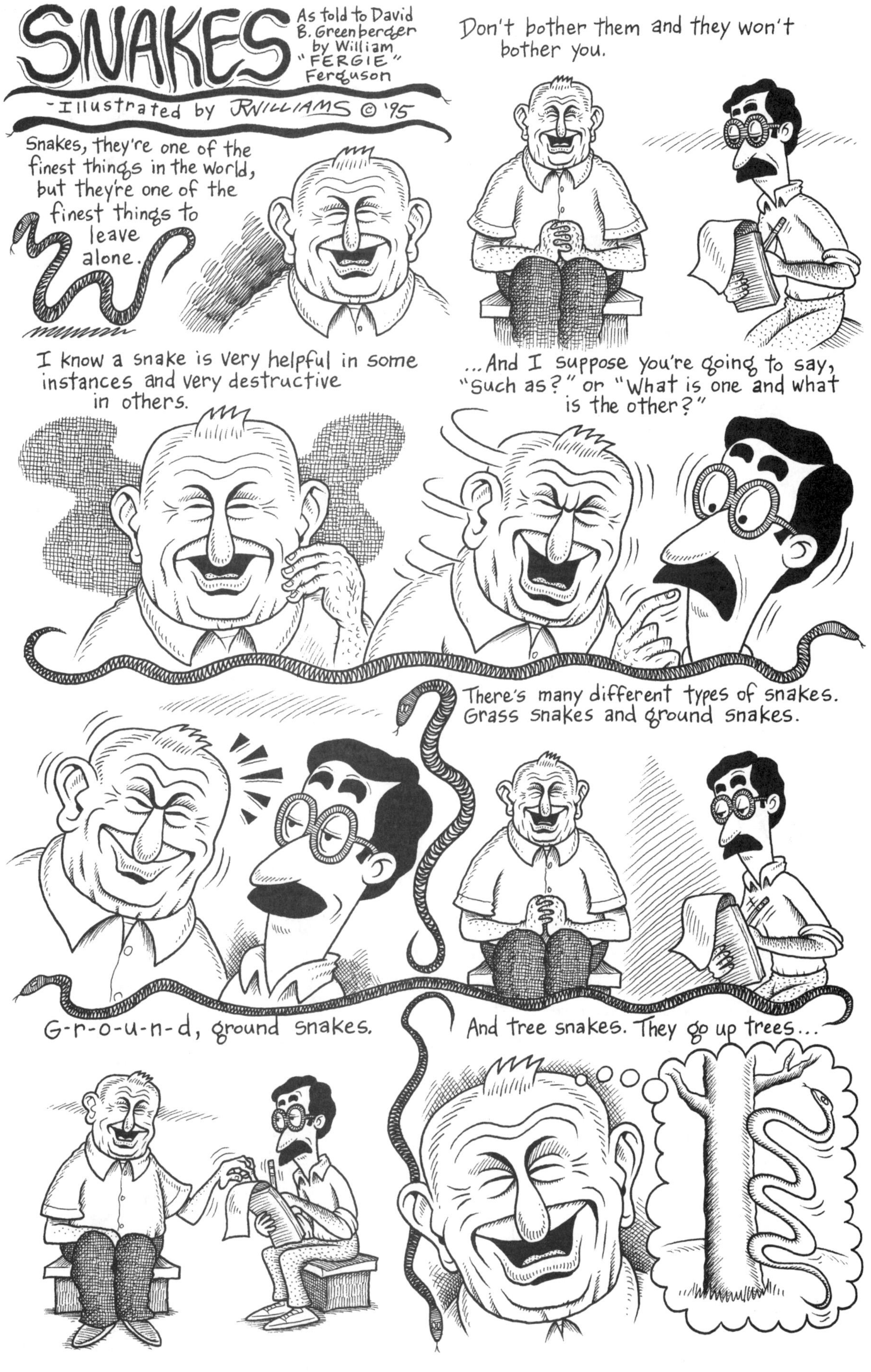
SNAKES
As told to David B. Greenberger by William "FERGIE" Ferguson
-Illustrated by JRWILLIAMS © '95
Snakes, they're one of the finest things in the world, but they're one of the finest things to leave alone.
Don't bother them and they won't bother you.
I know a snake is very helpful in some instances and very destructive in others.
...And I suppose you're going to say, "Such as?" or "What is one and what is the other?"
There's many different types of snakes. Grass snakes and ground snakes.
G-r-o-u-n-d, ground snakes.
And tree snakes. They go up trees...

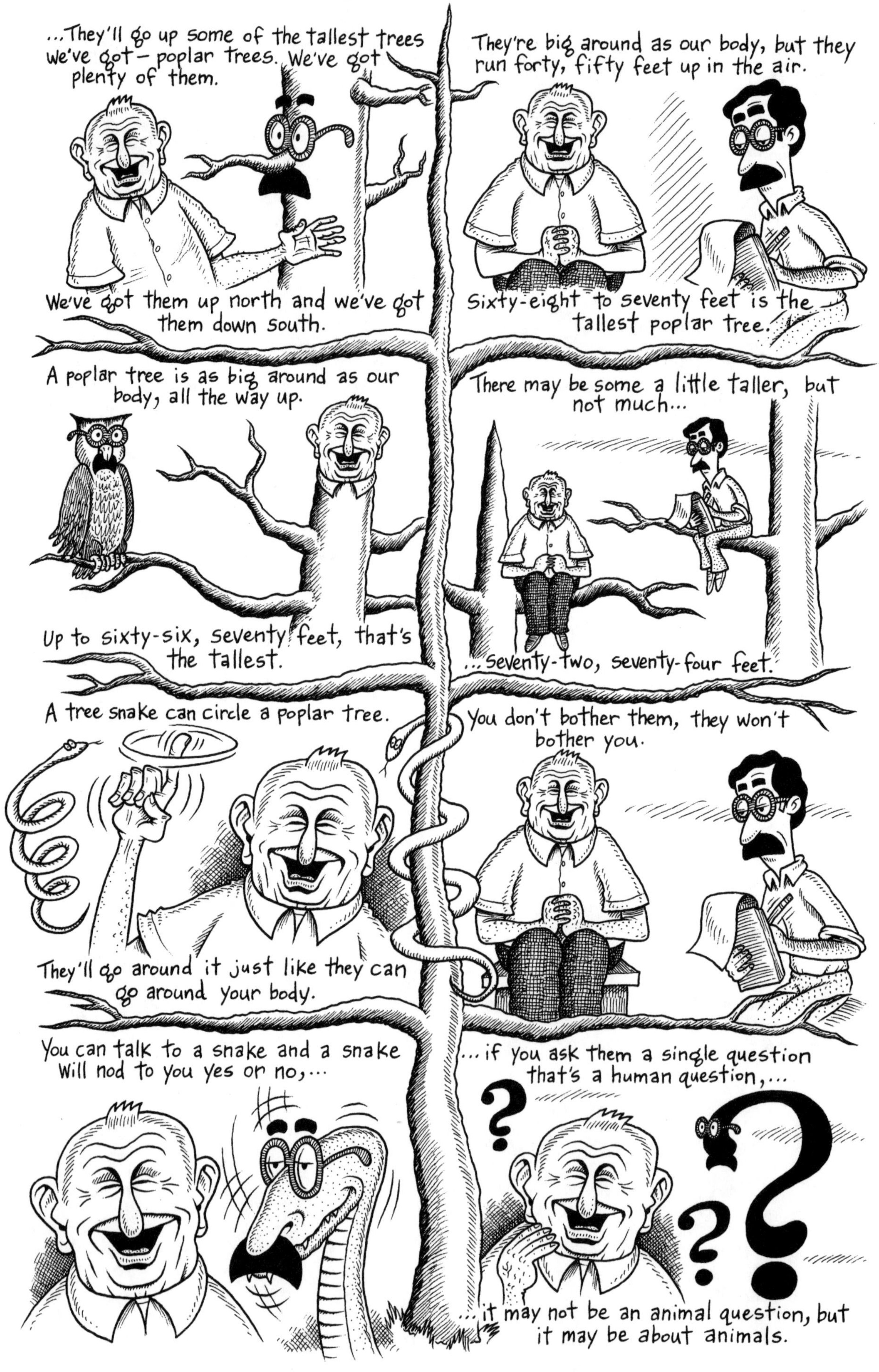
...They'll go up some of the tallest trees we've got—poplar trees. We've got plenty of them.
We've got them up north and we've got them down south.
They're big around as our body, but they run forty, fifty feet up in the air.
Sixty-eight to seventy feet is the tallest poplar tree.
A poplar tree is as big around as our body, all the way up.
Up to sixty-six, seventy feet, that's the tallest.
There may be some a little taller, but not much...
...seventy-two, seventy-four feet.
A tree snake can circle a poplar tree.
They'll go around it just like they can go around your body.
You don't bother them, they won't bother you.
You can talk to a snake and a snake will nod to you yes or no,...
...if you ask them a single question that's a human question,...
...it may not be an animal question, but it may be about animals.

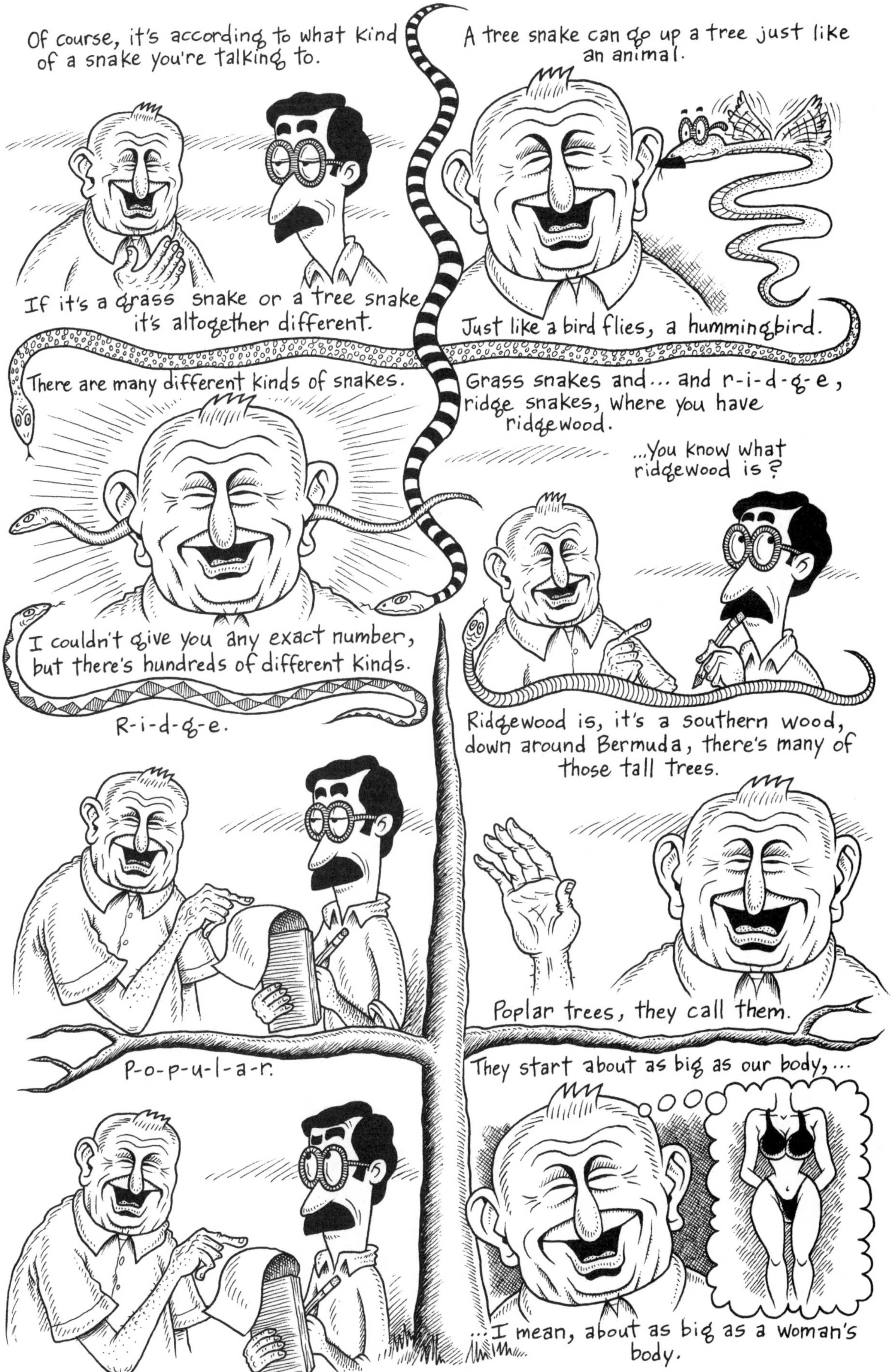
Of course, it's according to what kind of a snake you're talking to.
If it's a grass snake or a tree snake it's altogether different.
A tree snake can go up a tree just like an animal.
Just like a bird flies, a hummingbird.
There are many different kinds of snakes.
I couldn't give you any exact number, but there's hundreds of different kinds.
Grass snakes and... and r-i-d-g-e, ridge snakes, where you have ridgewood.
...You know what ridgewood is?
R-i-d-g-e.
Ridgewood is, it's a southern wood, down around Bermuda, there's many of those tall trees.
Poplar trees, they call them.
P-o-p-u-l-a-r.
They start about as big as our body,...
...I mean, about as big as a woman's body.

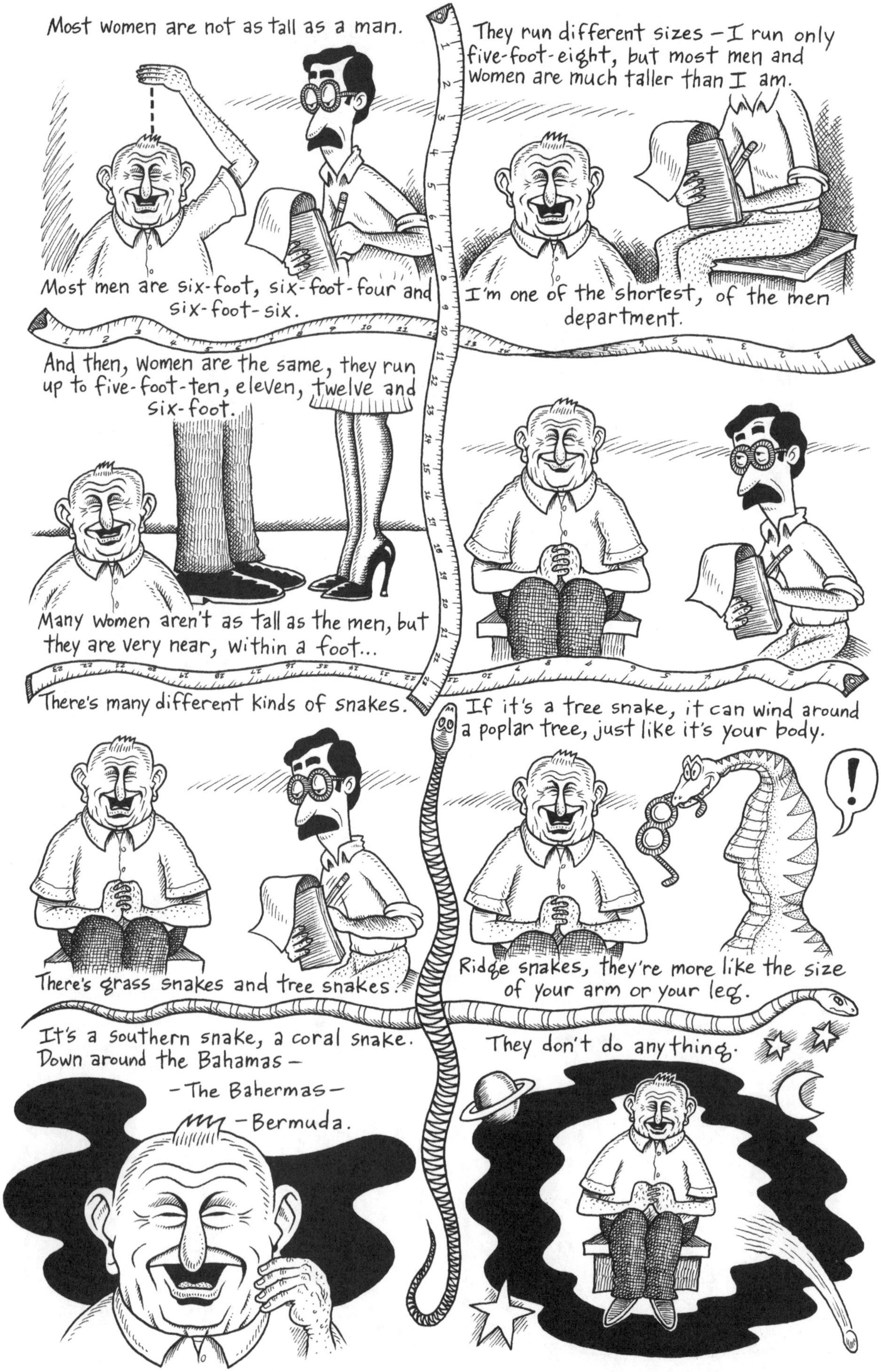

Most women are not as tall as a man.
Most men are six-foot, six-foot-four and six-foot-six.
They run different sizes — I run only five-foot-eight, but most men and women are much taller than I am.
I'm one of the shortest, of the men department.
And then, women are the same, they run up to five-foot-ten, eleven, twelve and six-foot.
Many women aren't as tall as the men, but they are very near, within a foot...
There's many different kinds of snakes.
There's grass snakes and tree snakes.
If it's a tree snake, it can wind around a poplar tree, just like it's your body.
!
Ridge snakes, they're more like the size of your arm or your leg.
It's a southern snake, a coral snake. Down around the Bahamas —
— The Bahermas —
— Bermuda.
They don't do anything.

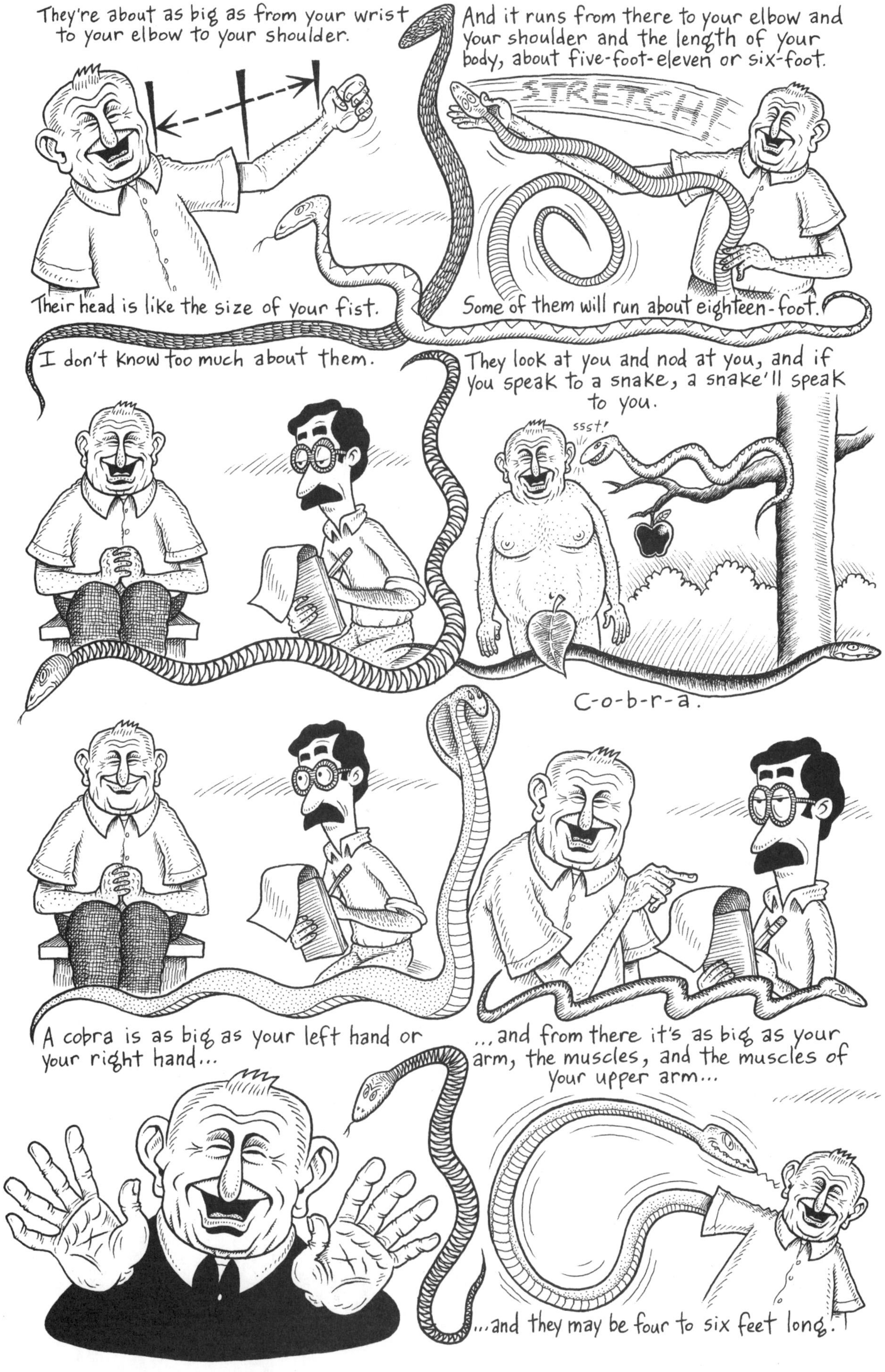
They're about as big as from your wrist to your elbow to your shoulder.
Their head is like the size of your fist.
And it runs from there to your elbow and your shoulder and the length of your body, about five-foot-eleven or six-foot.
STRETCH!
Some of them will run about eighteen-foot.
I don't know too much about them.
They look at you and nod at you, and if you speak to a snake, a snake'll speak to you.
ssst!
C-o-b-r-a.
A cobra is as big as your left hand or your right hand...
...and from there it's as big as your arm, the muscles, and the muscles of your upper arm...
...and they may be four to six feet long.

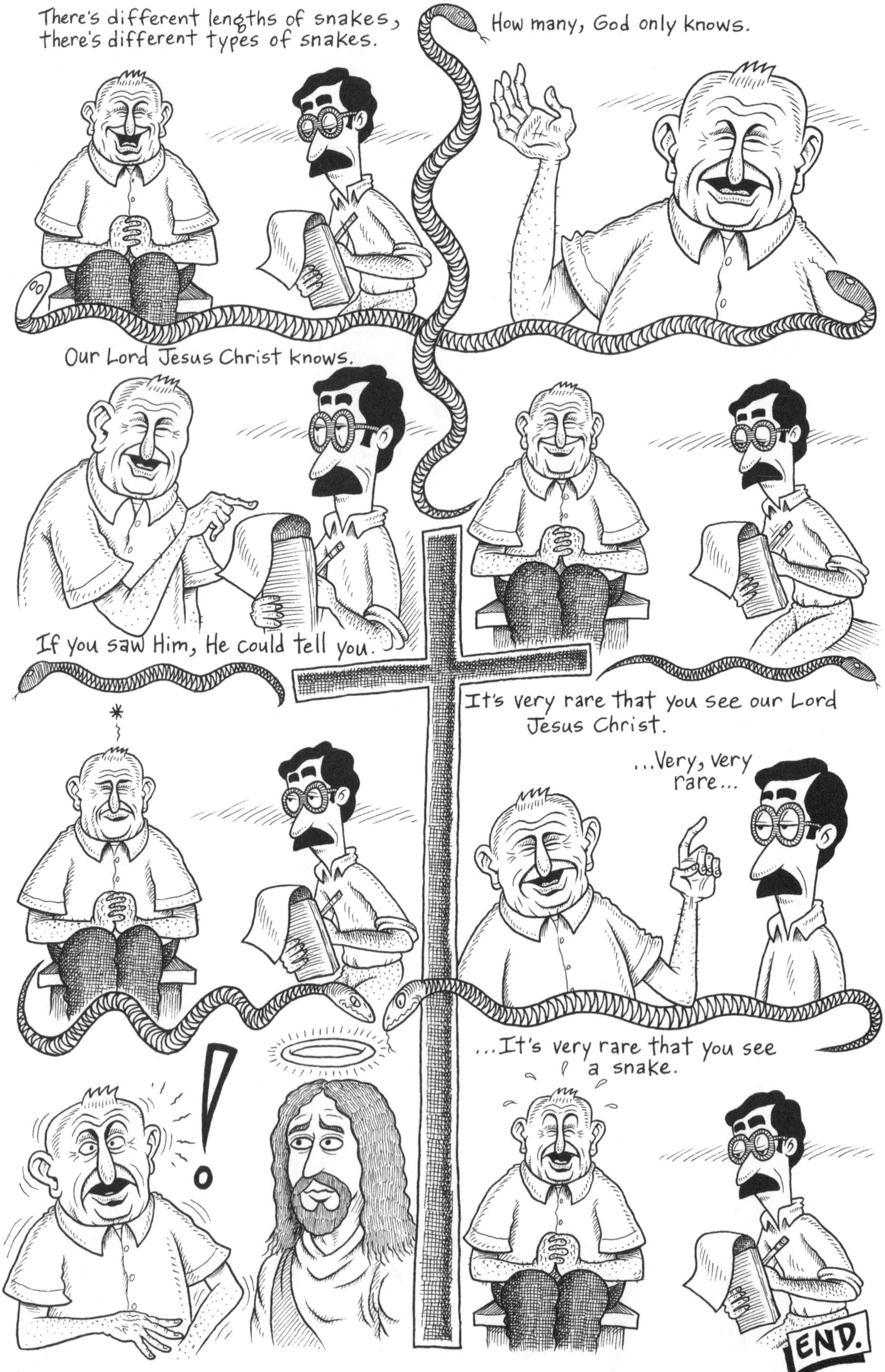
There's different lengths of snakes, there's different types of snakes.
How many, God only knows.
Our Lord Jesus Christ knows.
If you saw Him, He could tell you.
It's very rare that you see our Lord Jesus Christ.
...Very, very rare...
...It's very rare that you see a snake.
END.

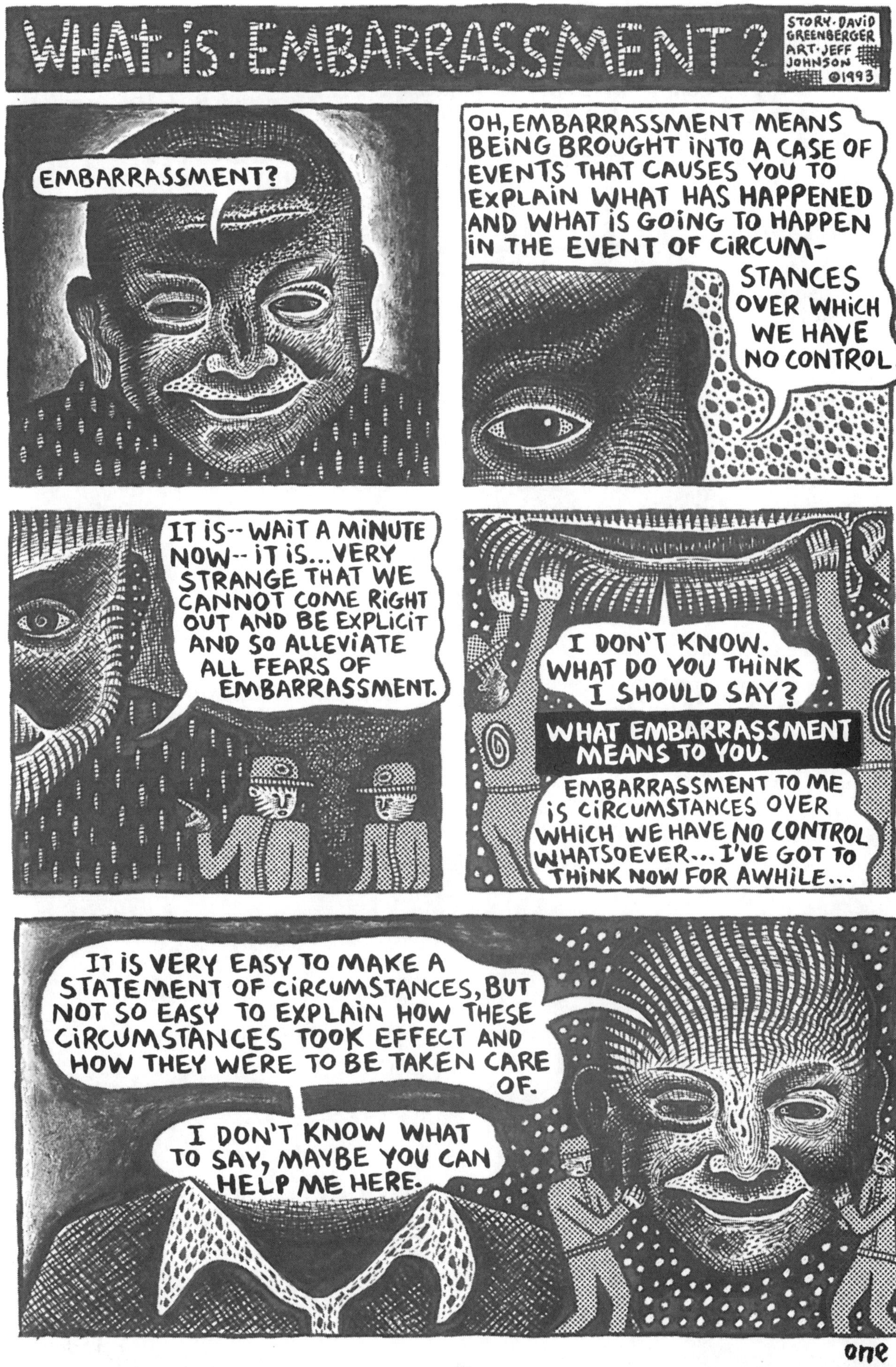
WHAT·IS·EMBARRASSMENT?
STORY·DAVID GREENBERGER ART·JEFF JOHNSON ©1993
EMBARRASSMENT?
OH, EMBARRASSMENT MEANS BEING BROUGHT INTO A CASE OF EVENTS THAT CAUSES YOU TO EXPLAIN WHAT HAS HAPPENED AND WHAT IS GOING TO HAPPEN IN THE EVENT OF CIRCUM-STANCES OVER WHICH WE HAVE NO CONTROL.
IT IS-- WAIT A MINUTE NOW-- IT IS... VERY STRANGE THAT WE CANNOT COME RIGHT OUT AND BE EXPLICIT AND SO ALLEVIATE ALL FEARS OF EMBARRASSMENT.
I DON'T KNOW. WHAT DO YOU THINK I SHOULD SAY?
WHAT EMBARRASSMENT MEANS TO YOU.
EMBARRASSMENT TO ME IS CIRCUMSTANCES OVER WHICH WE HAVE NO CONTROL WHATSOEVER... I'VE GOT TO THINK NOW FOR AWHILE...
IT IS VERY EASY TO MAKE A STATEMENT OF CIRCUMSTANCES, BUT NOT SO EASY TO EXPLAIN HOW THESE CIRCUMSTANCES TOOK EFFECT AND HOW THEY WERE TO BE TAKEN CARE OF.
I DON'T KNOW WHAT TO SAY, MAYBE YOU CAN HELP ME HERE.
one

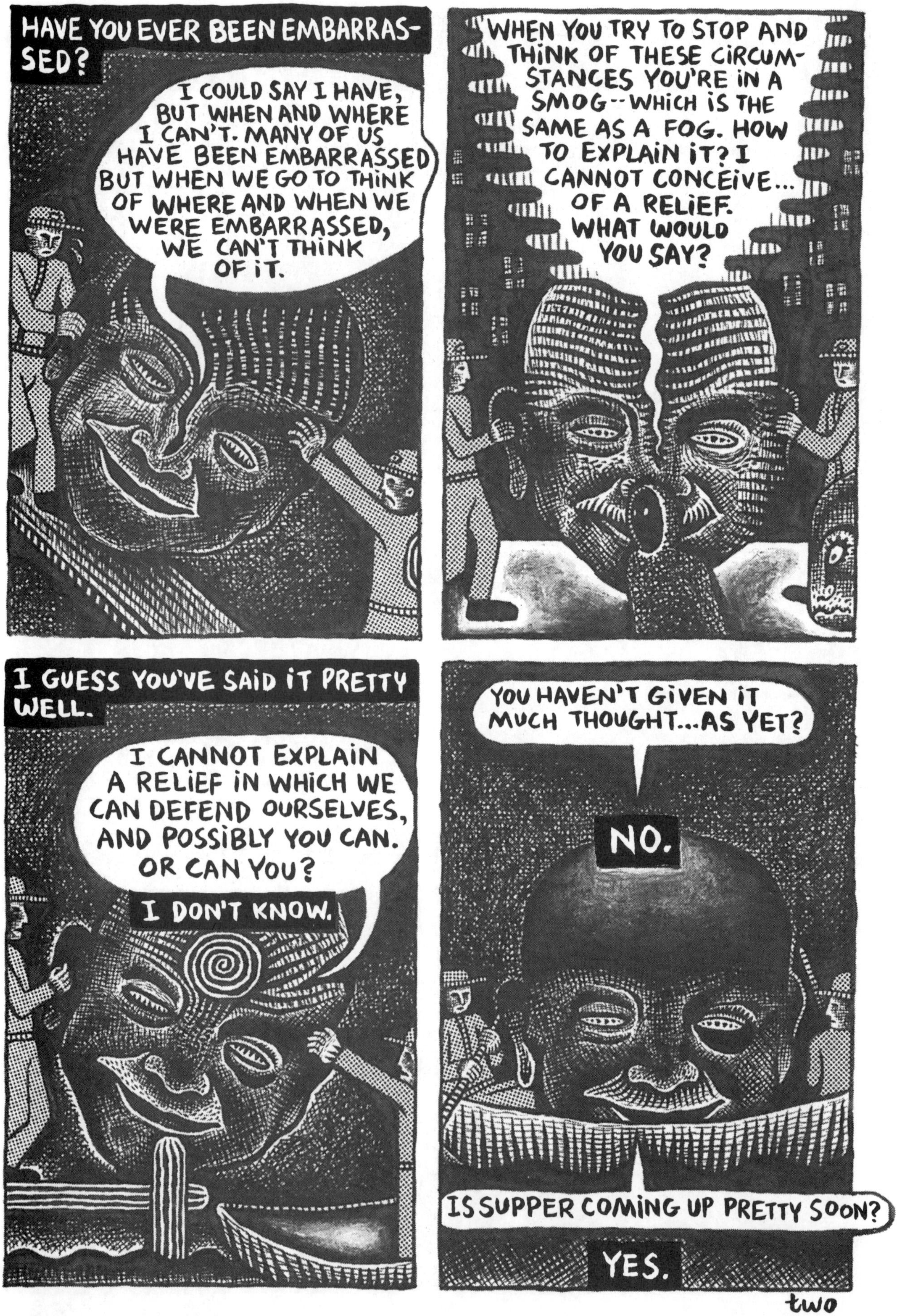
HAVE YOU EVER BEEN EMBARRASSED?
I COULD SAY I HAVE, BUT WHEN AND WHERE I CAN'T. MANY OF US HAVE BEEN EMBARRASSED BUT WHEN WE GO TO THINK OF WHERE AND WHEN WE WERE EMBARRASSED, WE CAN'T THINK OF IT.
WHEN YOU TRY TO STOP AND THINK OF THESE CIRCUMSTANCES YOU'RE IN A SMOG--WHICH IS THE SAME AS A FOG. HOW TO EXPLAIN IT? I CANNOT CONCEIVE... OF A RELIEF. WHAT WOULD YOU SAY?
I GUESS YOU'VE SAID IT PRETTY WELL.
I CANNOT EXPLAIN A RELIEF IN WHICH WE CAN DEFEND OURSELVES, AND POSSIBLY YOU CAN. OR CAN YOU?
I DON'T KNOW.
YOU HAVEN'T GIVEN IT MUCH THOUGHT...AS YET?
NO.
IS SUPPER COMING UP PRETTY SOON?
YES.
two

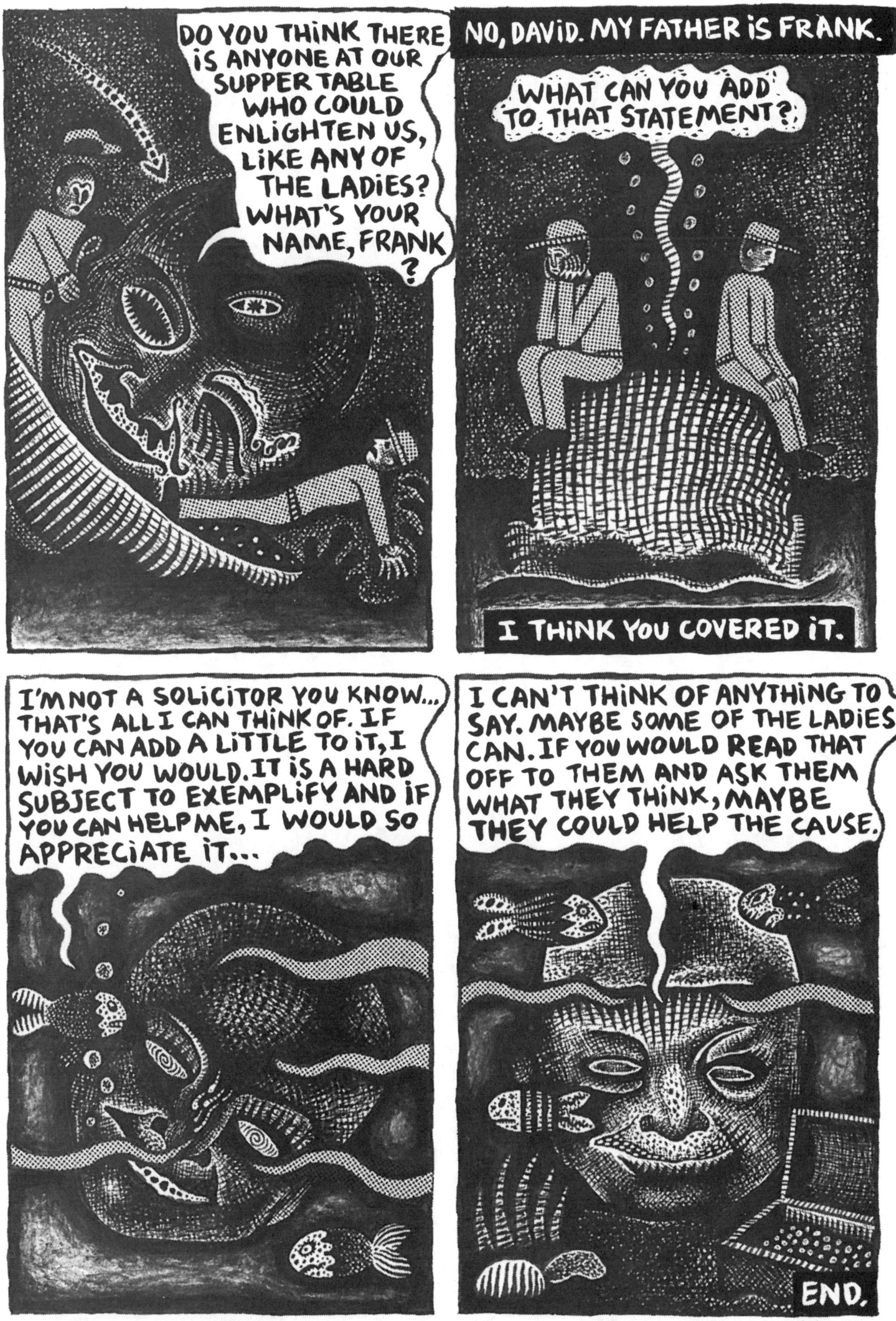
DO YOU THINK THERE IS ANYONE AT OUR SUPPER TABLE WHO COULD ENLIGHTEN US, LIKE ANY OF THE LADIES? WHAT'S YOUR NAME, FRANK ?
NO, DAVID. MY FATHER IS FRANK.
WHAT CAN YOU ADD TO THAT STATEMENT?
I THINK YOU COVERED IT.
I'M NOT A SOLICITOR YOU KNOW... THAT'S ALL I CAN THINK OF. IF YOU CAN ADD A LITTLE TO IT, I WISH YOU WOULD. IT IS A HARD SUBJECT TO EXEMPLIFY AND IF YOU CAN HELP ME, I WOULD SO APPRECIATE IT...
I CAN'T THINK OF ANYTHING TO SAY. MAYBE SOME OF THE LADIES CAN. IF YOU WOULD READ THAT OFF TO THEM AND ASK THEM WHAT THEY THINK, MAYBE THEY COULD HELP THE CAUSE.
END.
three

Baseball Damage

by William Ferguson

as told to David Greenberger
drawn by Oscar Stern

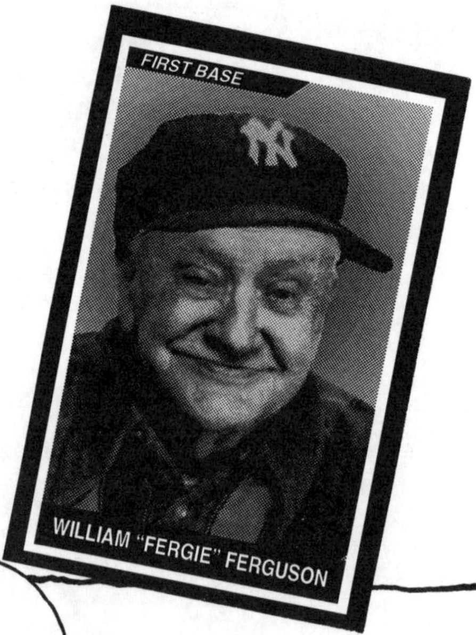
FIRST BASE
WILLIAM "FERGIE" FERGUSON

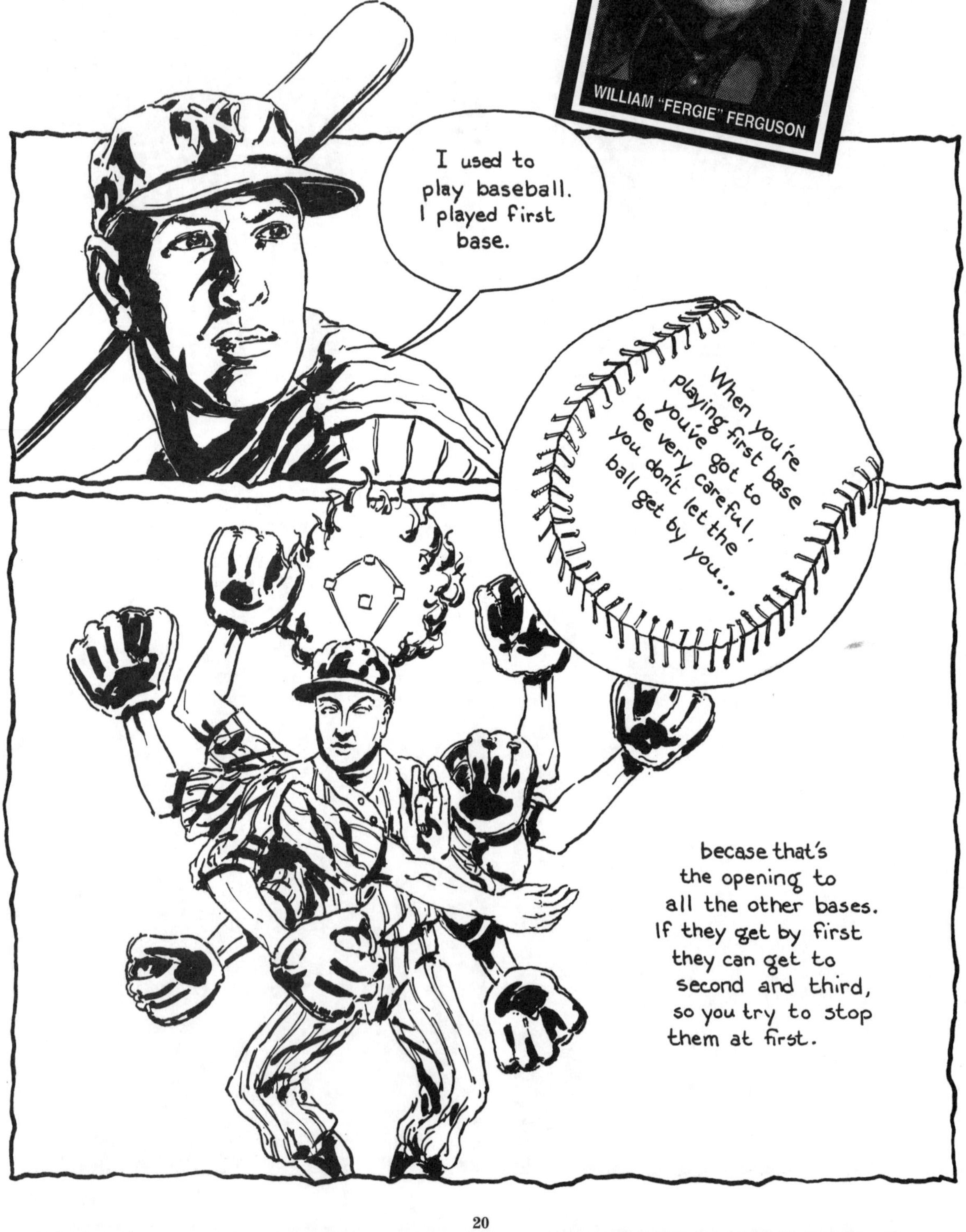
I used to play baseball. I played first base.
When you're playing first base you've got to be very careful, you don't let the ball get by you...
becase that's the opening to all the other bases. If they get by first they can get to second and third, so you try to stop them at first.

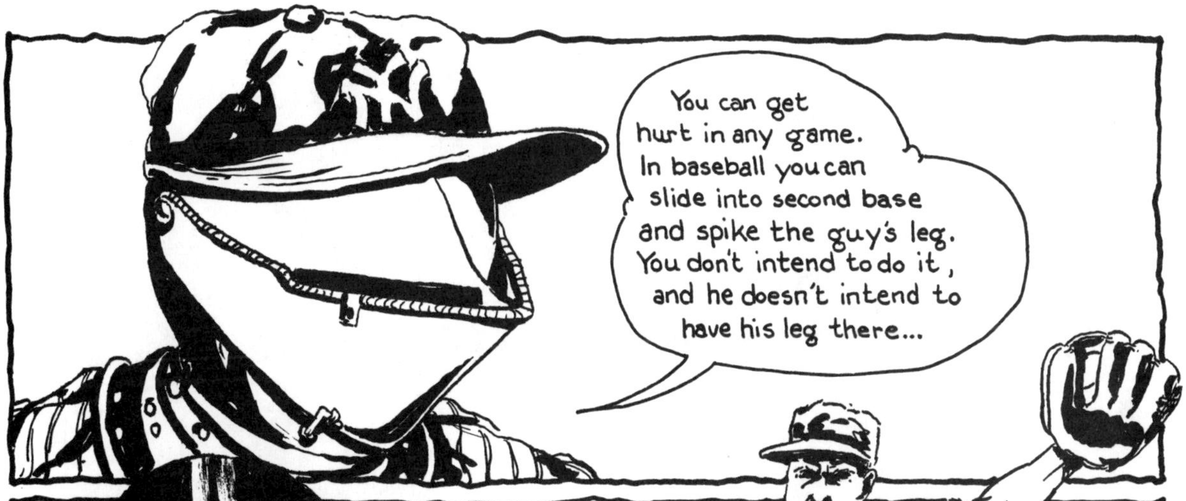
You can get hurt in any game. In baseball you can slide into second base and spike the guy's leg. You don't intend to do it, and he doesn't intend to have his leg there...

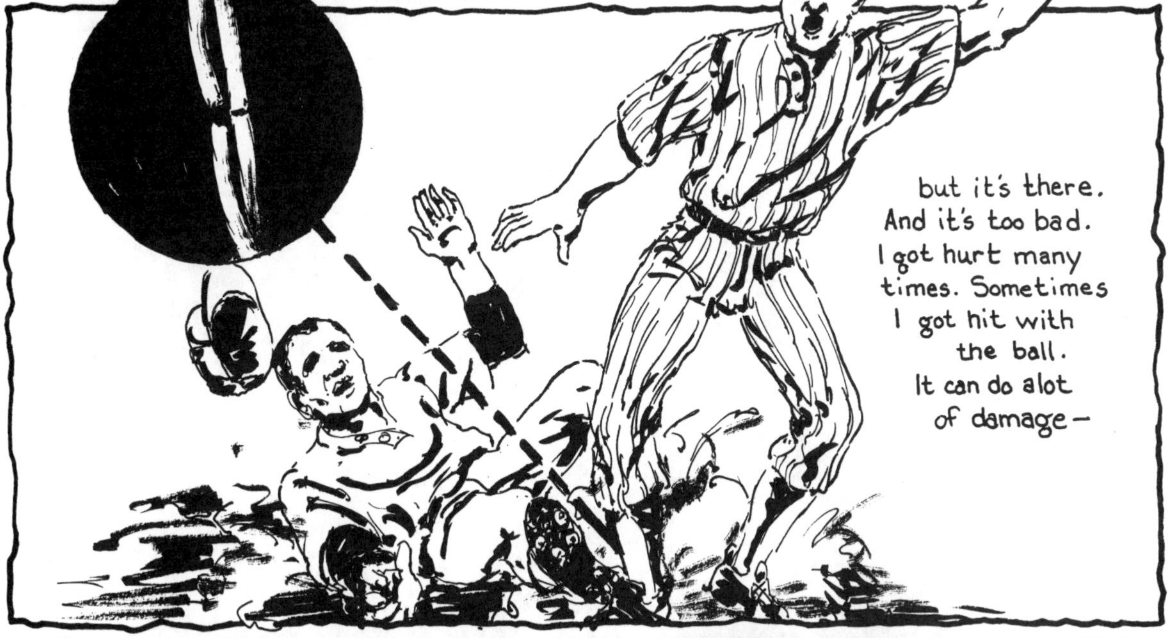
but it's there. And it's too bad. I got hurt many times. Sometimes I got hit with the ball. It can do alot of damage—

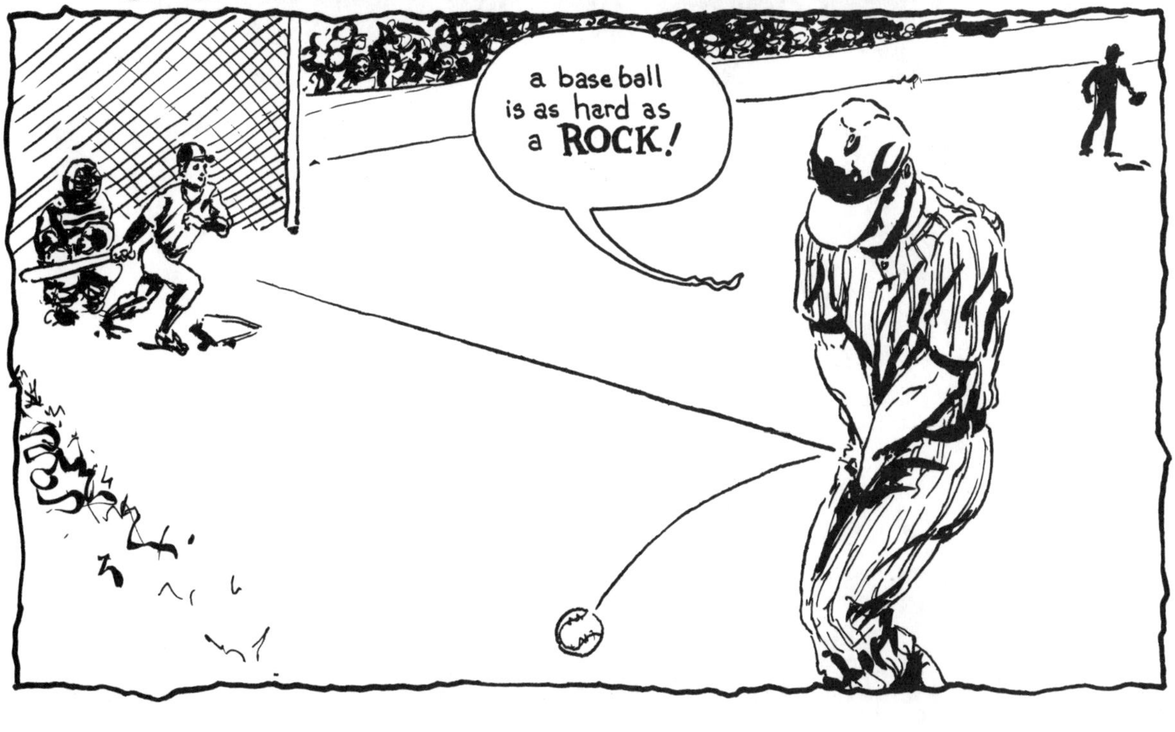
a base ball is as hard as a ROCK!

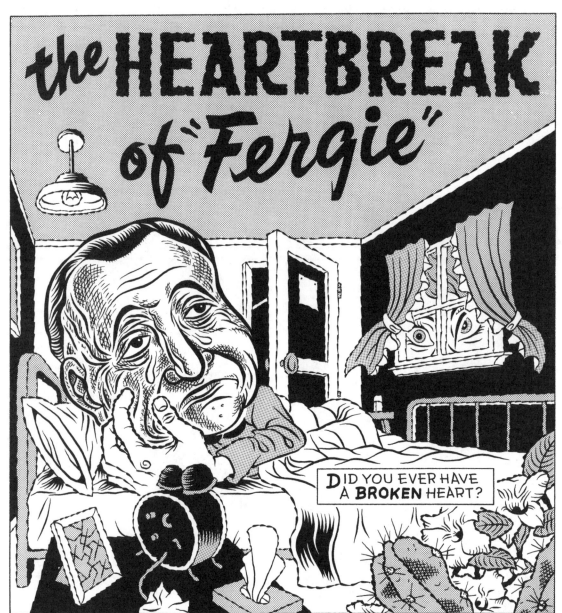

the HEARTBREAK of "Fergie"

DID YOU EVER HAVE A **BROKEN** HEART?

THE LAST TIME MY **MOTHER** WENT AND GAVE ME ALL HER **MONEY**. ONE-HUNDRED MILLION DOLLARS.

DID YOU HEAR THAT? ONE-HUNDRED **MILLION** DOLLARS SHE GAVE ME.

WRITTEN BY DAVID GREENBERGER   DRAWN BY TIM HENSLEY

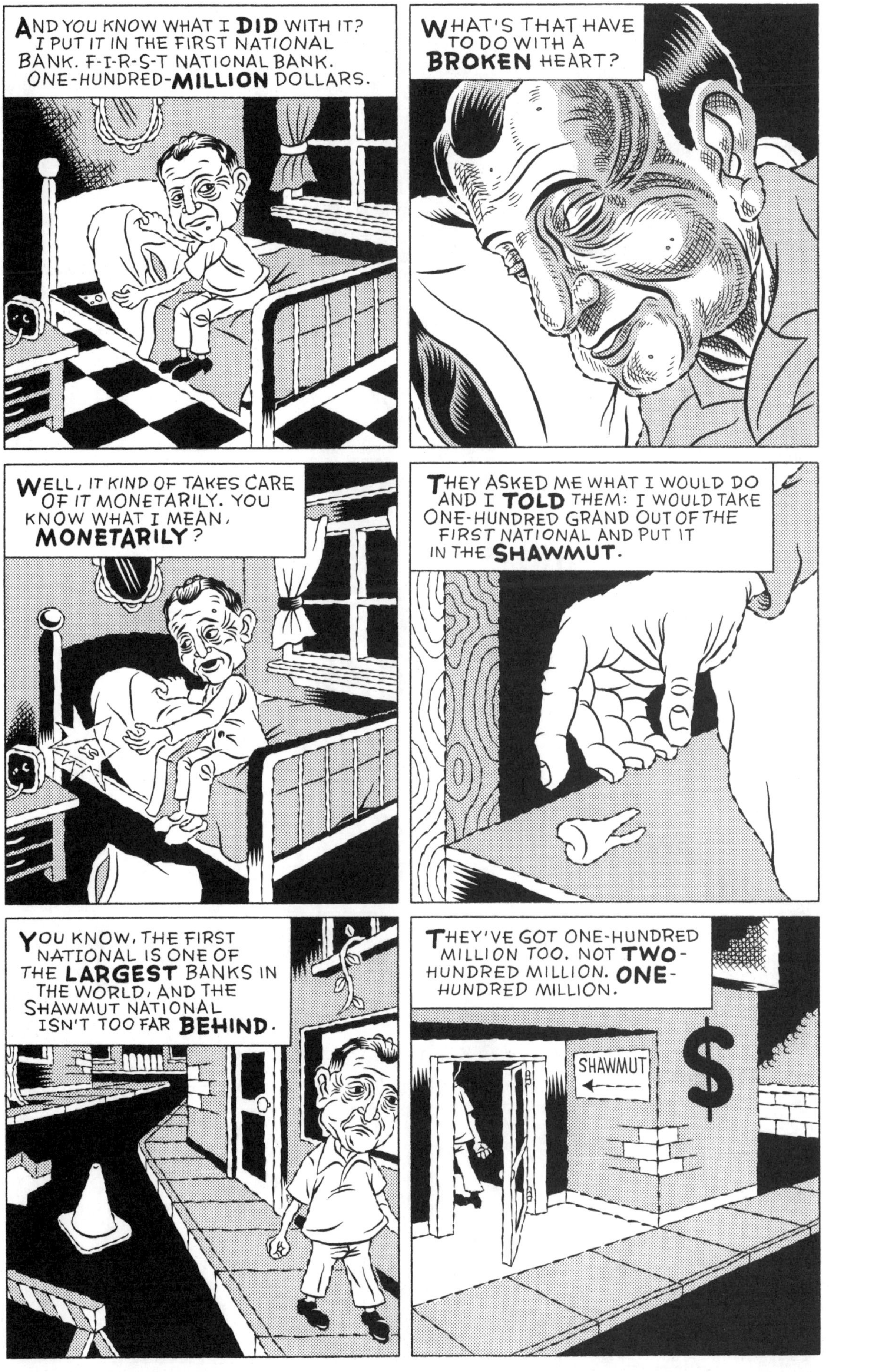
AND YOU KNOW WHAT I DID WITH IT? I PUT IT IN THE FIRST NATIONAL BANK. F-I-R-S-T NATIONAL BANK. ONE-HUNDRED-MILLION DOLLARS.
WHAT'S THAT HAVE TO DO WITH A BROKEN HEART?
WELL, IT KIND OF TAKES CARE OF IT MONETARILY. YOU KNOW WHAT I MEAN, MONETARILY?
THEY ASKED ME WHAT I WOULD DO AND I TOLD THEM: I WOULD TAKE ONE-HUNDRED GRAND OUT OF THE FIRST NATIONAL AND PUT IT IN THE SHAWMUT.
YOU KNOW, THE FIRST NATIONAL IS ONE OF THE LARGEST BANKS IN THE WORLD, AND THE SHAWMUT NATIONAL ISN'T TOO FAR BEHIND.
THEY'VE GOT ONE-HUNDRED MILLION TOO. NOT TWO-HUNDRED MILLION. ONE-HUNDRED MILLION.
SHAWMUT
$

WHO BROKE YOUR HEART?

MY MOTHER.

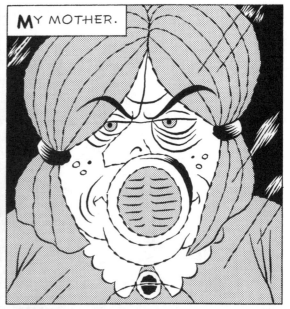

SHE SAID,

WHAT ARE YOU GOING TO **DO** WITH A HUNDRED MILLION DOLLARS IF I GIVE IT TO YOU?

I'LL SPEND IT ON **YOU**.

WELL, GO AHEAD AND START **SPENDING**.

WHERE ARE YOU GOING TO **SPEND** ALL THIS MONEY?

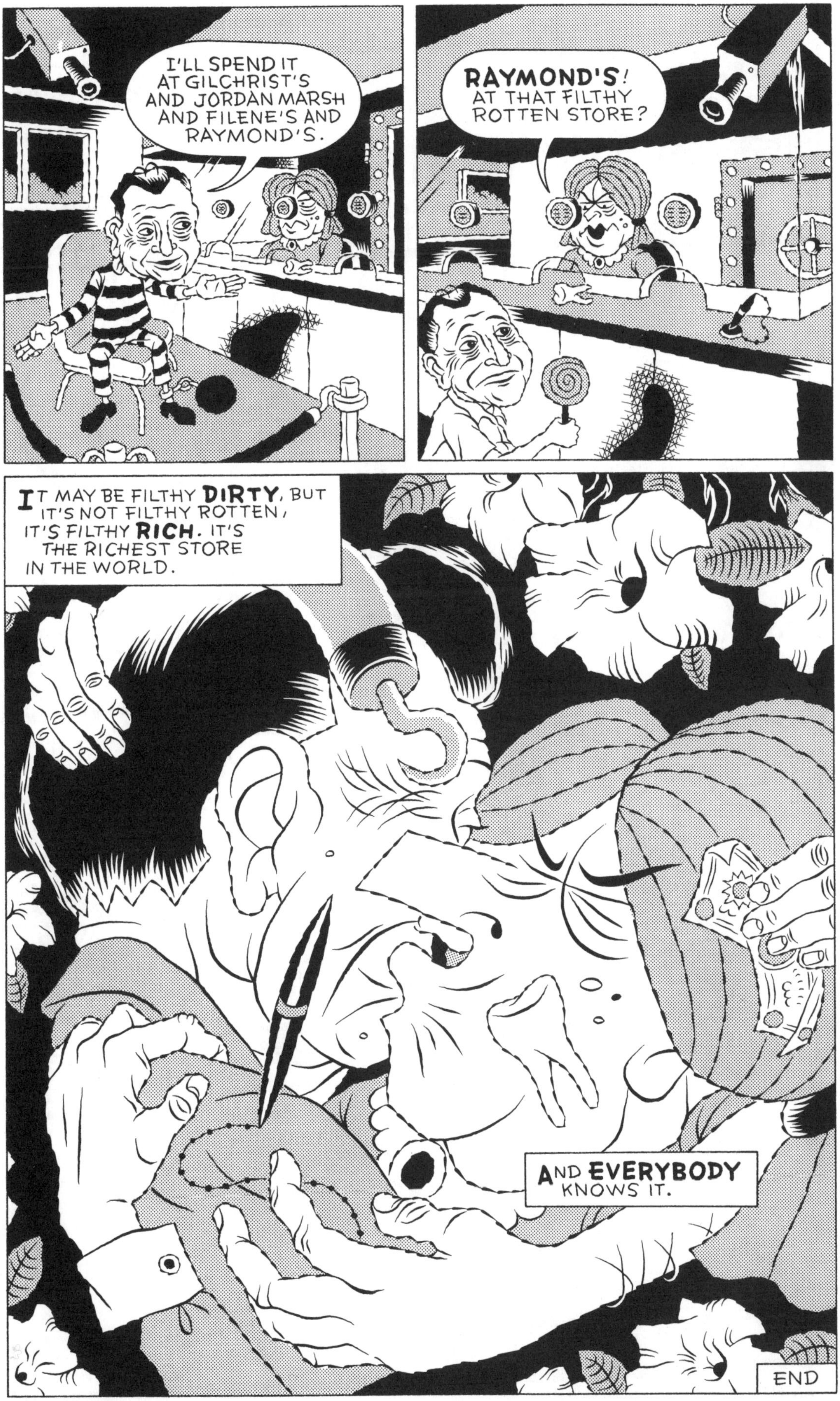
I'LL SPEND IT AT GILCHRIST'S AND JORDAN MARSH AND FILENE'S AND RAYMOND'S.
RAYMOND'S! AT THAT FILTHY ROTTEN STORE?
IT MAY BE FILTHY DIRTY, BUT IT'S NOT FILTHY ROTTEN, IT'S FILTHY RICH. IT'S THE RICHEST STORE IN THE WORLD.
AND EVERYBODY KNOWS IT.
END

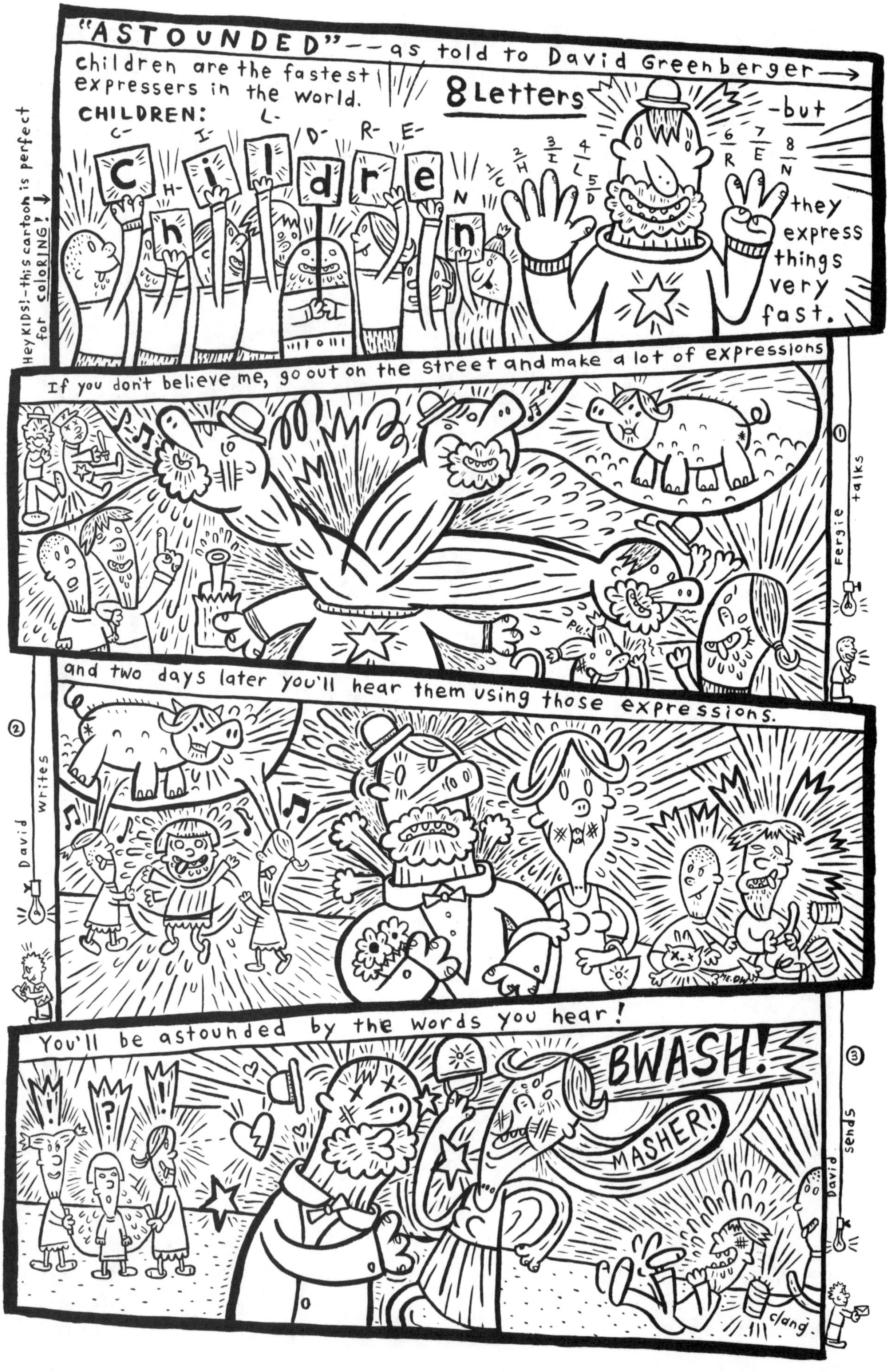
"ASTOUNDED"--as told to David Greenberger→
children are the fastest expressers in the world.
CHILDREN:
C- H- I- L- D- R- E- N
children
8 Letters
-but
1 C 2 H 3 I 4 L 5 D 6 R 7 E 8 N
they express things very fast.
Hey KIDS!-this cartoon is perfect for COLORING!→
If you don't believe me, go out on the street and make a lot of expressions
① Fergie talks
and two days later you'll hear them using those expressions.
② David writes
You'll be astounded by the words you hear!
BWASH!
MASHER!
clang.
③ David sends

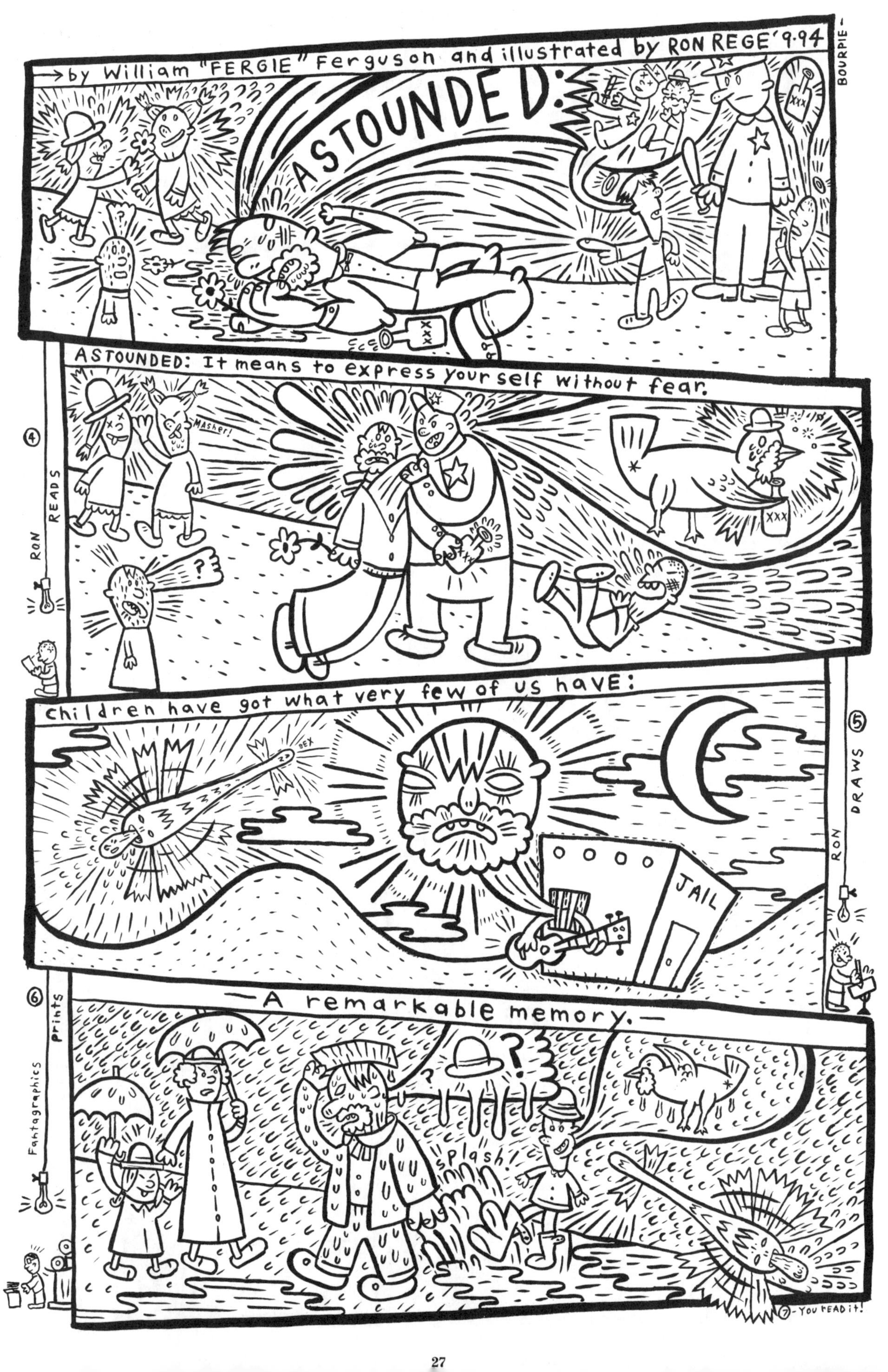

by William "FERGIE" Ferguson and illustrated by RON REGE' 9·94
BOURPIE-
ASTOUNDED:
ASTOUNDED: It means to express your self without fear.
Masher!
④ RON READS
children have got what very few of us have:
SEX
JAIL
⑤ RON DRAWS
—A remarkable memory.—
⑥ Fantagraphics prints
splash!
⑦-YOU READ it!

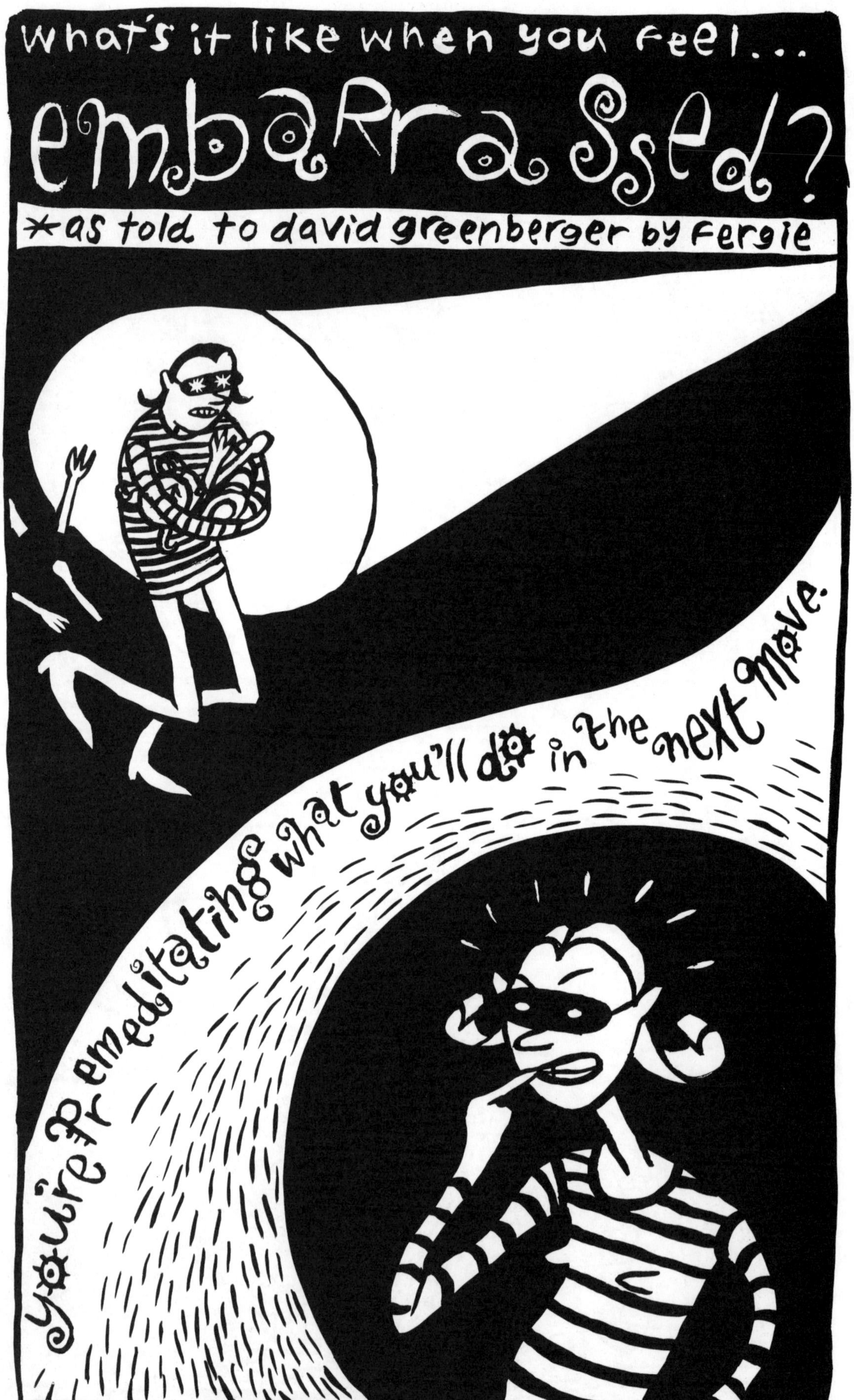

what's it like when you feel...
embarrassed?
*as told to david greenberger by fergie
you're premeditating what you'll do in the next move.

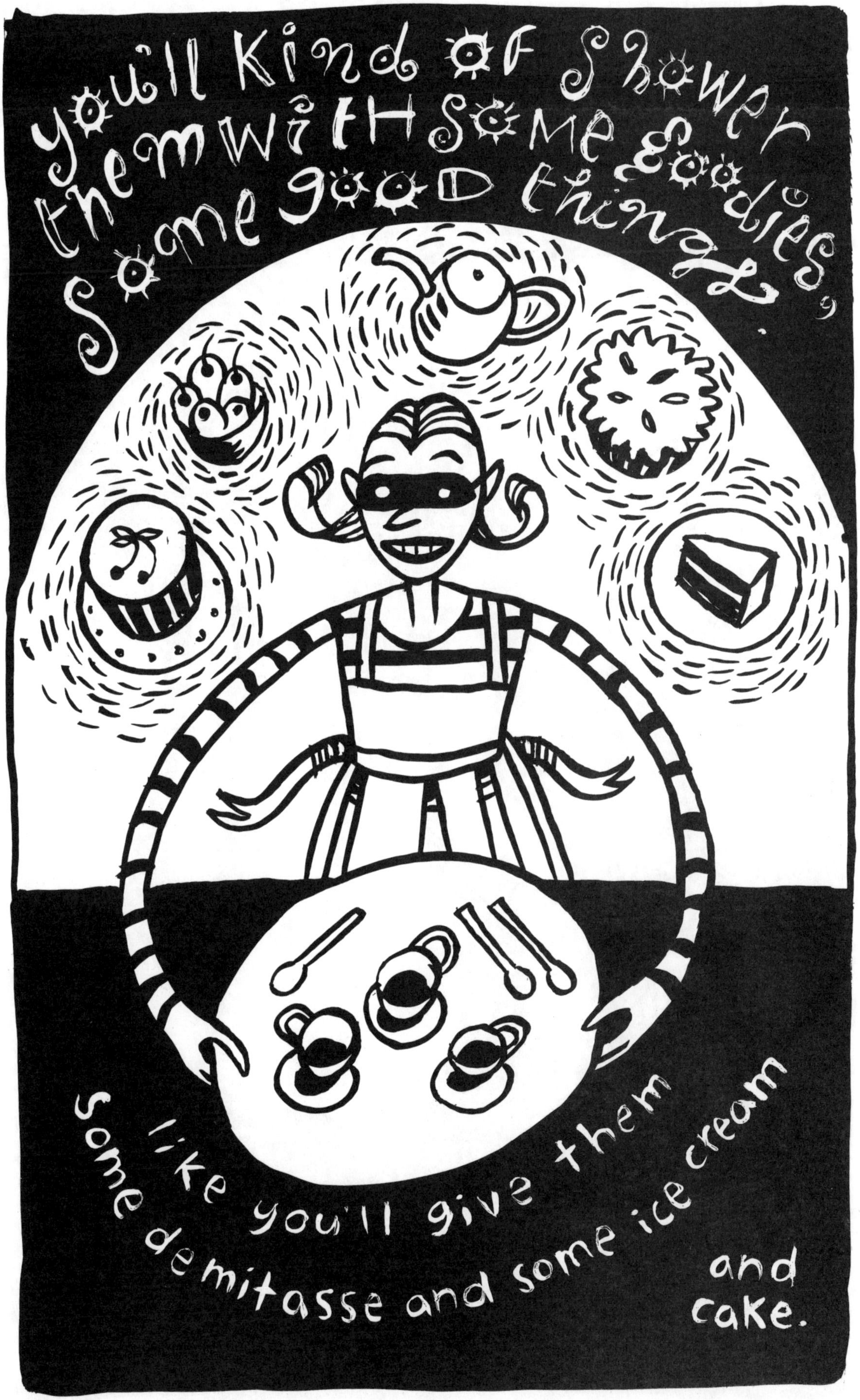
you'll kind of shower them with some goodies, some good things.
like you'll give them some demitasse and some ice cream and cake.

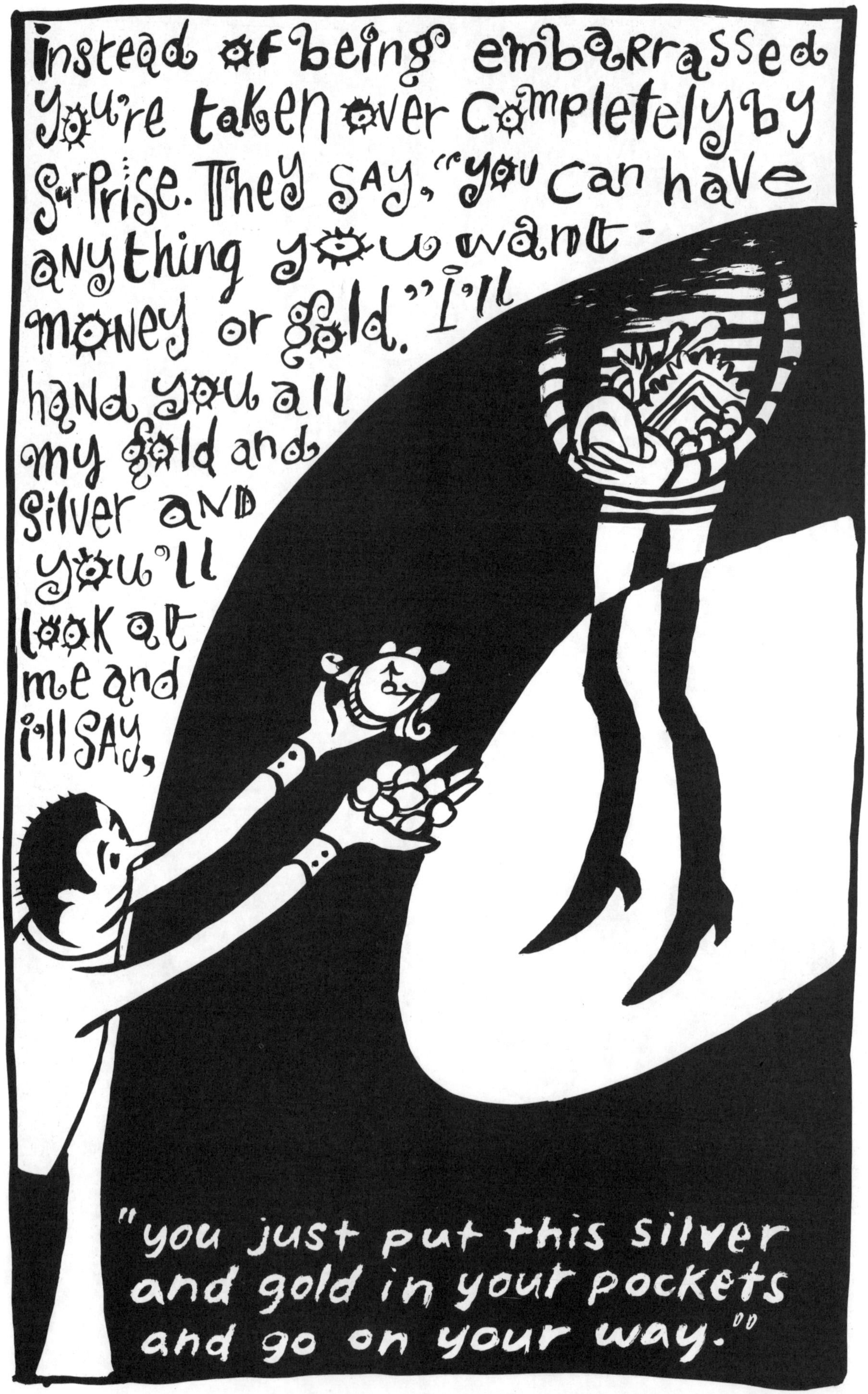
instead of being embarrassed you're taken over completely by surprise. They say, "you can have anything you want - money or gold." I'll hand you all my gold and silver and you'll look at me and i'll say,
"you just put this silver and gold in your pockets and go on your way."

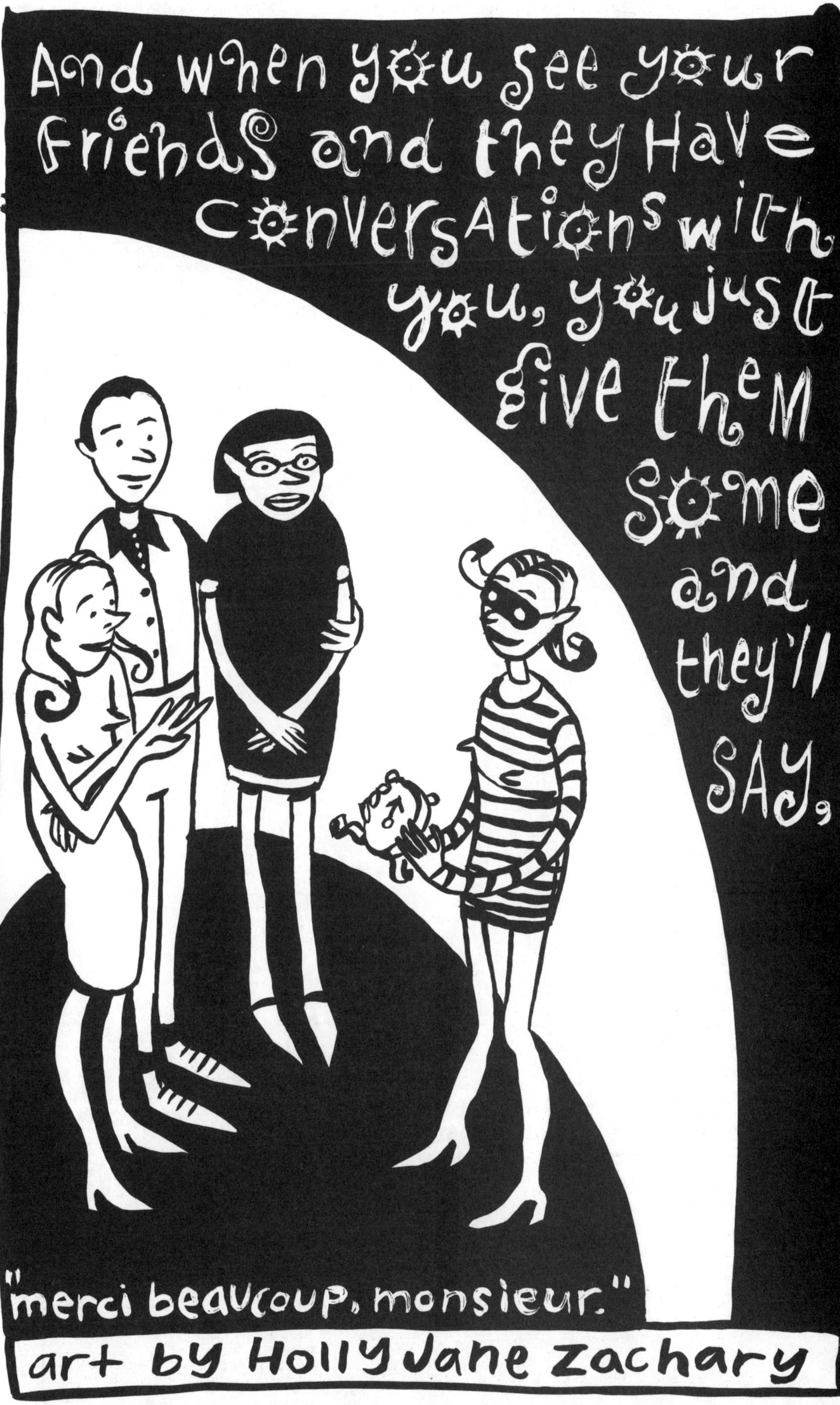
And when you see your friends and they have conversations with you, you just give them some and they'll say,
"merci beaucoup, monsieur."
art by Holly Jane Zachary

HIDING IN THE TREES

A story by William Ferguson ~ Recounted by David Greenberger
Images by Paul Nitsche

The best place to hide is in the top of a tree.

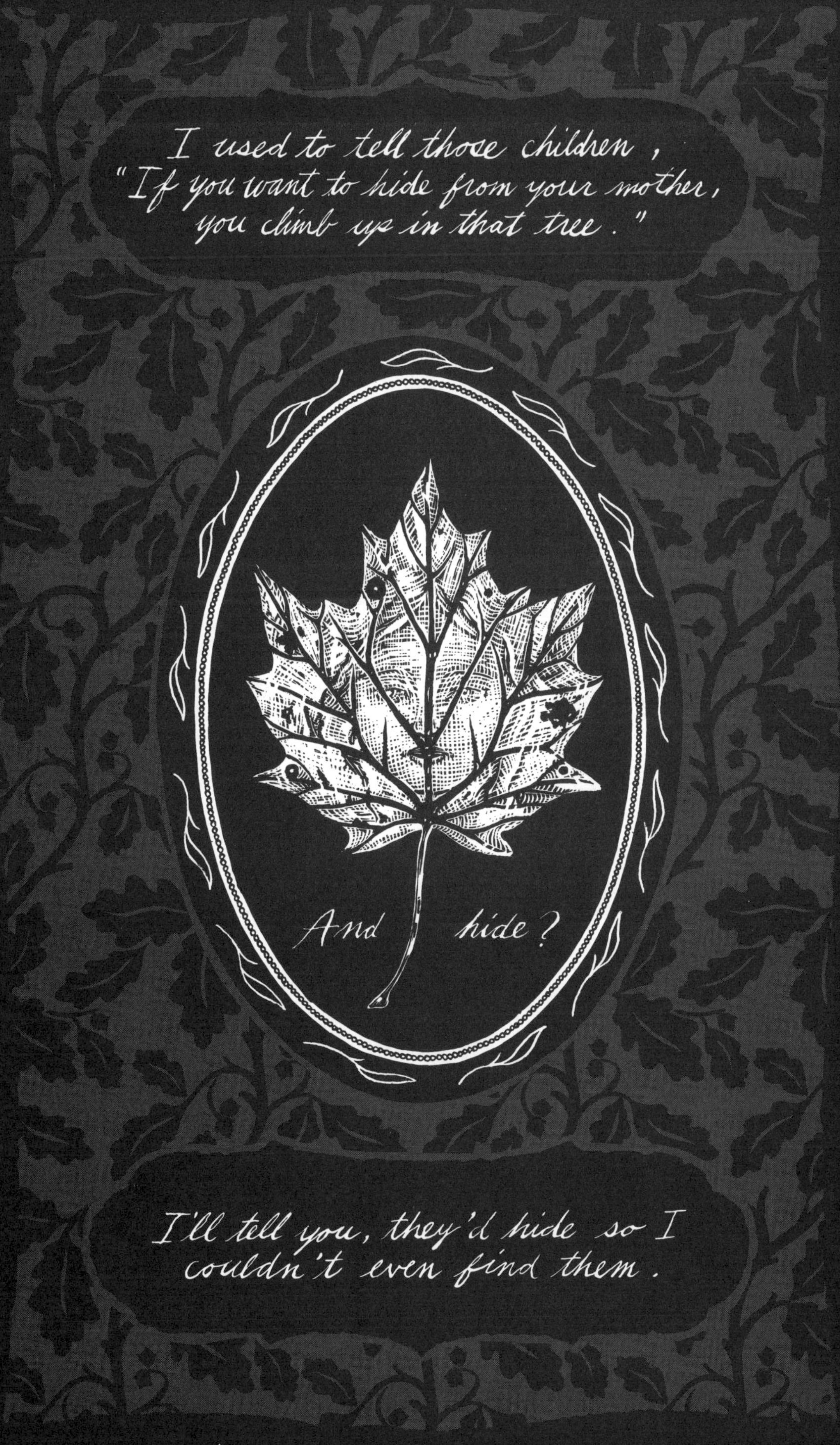
I used to tell those children, "If you want to hide from your mother, you climb up in that tree."
And hide?
I'll tell you, they'd hide so I couldn't even find them.

And I don't mean any small trees, I mean trees that were fifty, sixty feet.

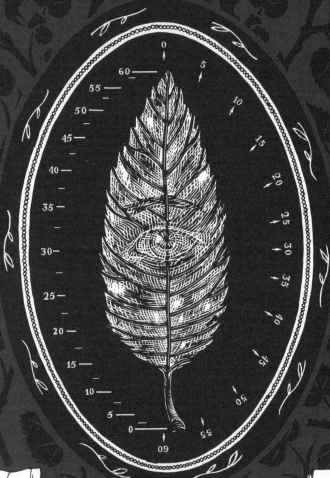

And they'd fall out of those trees...

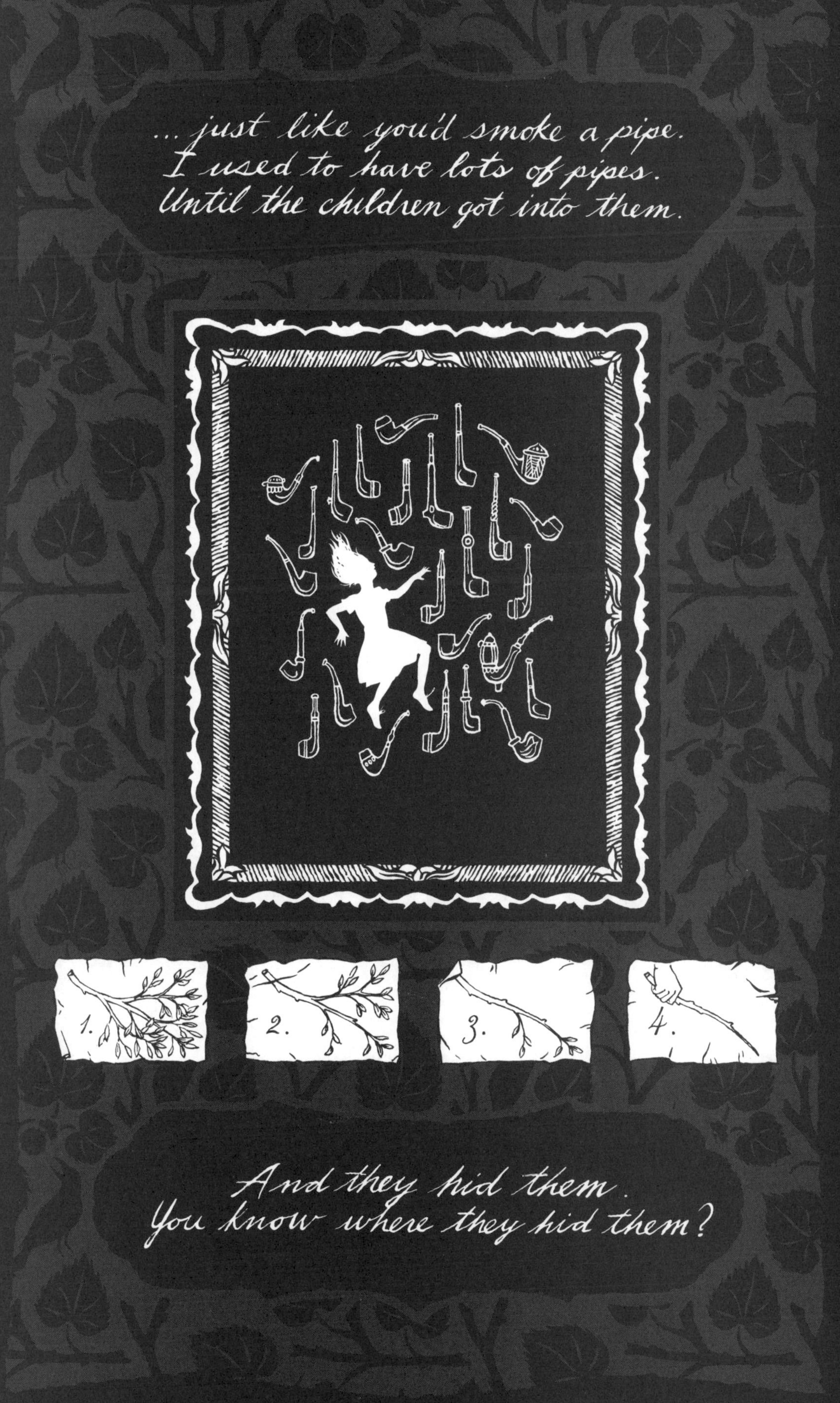
... just like you'd smoke a pipe. I used to have lots of pipes. Until the children got into them.
1.
2.
3.
4.
And they hid them. You know where they hid them?

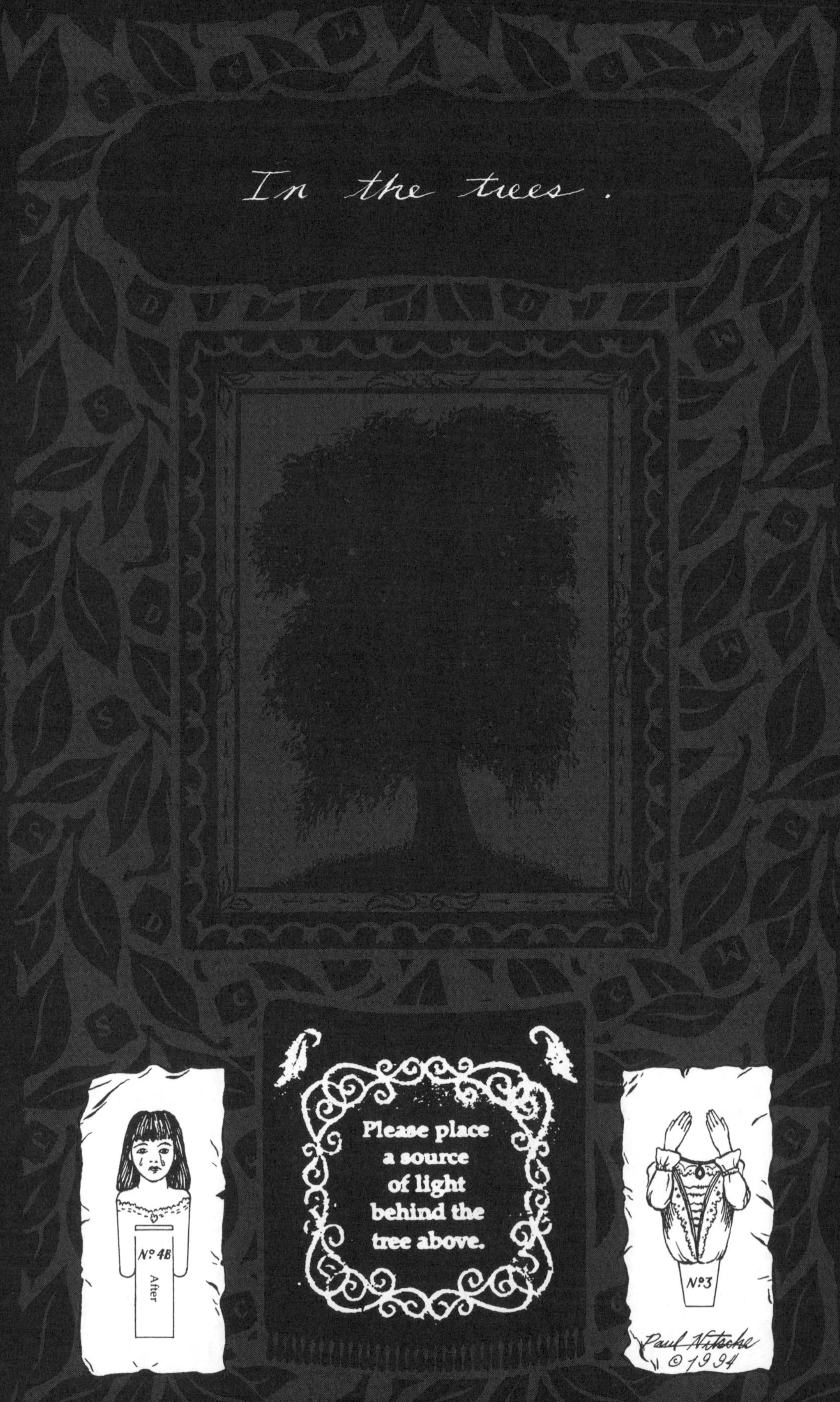

In the trees.
Nº 4B
After
Please place a source of light behind the tree above.
Nº 3
Paul Nitsche ©1994

Bill Niemi

1923—

You don't get many prizes for nothin' in this life.

◆

I doubt hell will freeze over, because people who say that or have that kind of personality or do the kind of things they do to earn their keep — it's probably something bad they do — that's where they'll end up, in that region.

◆

Ginger ale is supposed to taste good on a Friday.

◆

Pork, according to anyone who knows anything about cooking, you're supposed to have on Tuesdays. It tastes best on Tuesdays.

◆

Dishes are the hardest things to get clean nowadays.

◆

I was readin' some magazine in here a while back and there was a movie section in it and they said that Johnny Weismuller is a raving maniac in some hospital out in California.

◆

Nowadays you have to insist on everything.

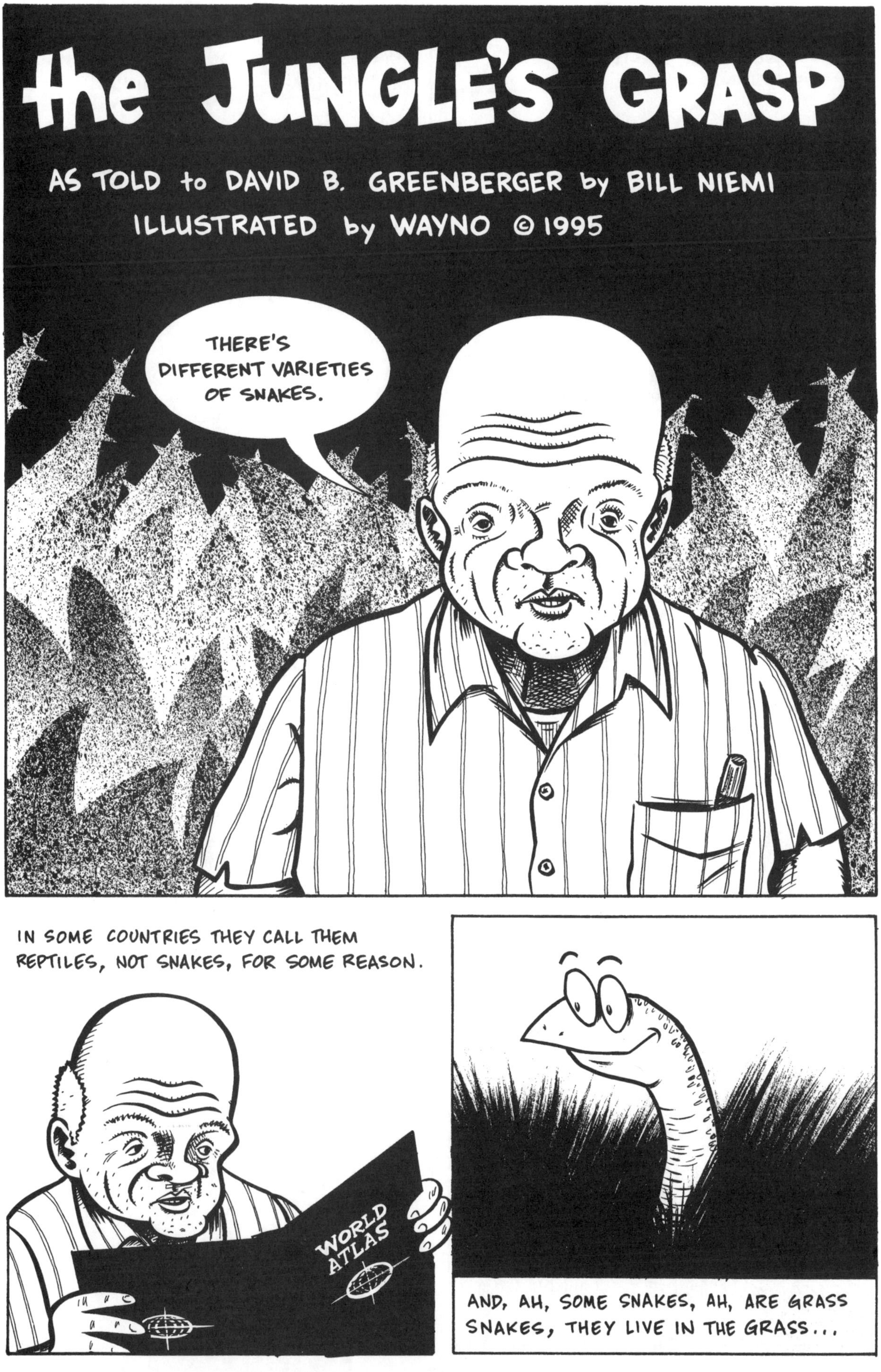
the JUNGLE'S GRASP
AS TOLD to DAVID B. GREENBERGER by BILL NIEMI
ILLUSTRATED by WAYNO © 1995
THERE'S DIFFERENT VARIETIES OF SNAKES.
IN SOME COUNTRIES THEY CALL THEM REPTILES, NOT SNAKES, FOR SOME REASON.
WORLD ATLAS
AND, AH, SOME SNAKES, AH, ARE GRASS SNAKES, THEY LIVE IN THE GRASS...

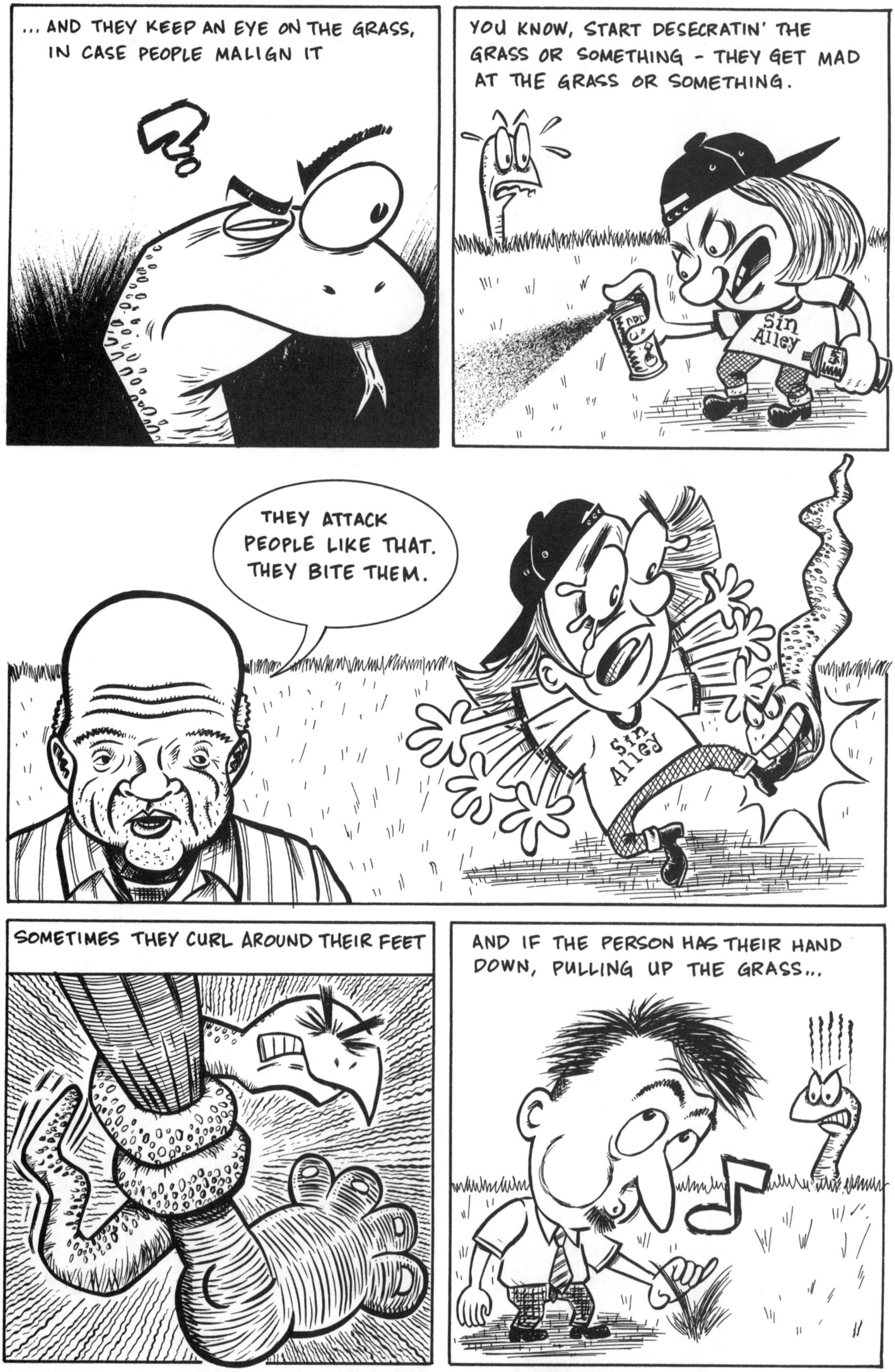
... AND THEY KEEP AN EYE ON THE GRASS, IN CASE PEOPLE MALIGN IT
YOU KNOW, START DESECRATIN' THE GRASS OR SOMETHING - THEY GET MAD AT THE GRASS OR SOMETHING.
Sin Alley
THEY ATTACK PEOPLE LIKE THAT. THEY BITE THEM.
Sin Alley
SOMETIMES THEY CURL AROUND THEIR FEET
AND IF THE PERSON HAS THEIR HAND DOWN, PULLING UP THE GRASS...

...THEY'RE LIABLE TO CURL AROUND THEIR WRIST

AND IF THEY ENTWINE THEMSELVES AROUND THE PERSON'S WRIST, THAT INTERFERES WITH YOUR BREATHING.

THEY'RE LIABLE TO CHOKE TO DEATH.

THERE'S WATER SNAKES

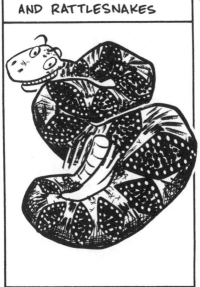

AND RATTLESNAKES

AND BOA CONSTRICTORS.

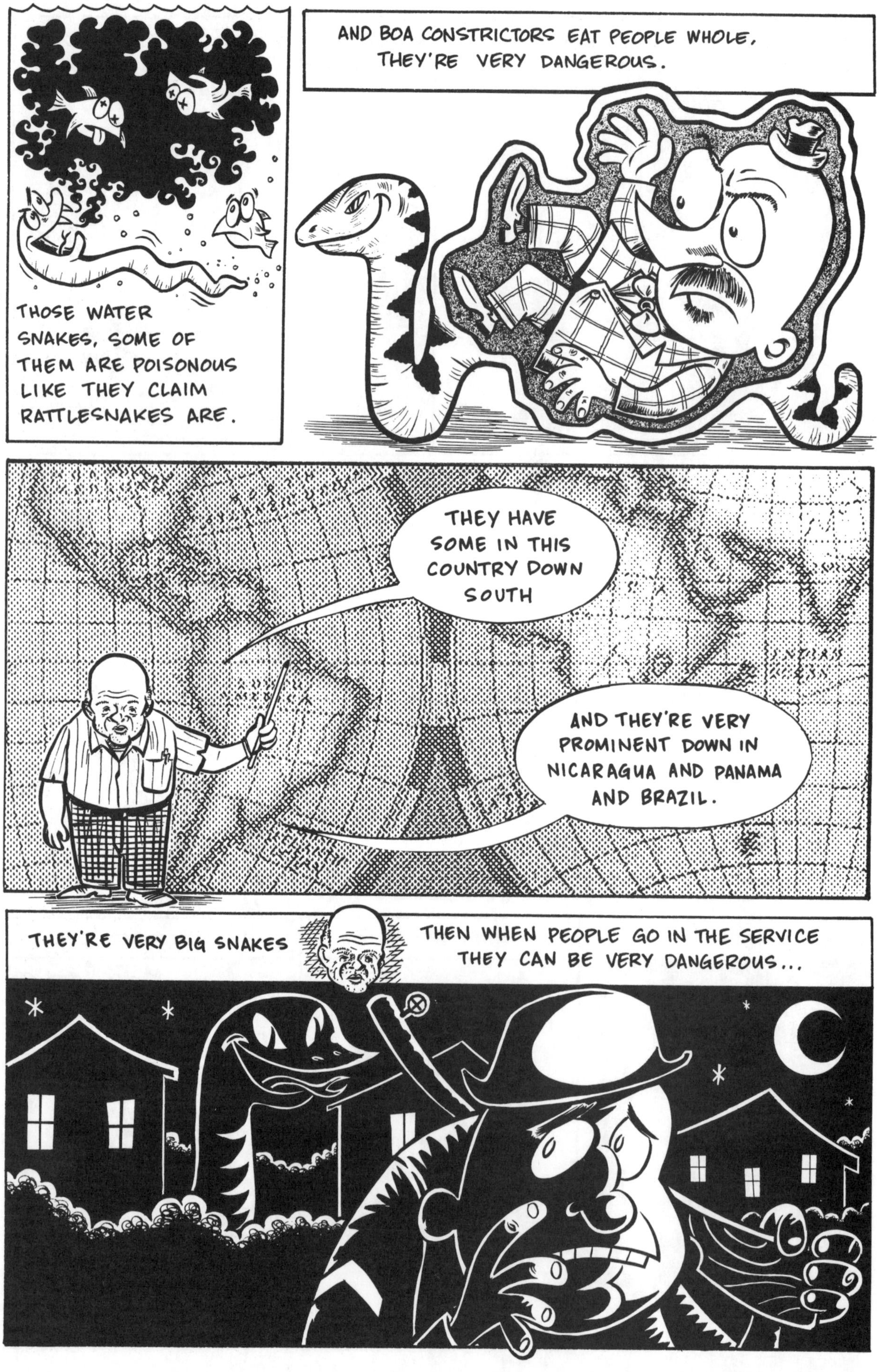
THOSE WATER SNAKES, SOME OF THEM ARE POISONOUS LIKE THEY CLAIM RATTLESNAKES ARE.
AND BOA CONSTRICTORS EAT PEOPLE WHOLE, THEY'RE VERY DANGEROUS.
THEY HAVE SOME IN THIS COUNTRY DOWN SOUTH
AND THEY'RE VERY PROMINENT DOWN IN NICARAGUA AND PANAMA AND BRAZIL.
THEY'RE VERY BIG SNAKES
THEN WHEN PEOPLE GO IN THE SERVICE THEY CAN BE VERY DANGEROUS...

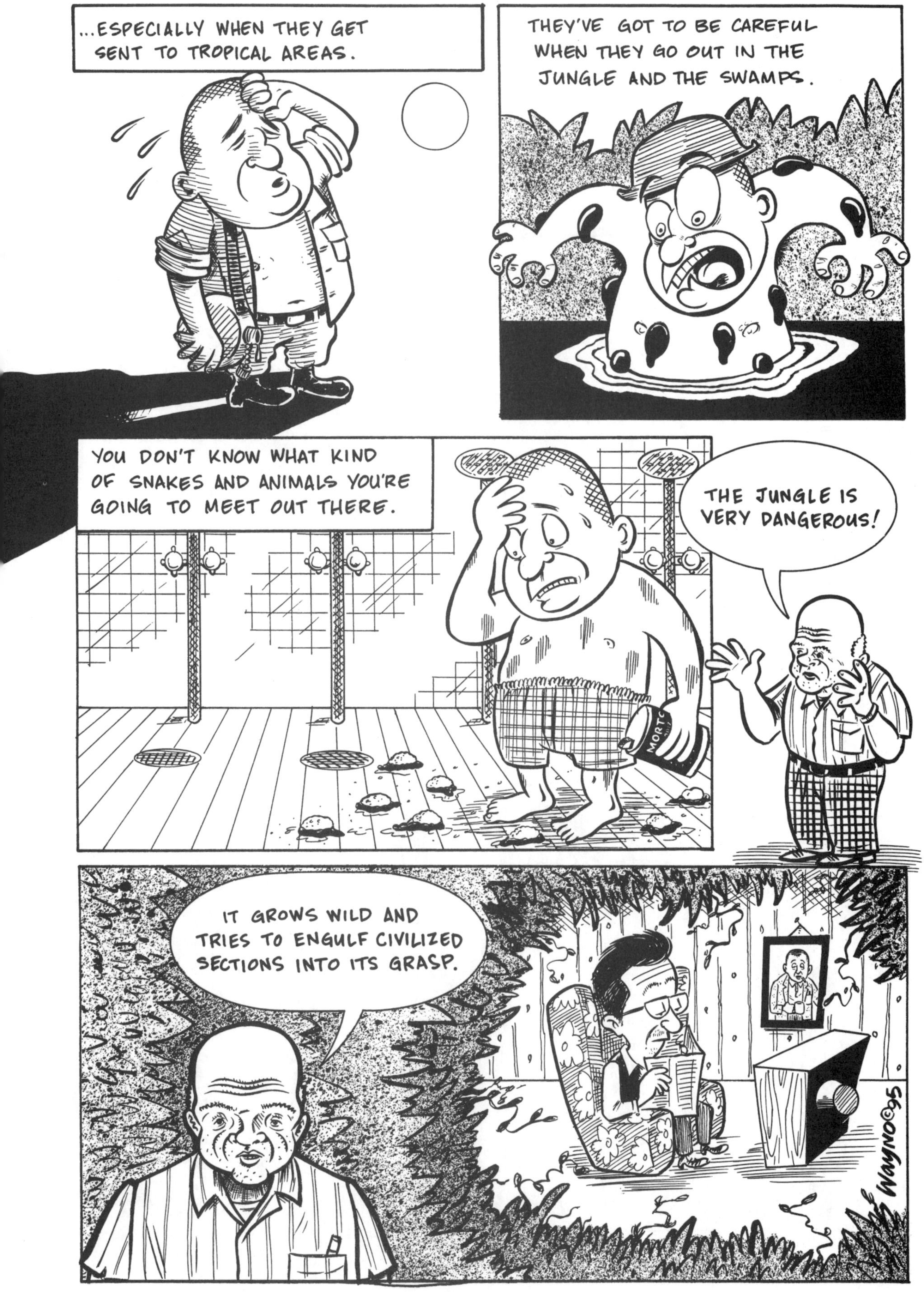
...ESPECIALLY WHEN THEY GET SENT TO TROPICAL AREAS.
THEY'VE GOT TO BE CAREFUL WHEN THEY GO OUT IN THE JUNGLE AND THE SWAMPS.
YOU DON'T KNOW WHAT KIND OF SNAKES AND ANIMALS YOU'RE GOING TO MEET OUT THERE.
THE JUNGLE IS VERY DANGEROUS!
IT GROWS WILD AND TRIES TO ENGULF CIVILIZED SECTIONS INTO ITS GRASP.
WAYNO©95

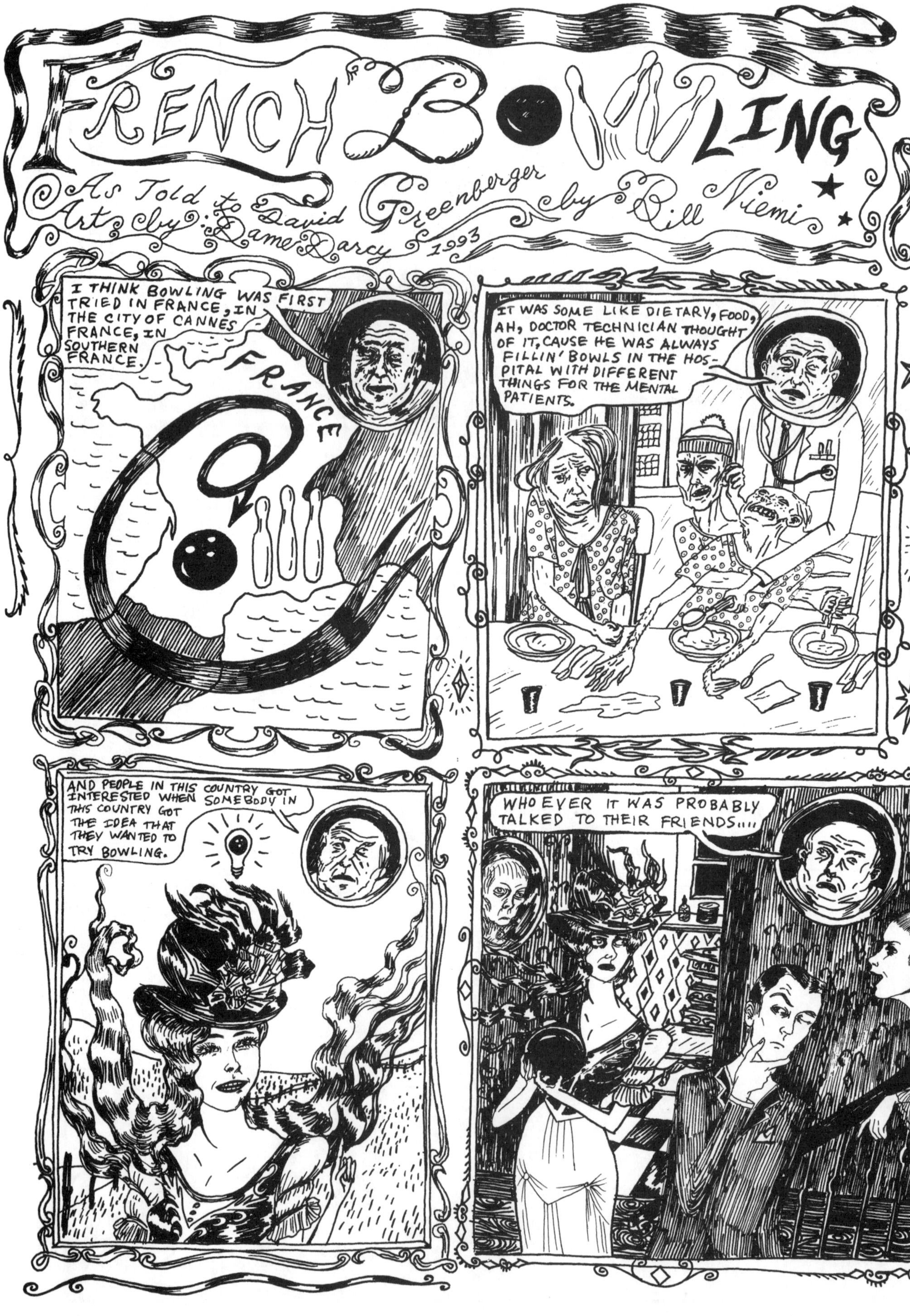
French Bowling
As Told to David Greenberger by Bill Niemi
Art by: Dame Darcy 1993
I THINK BOWLING WAS FIRST TRIED IN FRANCE, IN THE CITY OF CANNES FRANCE, IN SOUTHERN FRANCE.
FRANCE
IT WAS SOME LIKE DIETARY, FOOD, AH, DOCTOR TECHNICIAN THOUGHT OF IT, CAUSE HE WAS ALWAYS FILLIN' BOWLS IN THE HOSPITAL WITH DIFFERENT THINGS FOR THE MENTAL PATIENTS.
AND PEOPLE IN THIS COUNTRY GOT INTERESTED WHEN SOMEBODY IN THIS COUNTRY GOT THE IDEA THAT THEY WANTED TO TRY BOWLING.
WHO EVER IT WAS PROBABLY TALKED TO THEIR FRIENDS....

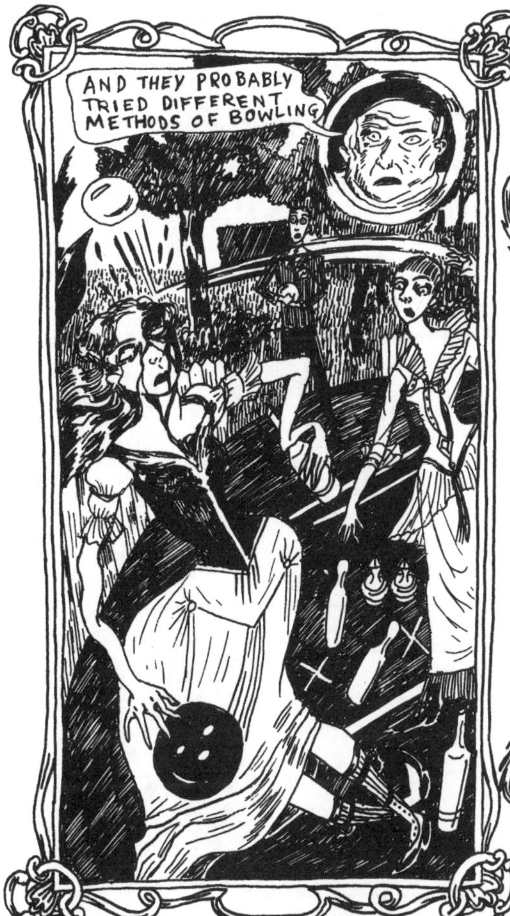
AND THEY PROBABLY TRIED DIFFERENT METHODS OF BOWLING

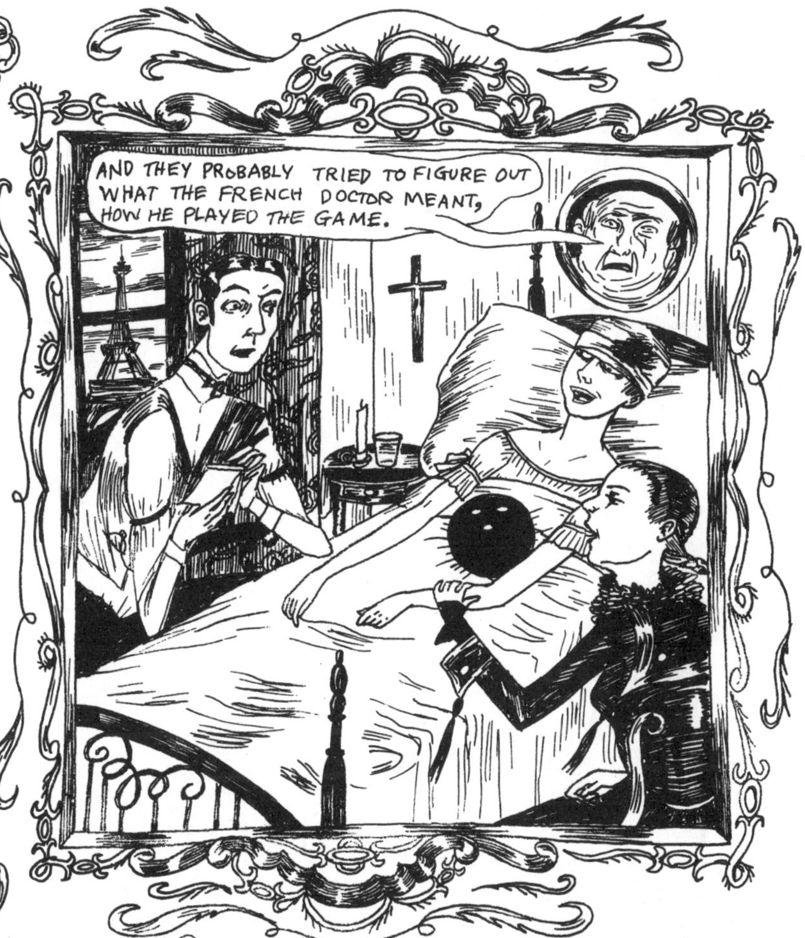
AND THEY PROBABLY TRIED TO FIGURE OUT WHAT THE FRENCH DOCTOR MEANT, HOW HE PLAYED THE GAME.

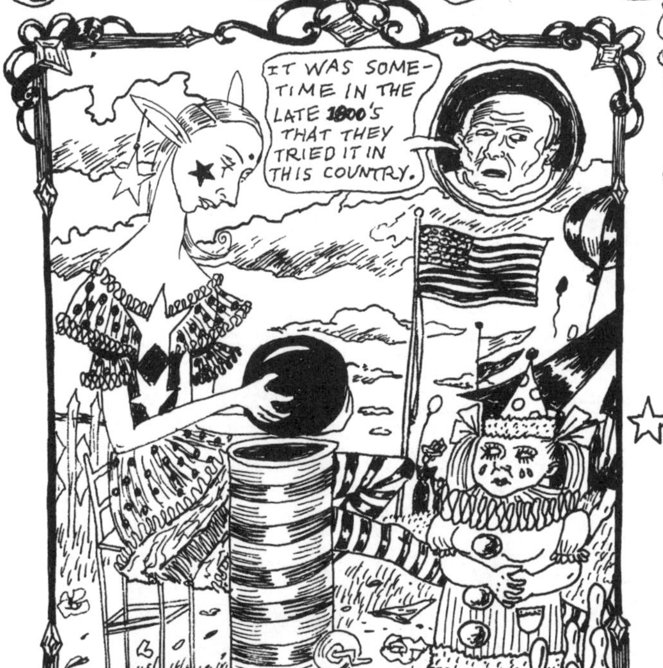
IT WAS SOMETIME IN THE LATE 1800'S THAT THEY TRIED IT IN THIS COUNTRY.

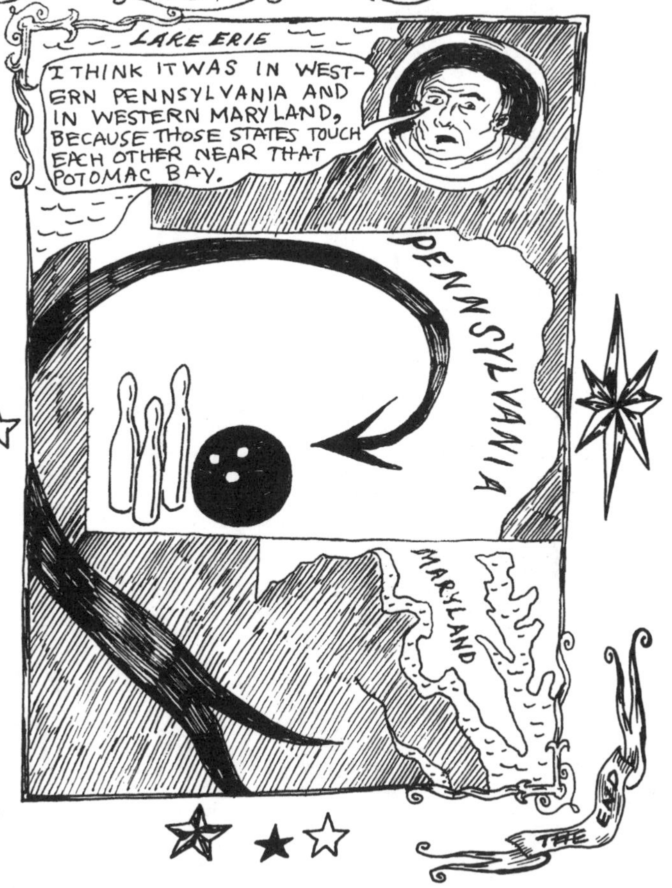
LAKE ERIE
I THINK IT WAS IN WESTERN PENNSYLVANIA AND IN WESTERN MARYLAND, BECAUSE THOSE STATES TOUCH EACH OTHER NEAR THAT POTOMAC BAY.
PENNSYLVANIA
MARYLAND
THE END

BILL NIEMI'S TANG THEORY

The Selective Service officials probably ended up with extra supplies of that drink Tang.

As told to David Greenberger and illustrated by Jason Lutes.

During the conflict years from 1936 to 1948, 1949 they were advertising that when you go into the Army, Navy, Coast Guard, Marines, or National Guard they'll supply the Tang for you, a glass every morning.

I never saw one glass of Tang.

It was probably some kind of gimmick to get younger men to go in the service.

Tang was supposed to be the best breakfast drink going, it might not go well if you drink it some other time, it's a breakfast drink.

You mix it up out of a jar,

it's supposed to taste like orange juice.

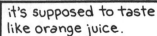

They still advertise it on television.

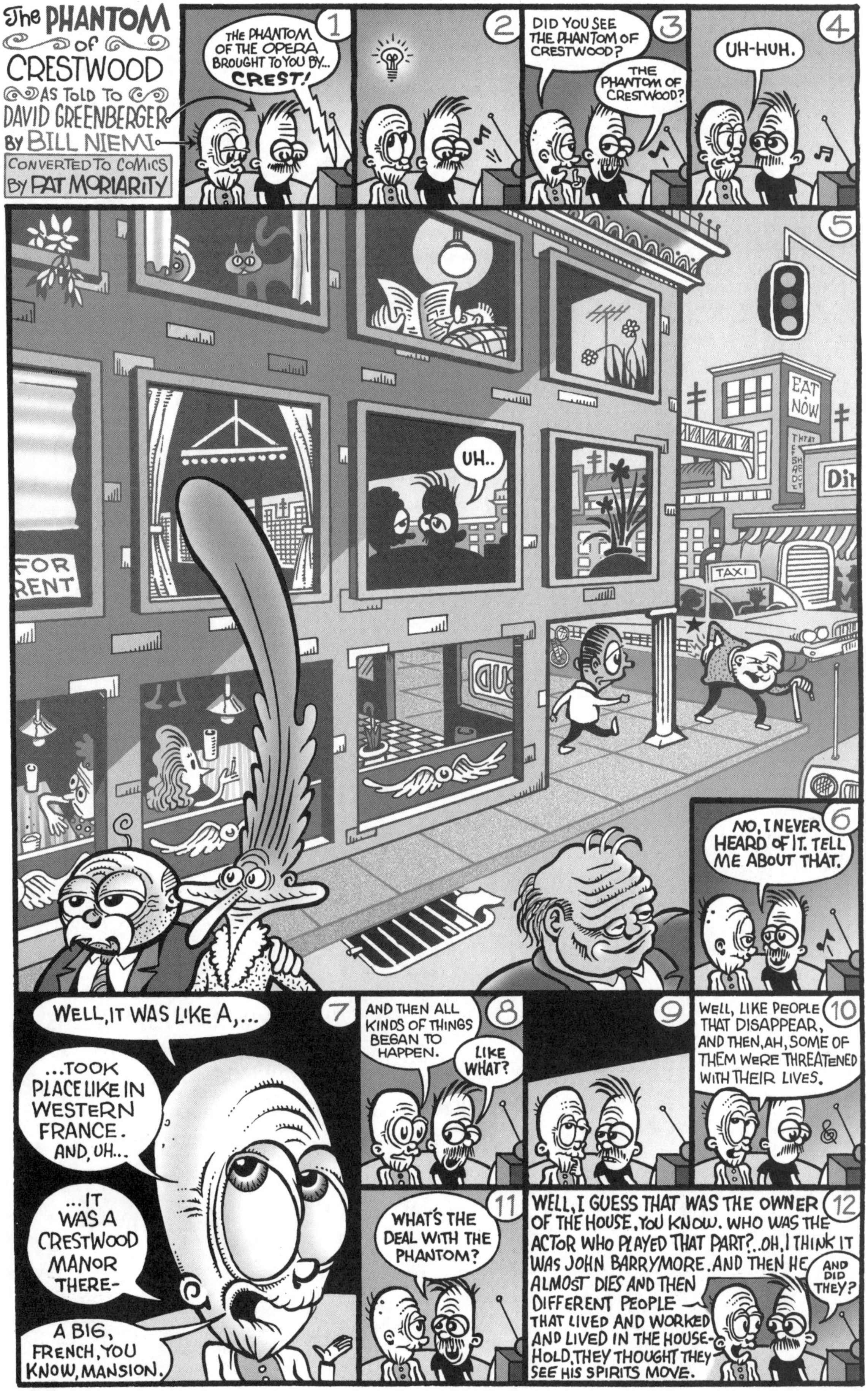

The PHANTOM of CRESTWOOD
AS TOLD TO DAVID GREENBERGER
BY BILL NIEMI
CONVERTED TO COMICS BY PAT MORIARITY
1
THE PHANTOM OF THE OPERA BROUGHT TO YOU BY... CREST!
2
3
DID YOU SEE THE PHANTOM OF CRESTWOOD?
THE PHANTOM OF CRESTWOOD?
4
UH-HUH.
5
UH..
EAT NOW
FOR RENT
TAXI
6
NO, I NEVER HEARD OF IT. TELL ME ABOUT THAT.
7
WELL, IT WAS LIKE A,...
...TOOK PLACE LIKE IN WESTERN FRANCE. AND, UH...
...IT WAS A CRESTWOOD MANOR THERE-
A BIG, FRENCH, YOU KNOW, MANSION.
8
AND THEN ALL KINDS OF THINGS BEGAN TO HAPPEN.
LIKE WHAT?
9
10
WELL, LIKE PEOPLE THAT DISAPPEAR, AND THEN, AH, SOME OF THEM WERE THREATENED WITH THEIR LIVES.
11
WHAT'S THE DEAL WITH THE PHANTOM?
12
WELL, I GUESS THAT WAS THE OWNER OF THE HOUSE, YOU KNOW. WHO WAS THE ACTOR WHO PLAYED THAT PART?.. OH, I THINK IT WAS JOHN BARRYMORE. AND THEN HE ALMOST DIES AND THEN DIFFERENT PEOPLE THAT LIVED AND WORKED AND LIVED IN THE HOUSEHOLD, THEY THOUGHT THEY SEE HIS SPIRITS MOVE.
AND DID THEY?

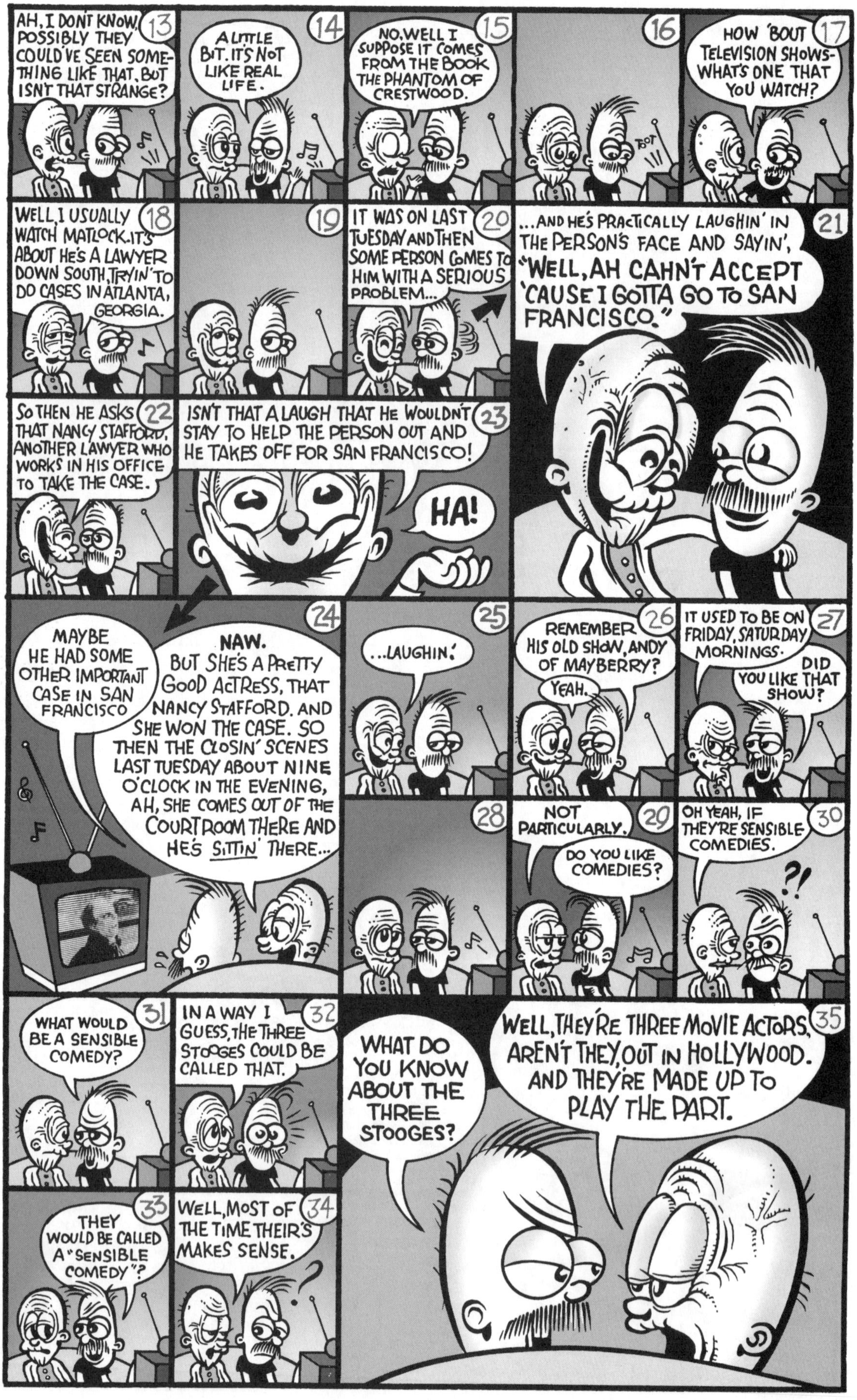

AH, I DON'T KNOW, POSSIBLY THEY COULD'VE SEEN SOMETHING LIKE THAT. BUT ISN'T THAT STRANGE?
A LITTLE BIT. IT'S NOT LIKE REAL LIFE.
NO. WELL I SUPPOSE IT COMES FROM THE BOOK THE PHANTOM OF CRESTWOOD.
TOOT
HOW 'BOUT TELEVISION SHOWS- WHAT'S ONE THAT YOU WATCH?
WELL, I USUALLY WATCH MATLOCK. IT'S ABOUT HE'S A LAWYER DOWN SOUTH, TRYIN' TO DO CASES IN ATLANTA, GEORGIA.
IT WAS ON LAST TUESDAY AND THEN SOME PERSON COMES TO HIM WITH A SERIOUS PROBLEM...
...AND HE'S PRACTICALLY LAUGHIN' IN THE PERSON'S FACE AND SAYIN', "WELL, AH CAHN'T ACCEPT 'CAUSE I GOTTA GO TO SAN FRANCISCO."
SO THEN HE ASKS THAT NANCY STAFFORD, ANOTHER LAWYER WHO WORKS IN HIS OFFICE TO TAKE THE CASE.
ISN'T THAT A LAUGH THAT HE WOULDN'T STAY TO HELP THE PERSON OUT AND HE TAKES OFF FOR SAN FRANCISCO!
HA!
MAYBE HE HAD SOME OTHER IMPORTANT CASE IN SAN FRANCISCO
NAW. BUT SHE'S A PRETTY GOOD ACTRESS, THAT NANCY STAFFORD. AND SHE WON THE CASE. SO THEN THE CLOSIN' SCENES LAST TUESDAY ABOUT NINE O'CLOCK IN THE EVENING, AH, SHE COMES OUT OF THE COURTROOM THERE AND HE'S SITTIN' THERE...
...LAUGHIN'.
REMEMBER HIS OLD SHOW, ANDY OF MAYBERRY?
YEAH.
IT USED TO BE ON FRIDAY, SATURDAY MORNINGS.
DID YOU LIKE THAT SHOW?
NOT PARTICULARLY.
DO YOU LIKE COMEDIES?
OH YEAH, IF THEY'RE SENSIBLE COMEDIES.
?!
WHAT WOULD BE A SENSIBLE COMEDY?
IN A WAY I GUESS, THE THREE STOOGES COULD BE CALLED THAT.
THEY WOULD BE CALLED A "SENSIBLE COMEDY"?
WELL, MOST OF THE TIME THEIR'S MAKES SENSE.
WHAT DO YOU KNOW ABOUT THE THREE STOOGES?
WELL, THEY'RE THREE MOVIE ACTORS, AREN'T THEY, OUT IN HOLLYWOOD. AND THEY'RE MADE UP TO PLAY THE PART.

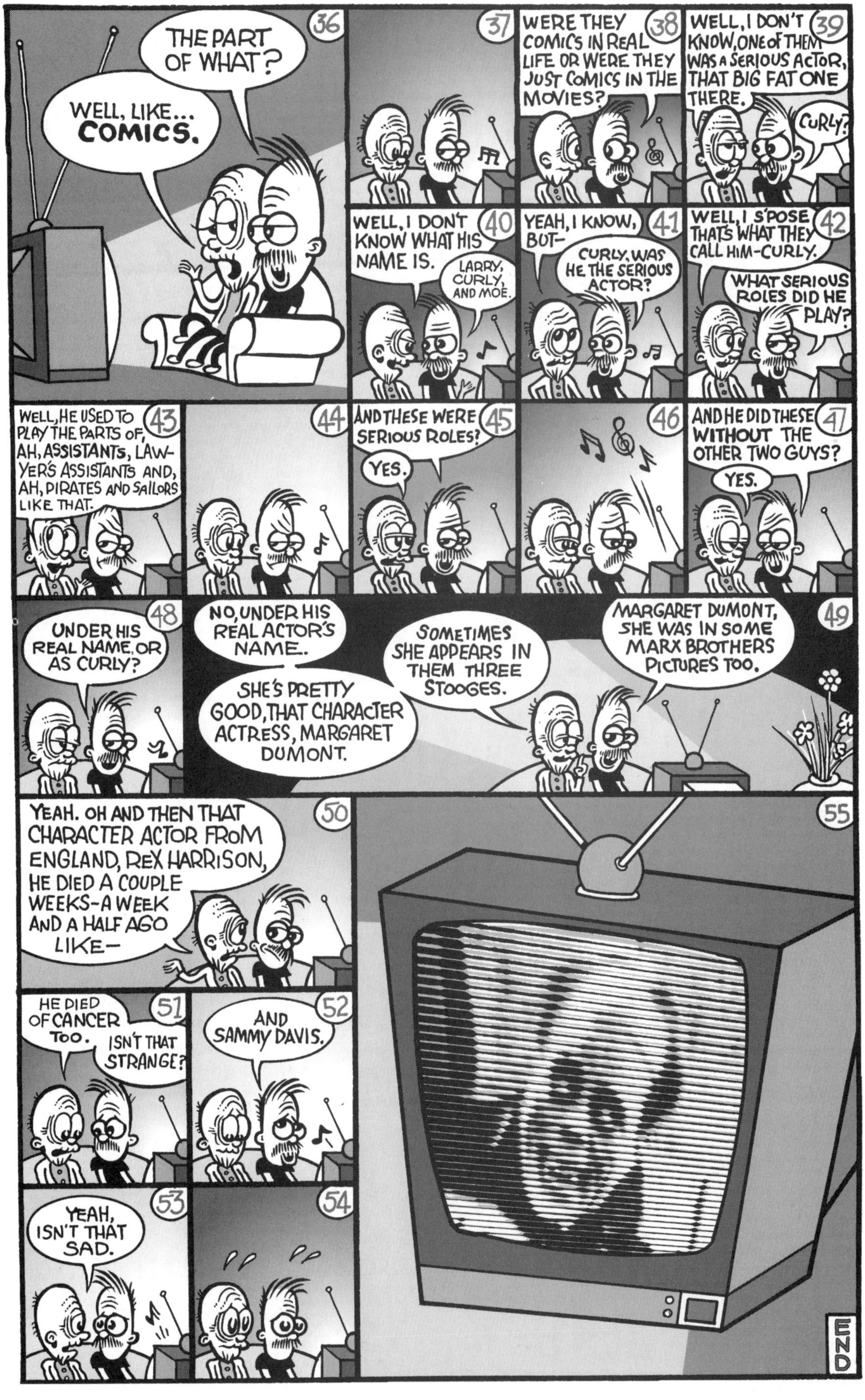
36
THE PART OF WHAT?
WELL, LIKE... COMICS.
37
38
WERE THEY COMICS IN REAL LIFE OR WERE THEY JUST COMICS IN THE MOVIES?
39
WELL, I DON'T KNOW, ONE OF THEM WAS A SERIOUS ACTOR, THAT BIG FAT ONE THERE.
CURLY?
40
WELL, I DON'T KNOW WHAT HIS NAME IS.
LARRY, CURLY, AND MOE.
41
YEAH, I KNOW, BUT-
CURLY, WAS HE THE SERIOUS ACTOR?
42
WELL, I S'POSE THAT'S WHAT THEY CALL HIM-CURLY.
WHAT SERIOUS ROLES DID HE PLAY?
43
WELL, HE USED TO PLAY THE PARTS OF, AH, ASSISTANTS, LAWYER'S ASSISTANTS AND, AH, PIRATES AND SAILORS LIKE THAT.
44
45
AND THESE WERE SERIOUS ROLES?
YES.
46
47
AND HE DID THESE WITHOUT THE OTHER TWO GUYS?
YES.
48
UNDER HIS REAL NAME, OR AS CURLY?
49
NO, UNDER HIS REAL ACTOR'S NAME.
SHE'S PRETTY GOOD, THAT CHARACTER ACTRESS, MARGARET DUMONT.
SOMETIMES SHE APPEARS IN THEM THREE STOOGES.
MARGARET DUMONT, SHE WAS IN SOME MARX BROTHERS PICTURES TOO.
50
YEAH. OH AND THEN THAT CHARACTER ACTOR FROM ENGLAND, REX HARRISON, HE DIED A COUPLE WEEKS-A WEEK AND A HALF AGO LIKE-
51
HE DIED OF CANCER TOO.
ISN'T THAT STRANGE?
52
AND SAMMY DAVIS.
53
YEAH, ISN'T THAT SAD.
54
55
END

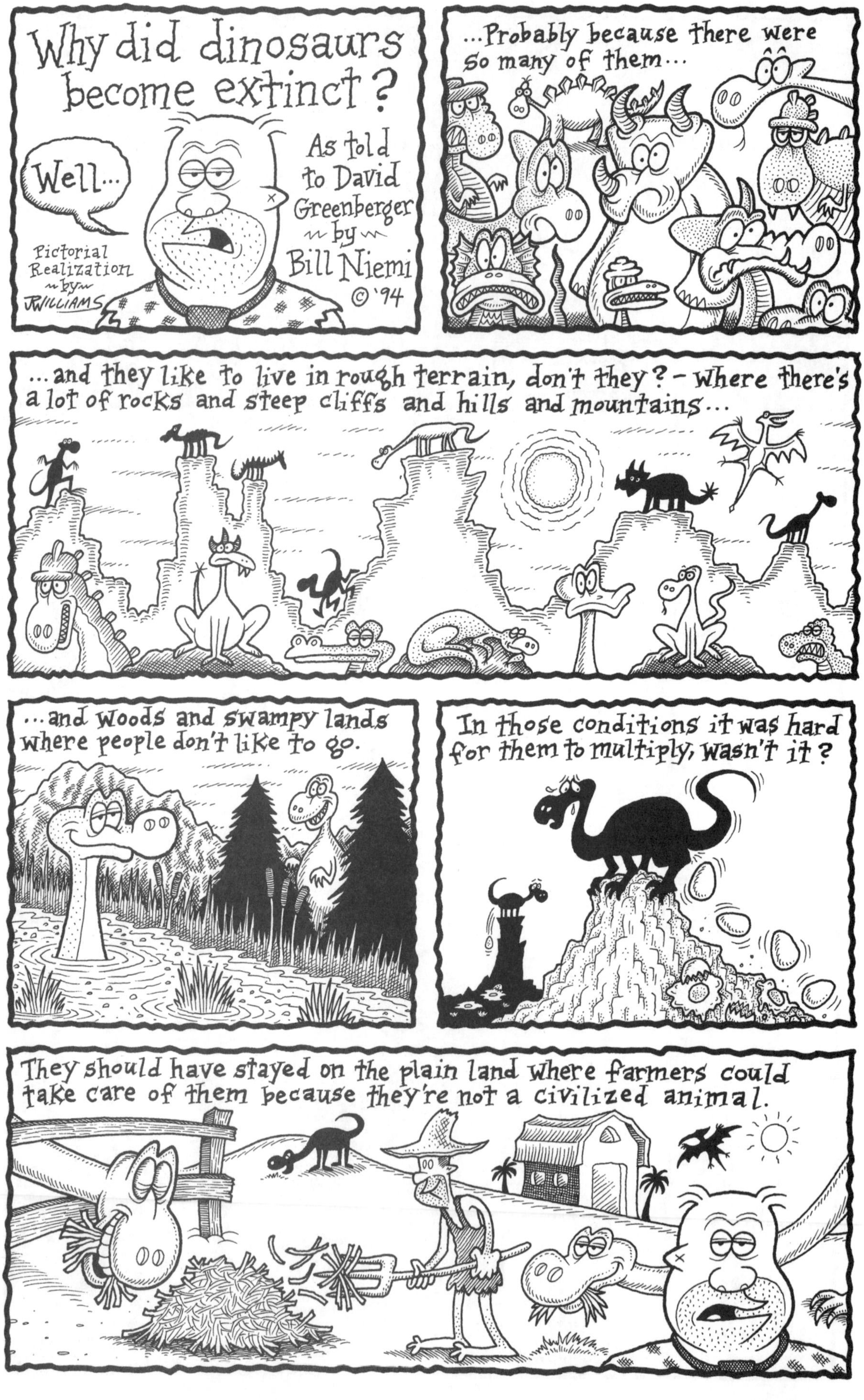
Why did dinosaurs become extinct?
Well...
As told to David Greenberger ~by~ Bill Niemi ©'94
Pictorial Realization ~by~ JWILLIAMS
...Probably because there were so many of them...
...and they like to live in rough terrain, don't they? - where there's a lot of rocks and steep cliffs and hills and mountains...
...and woods and swampy lands where people don't like to go.
In those conditions it was hard for them to multiply, wasn't it?
They should have stayed on the plain land where farmers could take care of them because they're not a civilized animal.

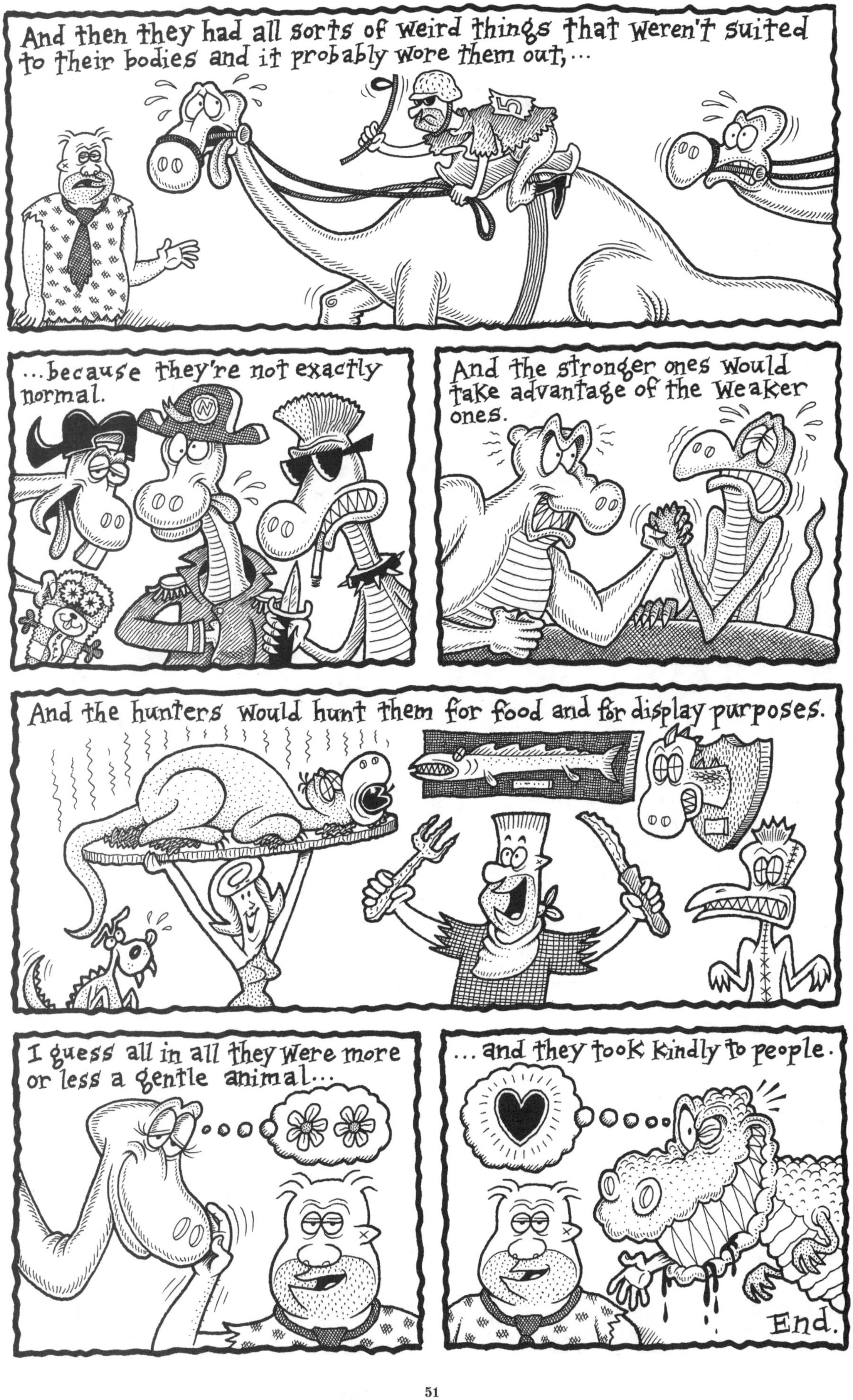
And then they had all sorts of weird things that weren't suited to their bodies and it probably wore them out,...
...because they're not exactly normal.
And the stronger ones would take advantage of the weaker ones.
And the hunters would hunt them for food and for display purposes.
I guess all in all they were more or less a gentle animal...
... and they took kindly to people.
End.

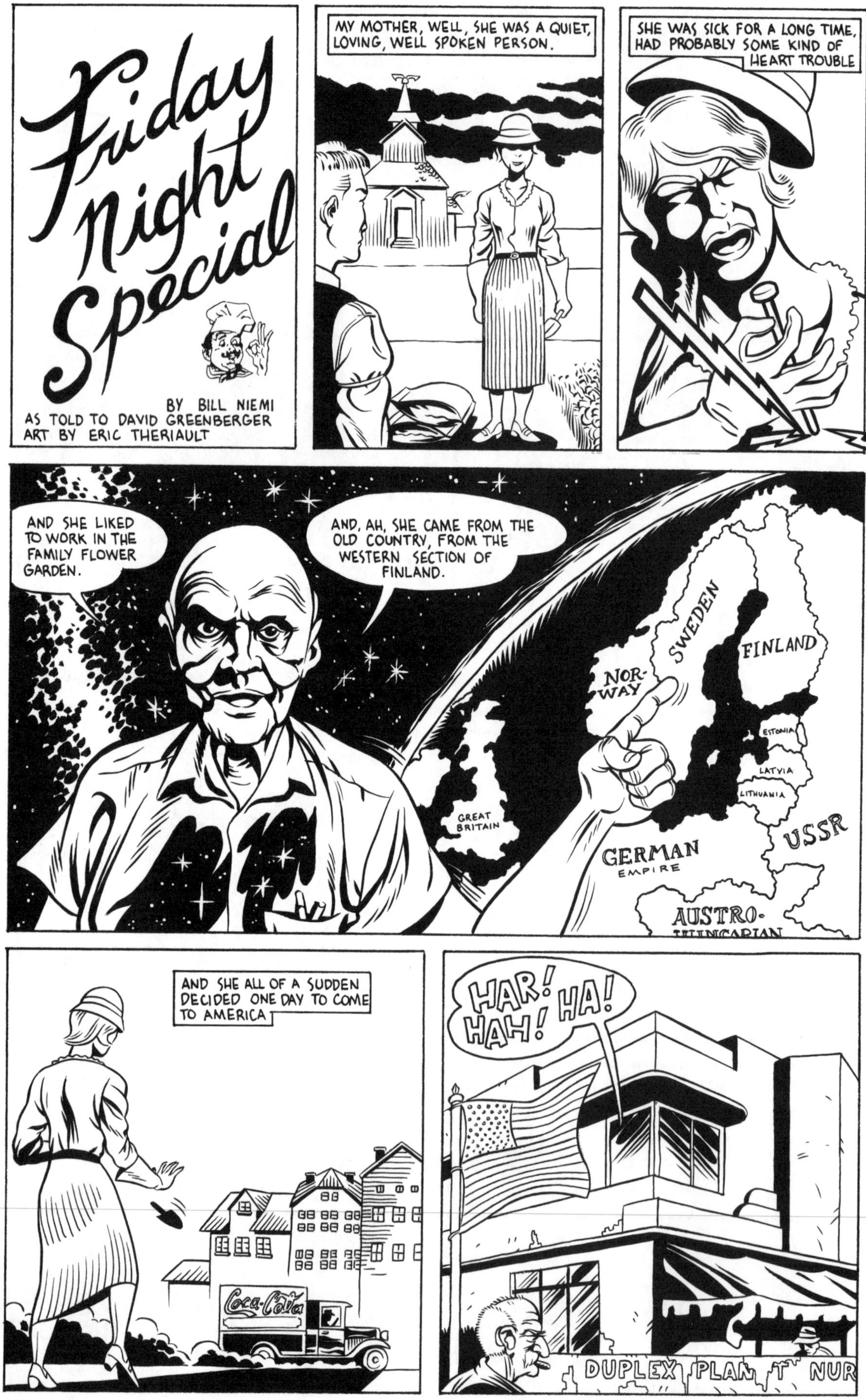

Friday Night Special
BY BILL NIEMI
AS TOLD TO DAVID GREENBERGER
ART BY ERIC THERIAULT
MY MOTHER, WELL, SHE WAS A QUIET, LOVING, WELL SPOKEN PERSON.
SHE WAS SICK FOR A LONG TIME, HAD PROBABLY SOME KIND OF HEART TROUBLE
AND SHE LIKED TO WORK IN THE FAMILY FLOWER GARDEN.
AND, AH, SHE CAME FROM THE OLD COUNTRY, FROM THE WESTERN SECTION OF FINLAND.
NOR-WAY
SWEDEN
FINLAND
ESTONIA
LATVIA
LITHUANIA
GREAT BRITAIN
USSR
GERMAN EMPIRE
AUSTRO-
AND SHE ALL OF A SUDDEN DECIDED ONE DAY TO COME TO AMERICA
Coca-Cola
HAR! HAH! HA!
DUPLEX PLAN T NUR

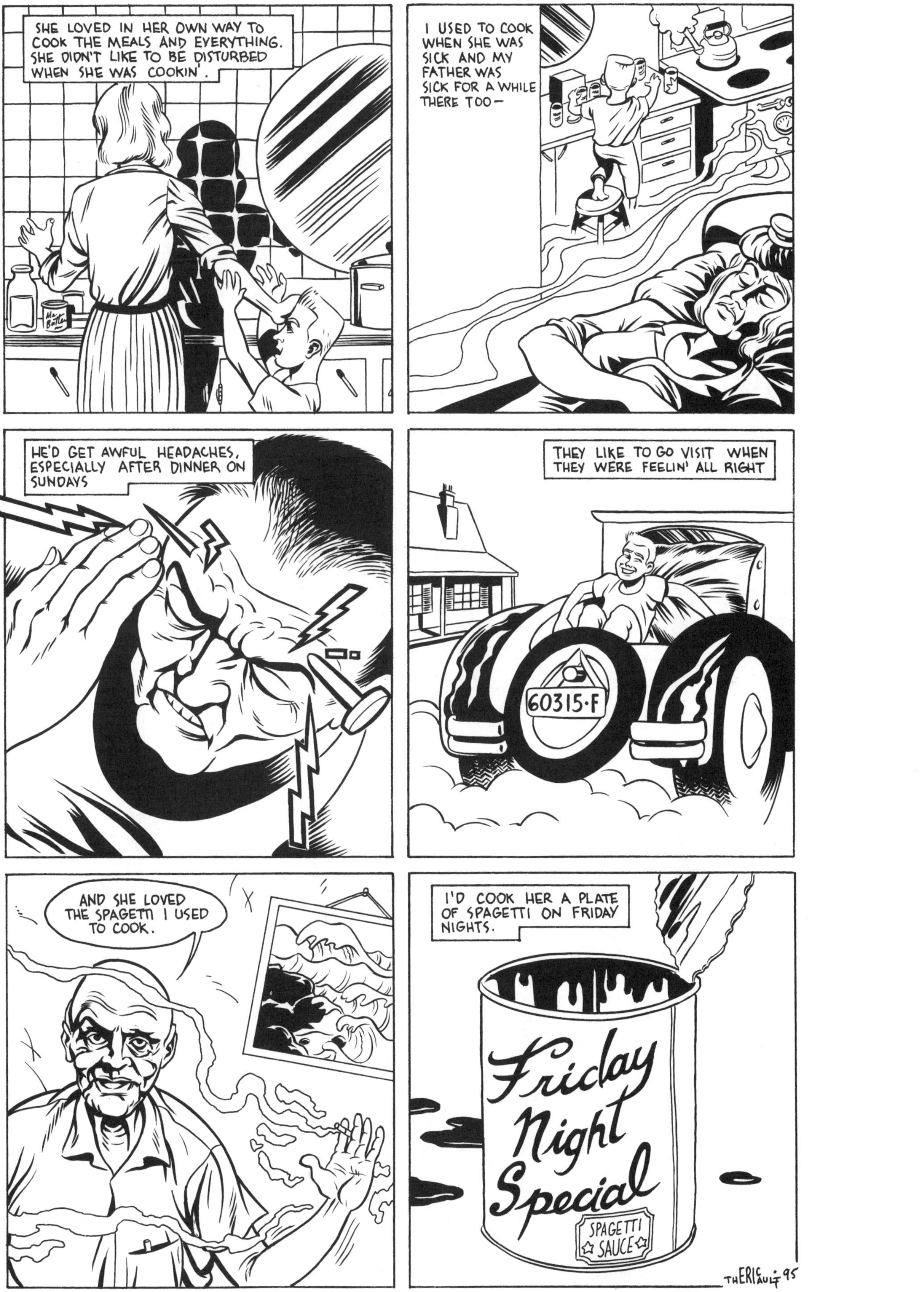
SHE LOVED IN HER OWN WAY TO COOK THE MEALS AND EVERYTHING. SHE DIDN'T LIKE TO BE DISTURBED WHEN SHE WAS COOKIN'.
I USED TO COOK WHEN SHE WAS SICK AND MY FATHER WAS SICK FOR A WHILE THERE TOO—
HE'D GET AWFUL HEADACHES, ESPECIALLY AFTER DINNER ON SUNDAYS
THEY LIKE TO GO VISIT WHEN THEY WERE FEELIN' ALL RIGHT
60315·F
AND SHE LOVED THE SPAGETTI I USED TO COOK.
I'D COOK HER A PLATE OF SPAGETTI ON FRIDAY NIGHTS.
Friday Night Special
SPAGETTI SAUCE
THERIAULT 95

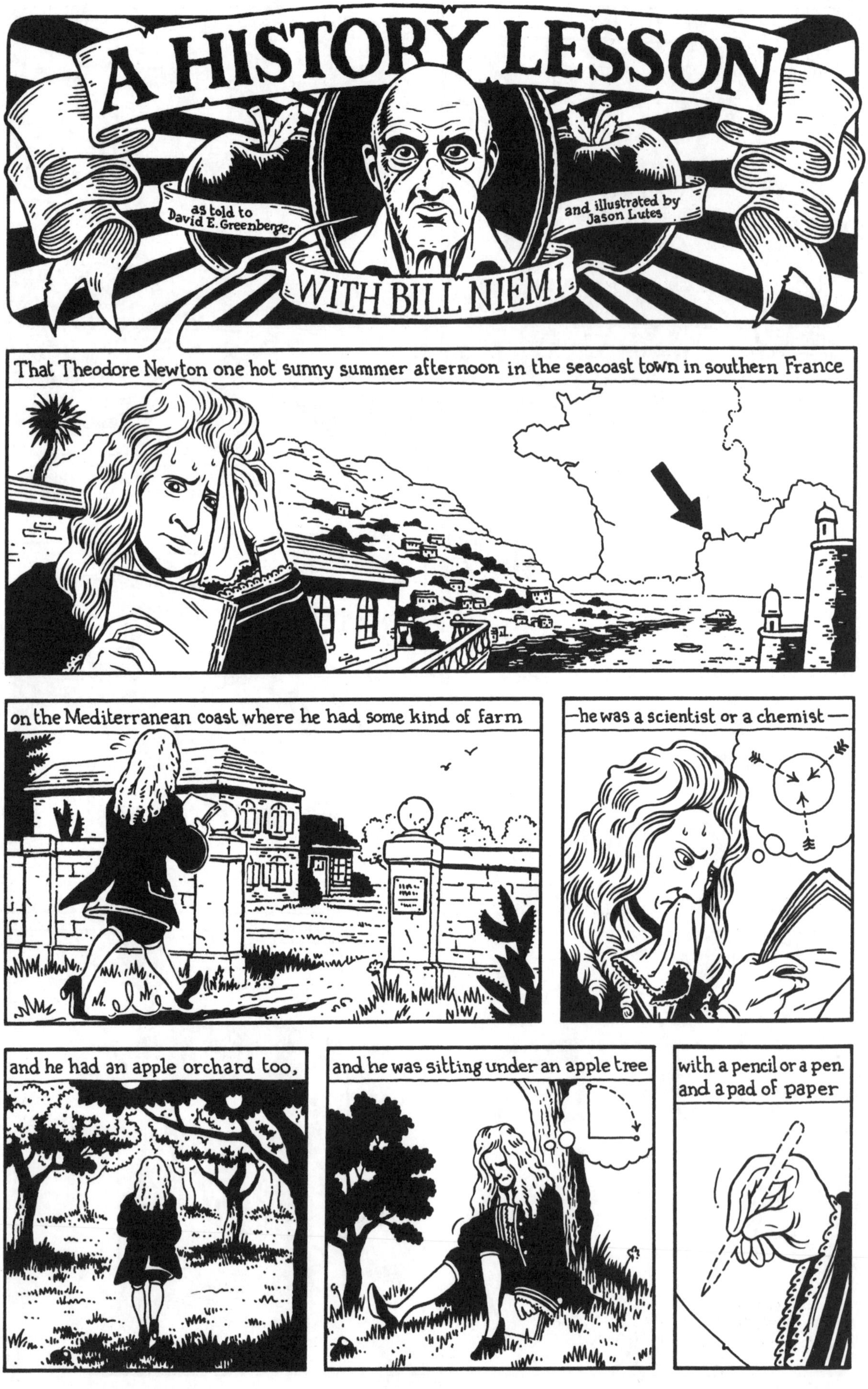
A HISTORY LESSON
as told to David E. Greenberger
and illustrated by Jason Lutes
WITH BILL NIEMI
That Theodore Newton one hot sunny summer afternoon in the seacoast town in southern France
on the Mediterranean coast where he had some kind of farm
—he was a scientist or a chemist—
and he had an apple orchard too,
and he was sitting under an apple tree
with a pencil or a pen and a pad of paper

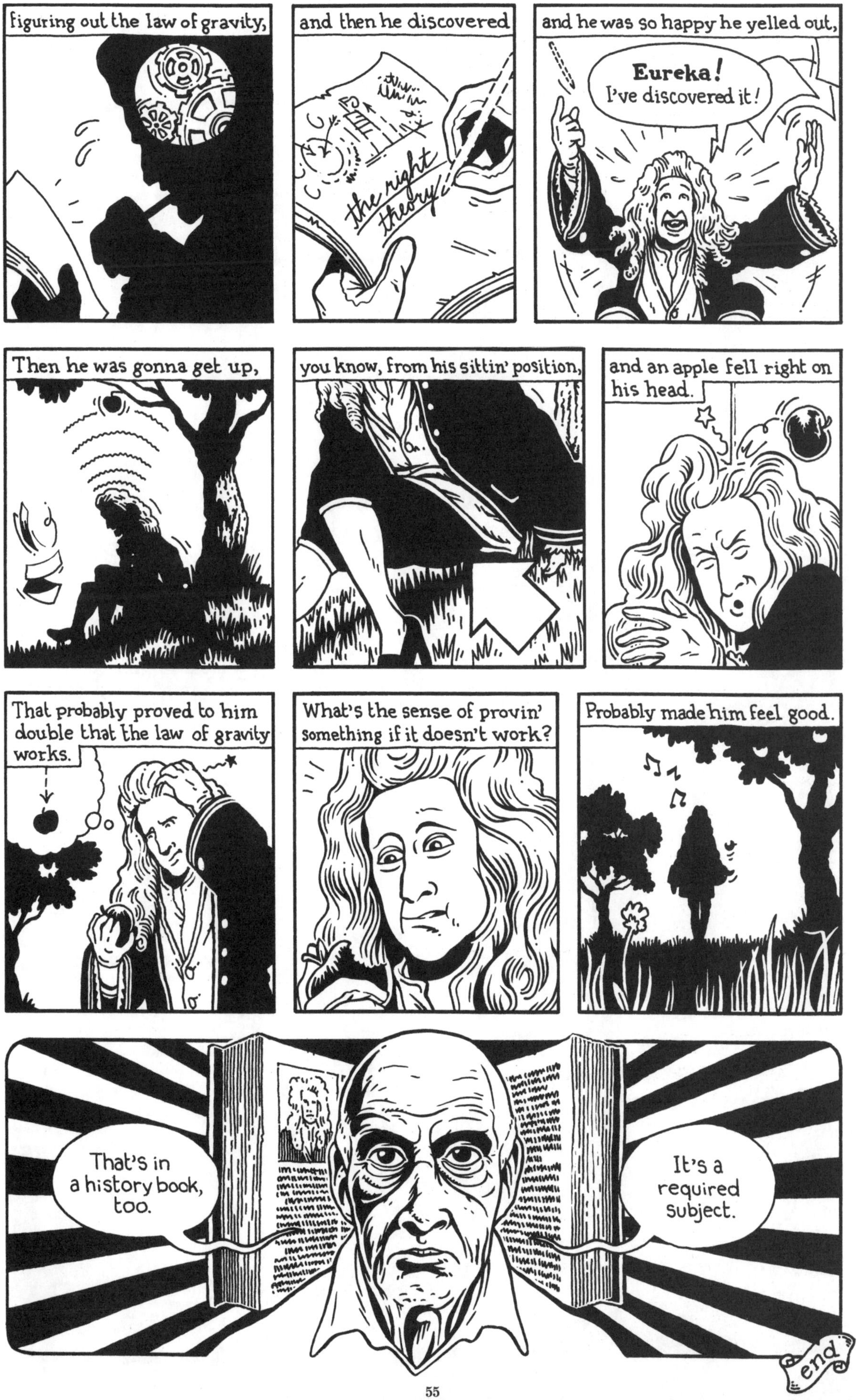
figuring out the law of gravity,
the right theory
and then he discovered
and he was so happy he yelled out,
Eureka! I've discovered it!
Then he was gonna get up,
you know, from his sittin' position,
and an apple fell right on his head.
That probably proved to him double that the law of gravity works.
What's the sense of provin' something if it doesn't work?
Probably made him feel good.
That's in a history book, too.
It's a required subject.
end

the Frankensteins of Bavaria

(as told to david greenberger by bill niemi then drawn by greg ruth)

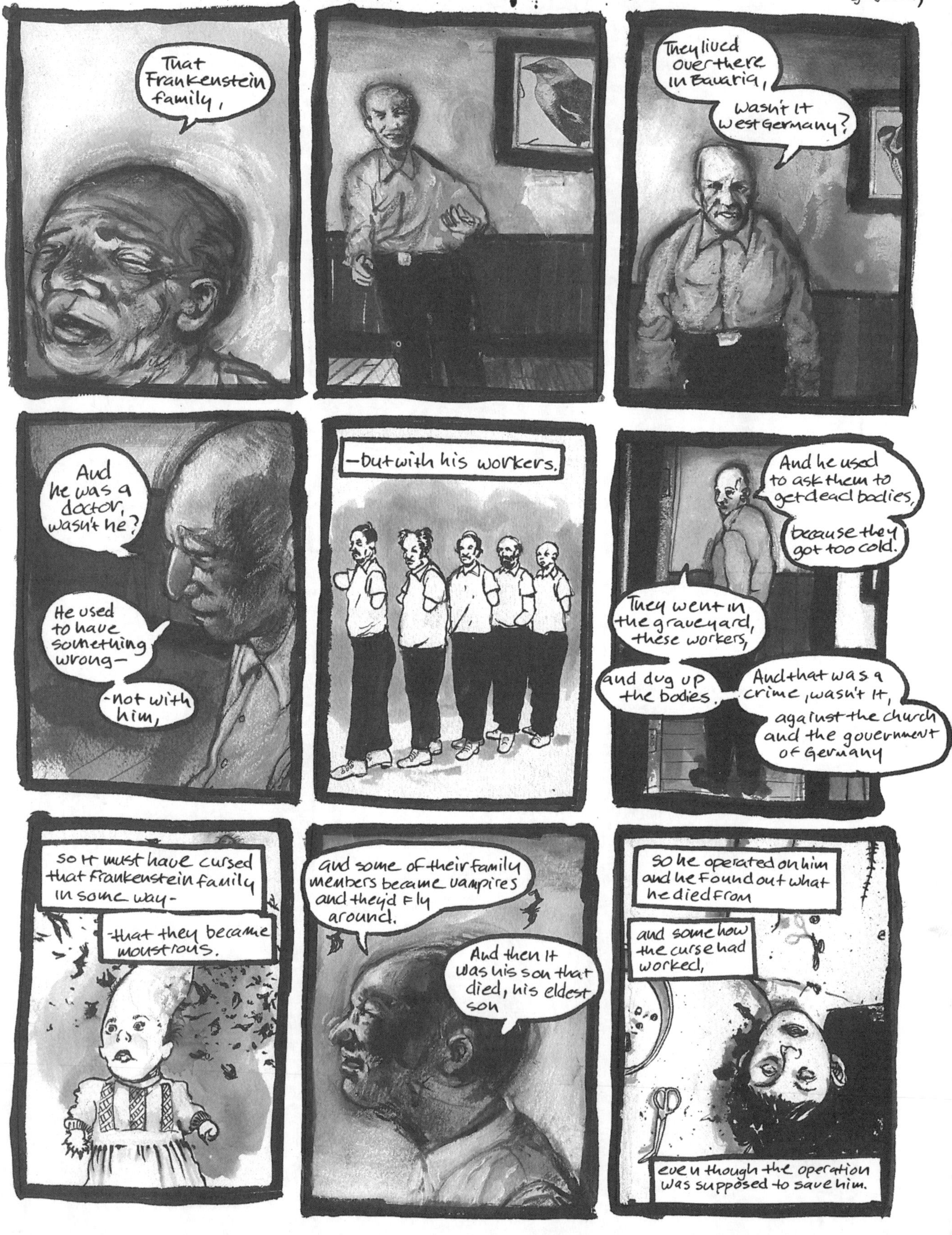

That Frankenstein family,
They lived over there in Bavaria,
wasn't it West Germany?
And he was a doctor, wasn't he?
He used to have something wrong—
-not with him,
—but with his workers.
And he used to ask them to get dead bodies,
because they got too cold.
They went in the graveyard, these workers,
and dug up the bodies.
And that was a crime, wasn't it,
against the church and the government of Germany
so it must have cursed that Frankenstein family in some way-
-that they became monstrous.
and some of their family members became vampires and they'd fly around.
And then it was his son that died, his eldest son
so he operated on him and he found out what he died from
and somehow the curse had worked,
even though the operation was supposed to save him.

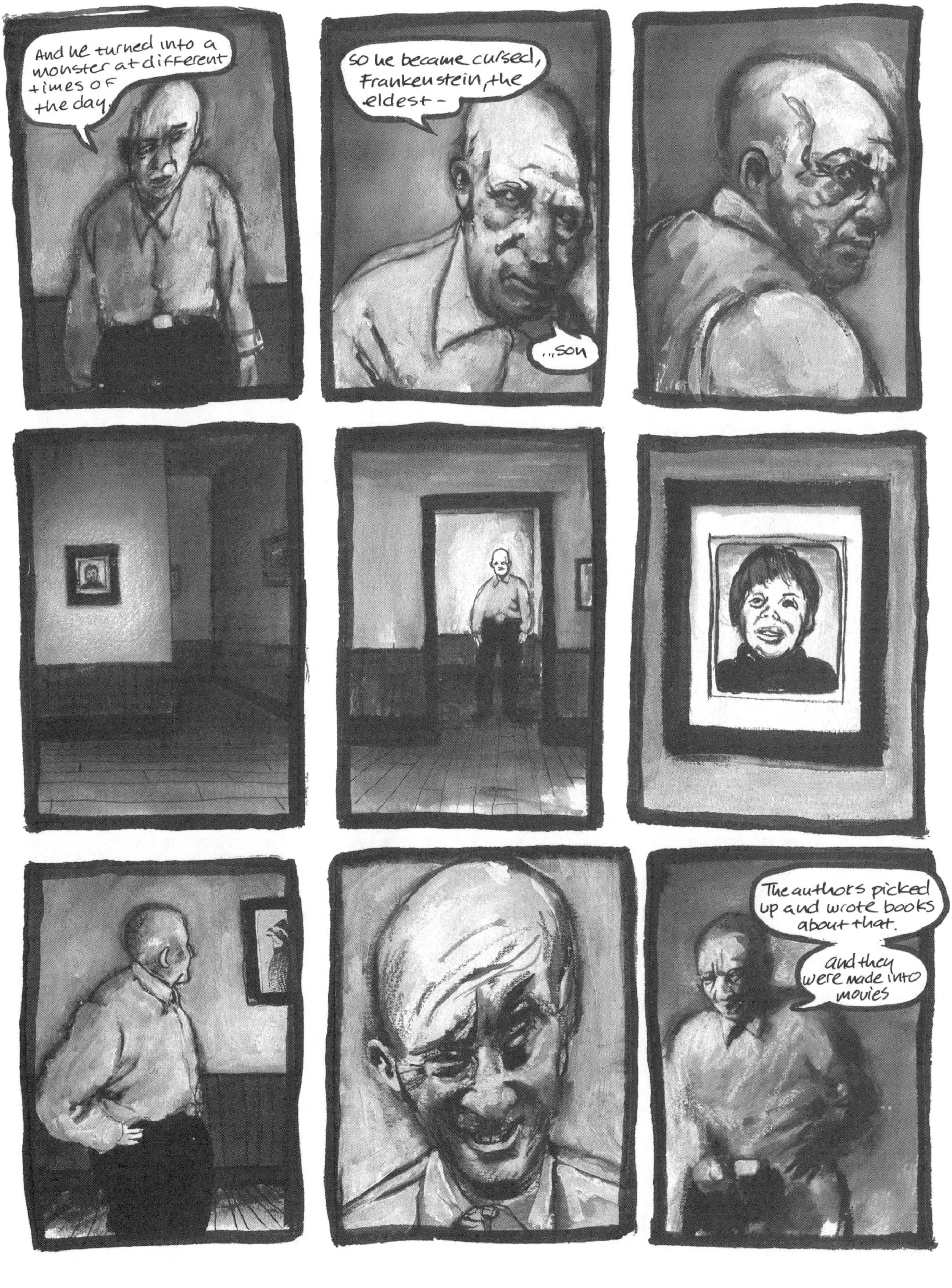
And he turned into a monster at different times of the day.
So he became cursed, Frankenstein, the eldest -
...son
The authors picked up and wrote books about that.
and they were made into movies

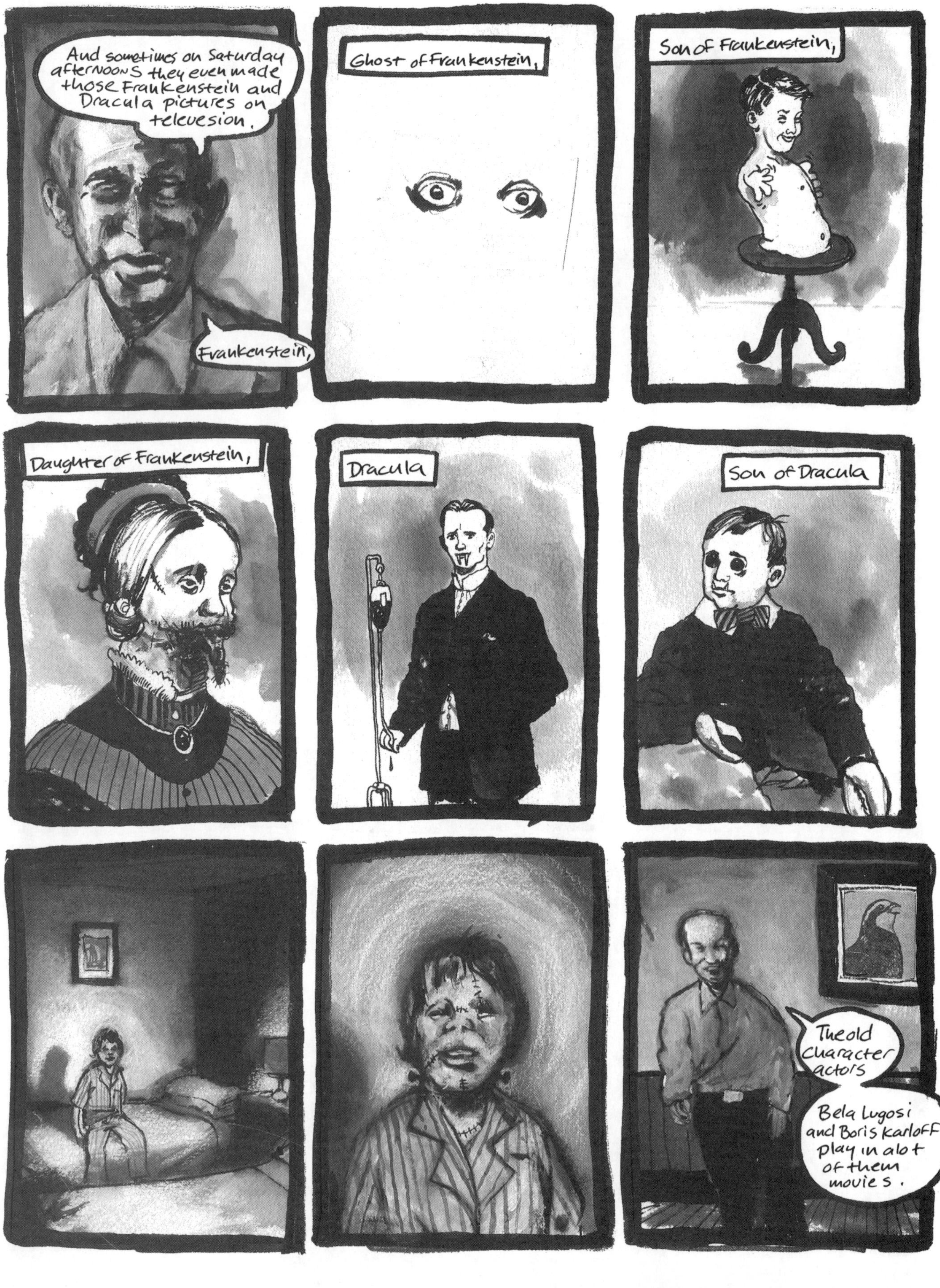
And sometimes on Saturday afternoons they even made those Frankenstein and Dracula pictures on televesion.
Frankenstein,
Ghost of Frankenstein,
Son of Frankenstein,
Daughter of Frankenstein,
Dracula
Son of Dracula
The old character actors
Bela Lugosi and Boris karloff play in alot of them movies.

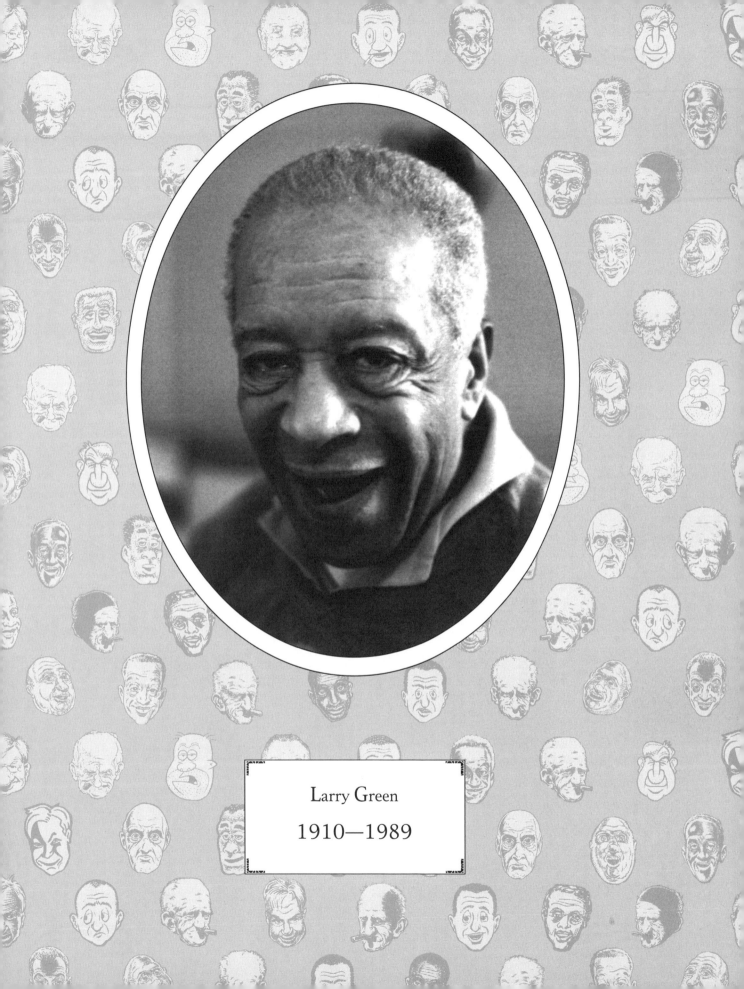

Larry Green

1910—1989

The Beatles were good singers. They're a good quartet. "Apple Blossom Time," "God Bless America" — Kate Smith sang that, she sang it way down yonder in New Orleans. I'll be seeing you in apple blossom time. You are my sunshine, my only sunshine. God bless America, land of the free, stand beside us and guide us — I forget all the words, I used to know them. "Apple Blossom time." "God Bless America."

◆

LARRY: Jesus, I'm glad to see you, Dave! What day is this?
DBG: Sunday.
LARRY: Sunday? Oh boy! Jesus, I'm glad to see you! I didn't know where the hell you was. Go swimmin'?
DBG: Yeah, last week.

◆

Robots are mechanical men. They walk around, they set the table and don't say nothin'. They bring you your underwear and they put you to bed. They take out a cigar and smoke cigars. They stand there and watch you. Mechanical men. Christ, they wash windows, shovel snow, give you a cigar, put out the lights, and then they wave good night.

◆

Guitars make good music. Banjo — plink, plink, plink. Guitars play at dances. Drink beer and wine, down at Pete's bar. Wake up with a big head. Guitar goes plink, plink, plinky, plink.

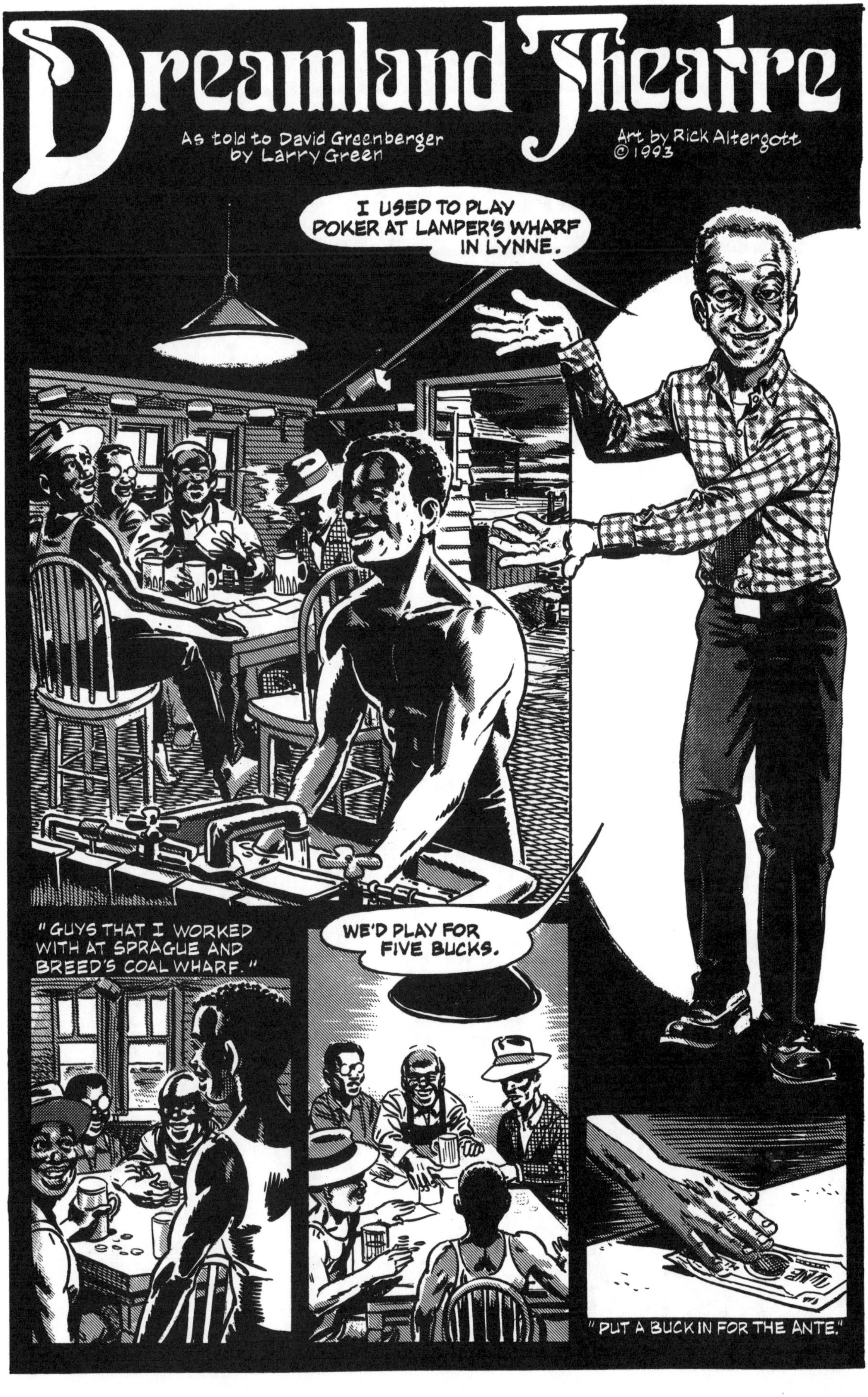

Dreamland Theatre
As told to David Greenberger by Larry Green
Art by Rick Altergott ©1993
I USED TO PLAY POKER AT LAMPER'S WHARF IN LYNNE.
"GUYS THAT I WORKED WITH AT SPRAGUE AND BREED'S COAL WHARF."
WE'D PLAY FOR FIVE BUCKS.
"PUT A BUCK IN FOR THE ANTE."

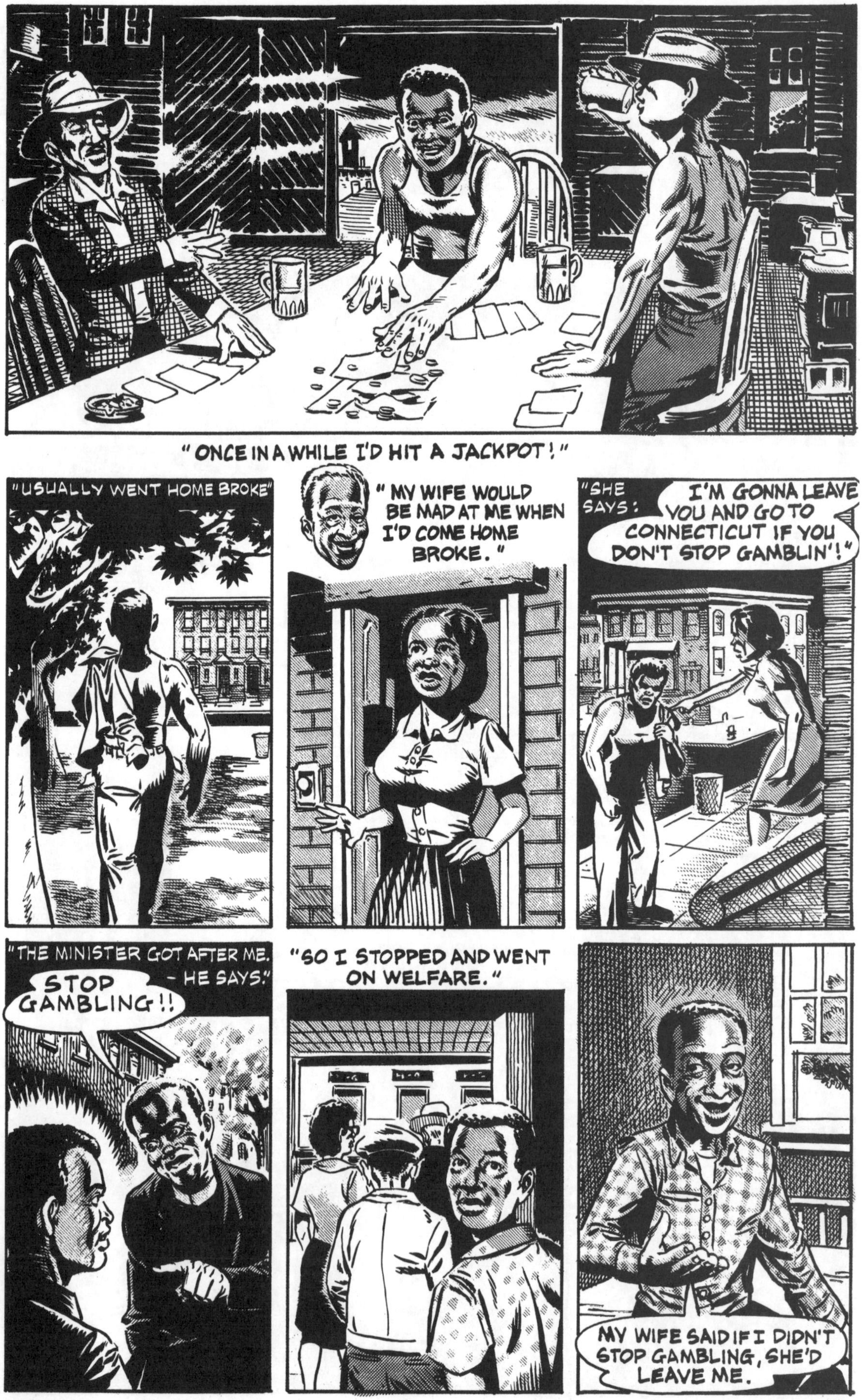
"ONCE IN A WHILE I'D HIT A JACKPOT!"
"USUALLY WENT HOME BROKE"
"MY WIFE WOULD BE MAD AT ME WHEN I'D COME HOME BROKE."
"SHE SAYS:
I'M GONNA LEAVE YOU AND GO TO CONNECTICUT IF YOU DON'T STOP GAMBLIN'!"
"THE MINISTER GOT AFTER ME. - HE SAYS:"
STOP GAMBLING!!
"SO I STOPPED AND WENT ON WELFARE."
MY WIFE SAID IF I DIDN'T STOP GAMBLING, SHE'D LEAVE ME.

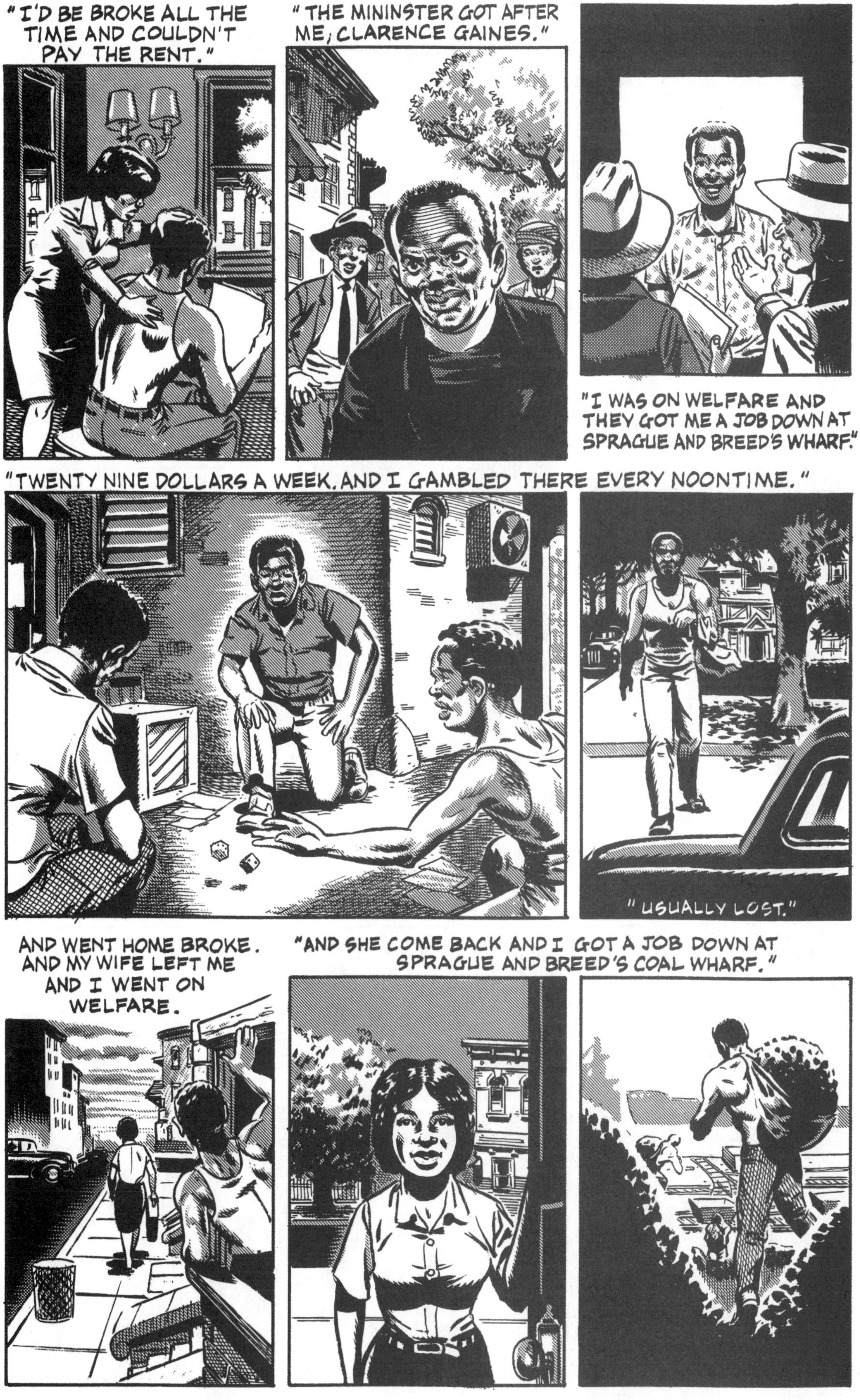
"I'D BE BROKE ALL THE TIME AND COULDN'T PAY THE RENT."
"THE MININSTER GOT AFTER ME; CLARENCE GAINES."
"I WAS ON WELFARE AND THEY GOT ME A JOB DOWN AT SPRAGUE AND BREED'S WHARF."
"TWENTY NINE DOLLARS A WEEK. AND I GAMBLED THERE EVERY NOONTIME."
"USUALLY LOST."
AND WENT HOME BROKE. AND MY WIFE LEFT ME AND I WENT ON WELFARE.
"AND SHE COME BACK AND I GOT A JOB DOWN AT SPRAGUE AND BREED'S COAL WHARF."

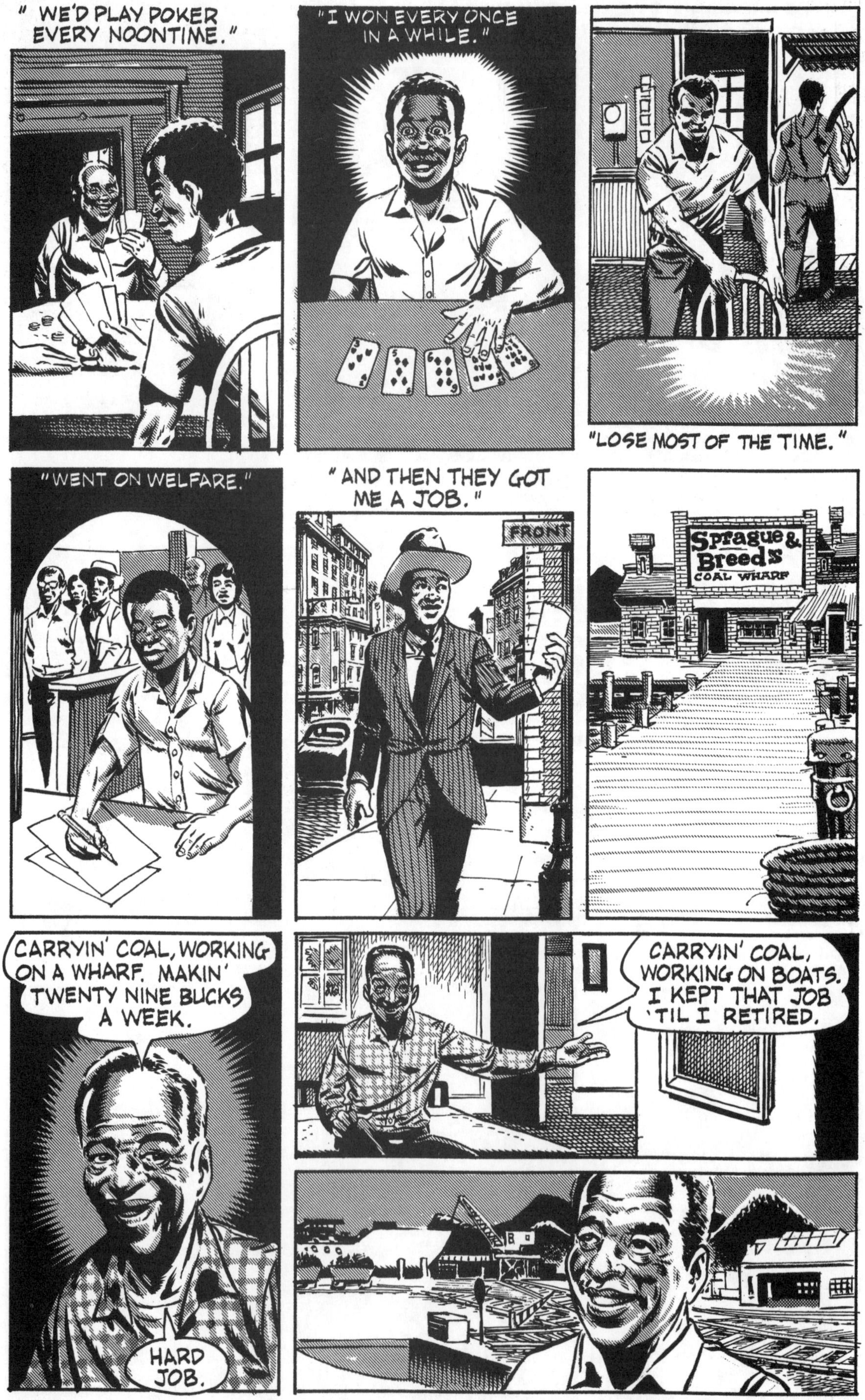
"WE'D PLAY POKER EVERY NOONTIME."
"I WON EVERY ONCE IN A WHILE."
"LOSE MOST OF THE TIME."
"WENT ON WELFARE."
"AND THEN THEY GOT ME A JOB."
FRONT
Sprague & Breed's COAL WHARF
CARRYIN' COAL, WORKING ON A WHARF. MAKIN' TWENTY NINE BUCKS A WEEK.
HARD JOB.
CARRYIN' COAL, WORKING ON BOATS. I KEPT THAT JOB 'TIL I RETIRED.

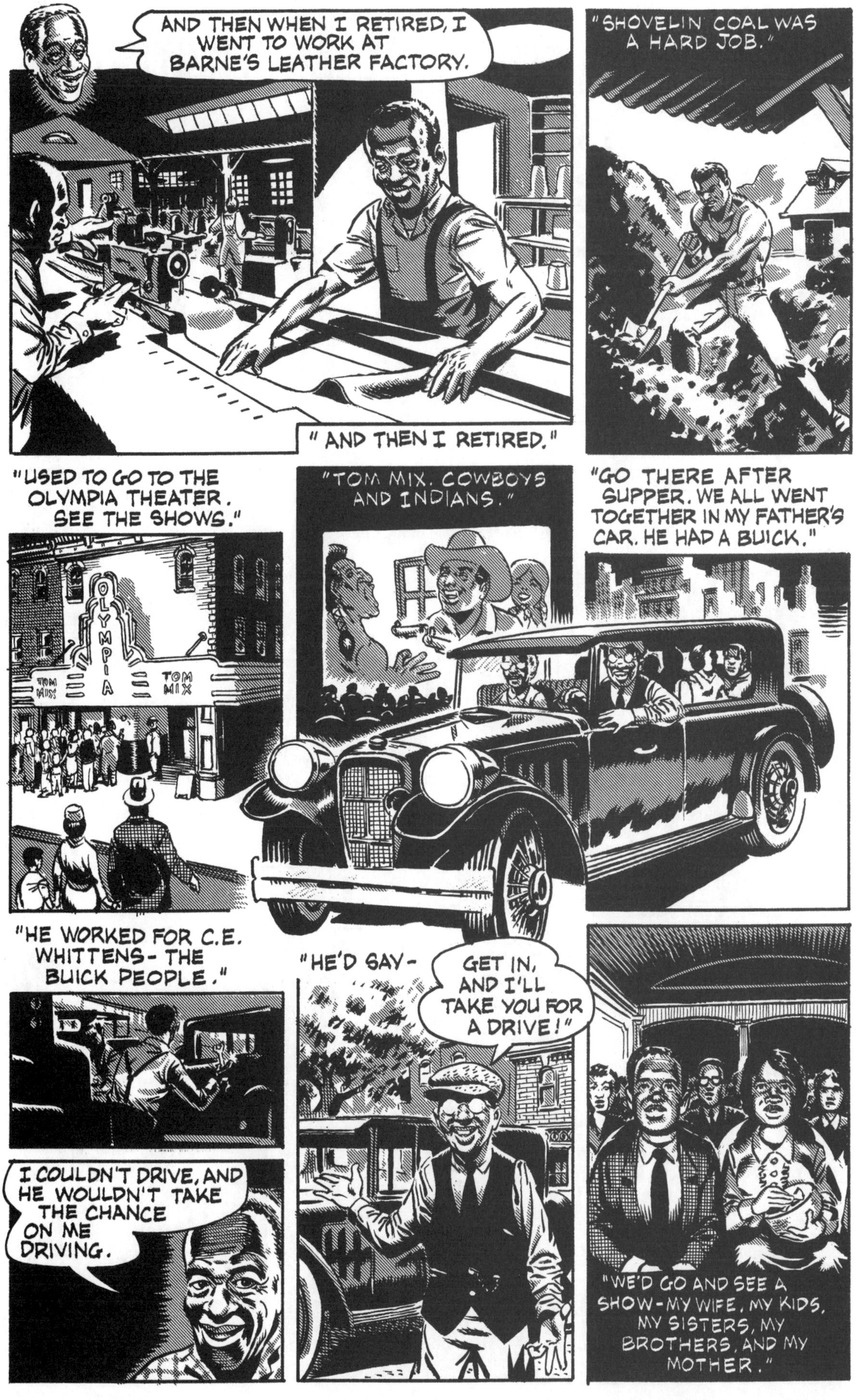
AND THEN WHEN I RETIRED, I WENT TO WORK AT BARNE'S LEATHER FACTORY.
" AND THEN I RETIRED."
"SHOVELIN' COAL WAS A HARD JOB."
"USED TO GO TO THE OLYMPIA THEATER. SEE THE SHOWS."
OLYMPIA
TOM MIX
TOM MIX
"TOM MIX. COWBOYS AND INDIANS."
"GO THERE AFTER SUPPER. WE ALL WENT TOGETHER IN MY FATHER'S CAR. HE HAD A BUICK."
"HE WORKED FOR C.E. WHITTENS- THE BUICK PEOPLE."
I COULDN'T DRIVE, AND HE WOULDN'T TAKE THE CHANCE ON ME DRIVING.
"HE'D SAY-
GET IN, AND I'LL TAKE YOU FOR A DRIVE!"
"WE'D GO AND SEE A SHOW-MY WIFE, MY KIDS, MY SISTERS, MY BROTHERS, AND MY MOTHER."

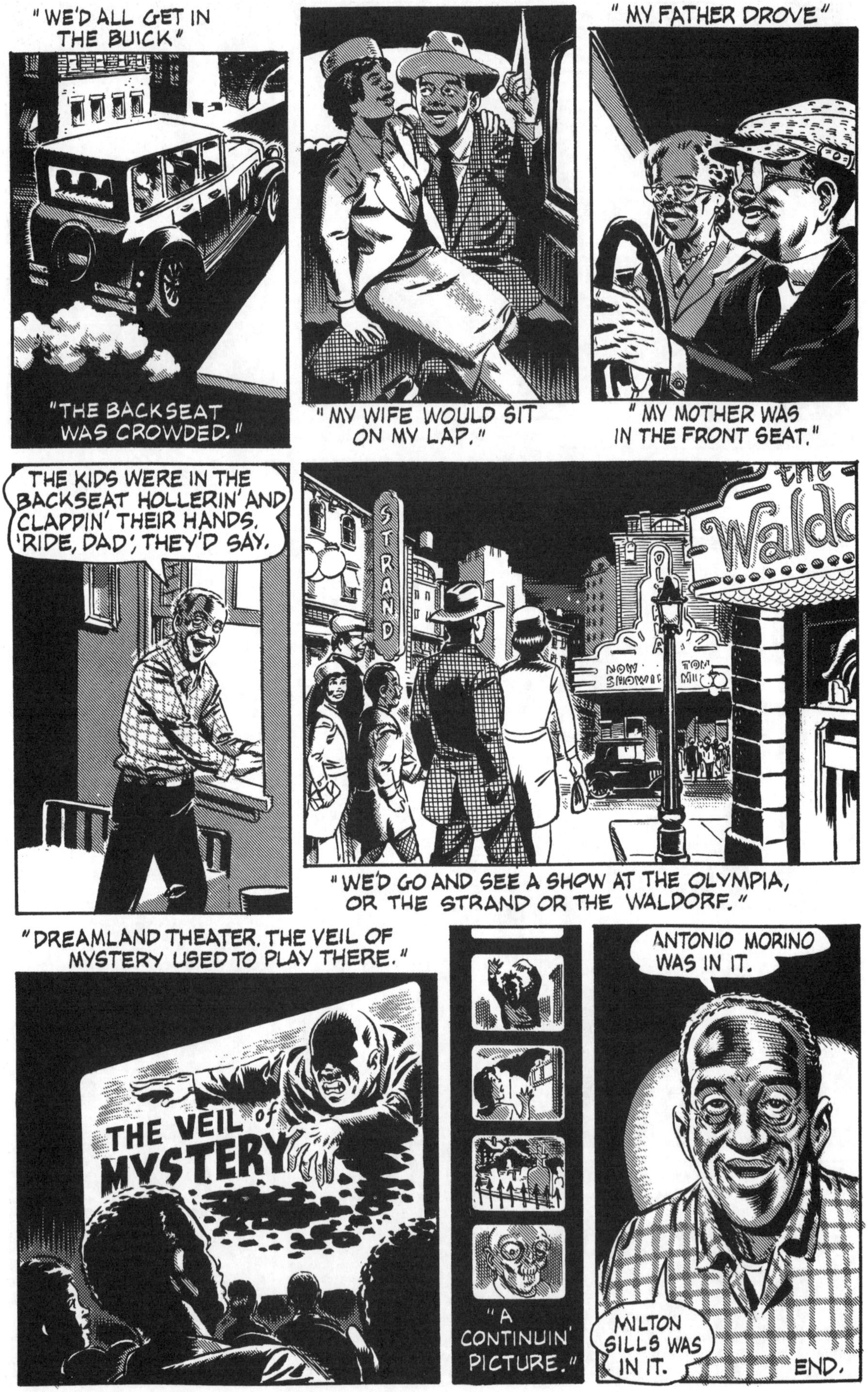
"WE'D ALL GET IN THE BUICK"
"THE BACKSEAT WAS CROWDED."
"MY WIFE WOULD SIT ON MY LAP."
"MY FATHER DROVE"
"MY MOTHER WAS IN THE FRONT SEAT."
THE KIDS WERE IN THE BACKSEAT HOLLERIN' AND CLAPPIN' THEIR HANDS. 'RIDE, DAD', THEY'D SAY.
STRAND
Waldo
NOW SHOWI
"WE'D GO AND SEE A SHOW AT THE OLYMPIA, OR THE STRAND OR THE WALDORF."
"DREAMLAND THEATER. THE VEIL OF MYSTERY USED TO PLAY THERE."
THE VEIL of MYSTERY
"A CONTINUIN' PICTURE."
ANTONIO MORINO WAS IN IT.
MILTON SILLS WAS IN IT.
END.

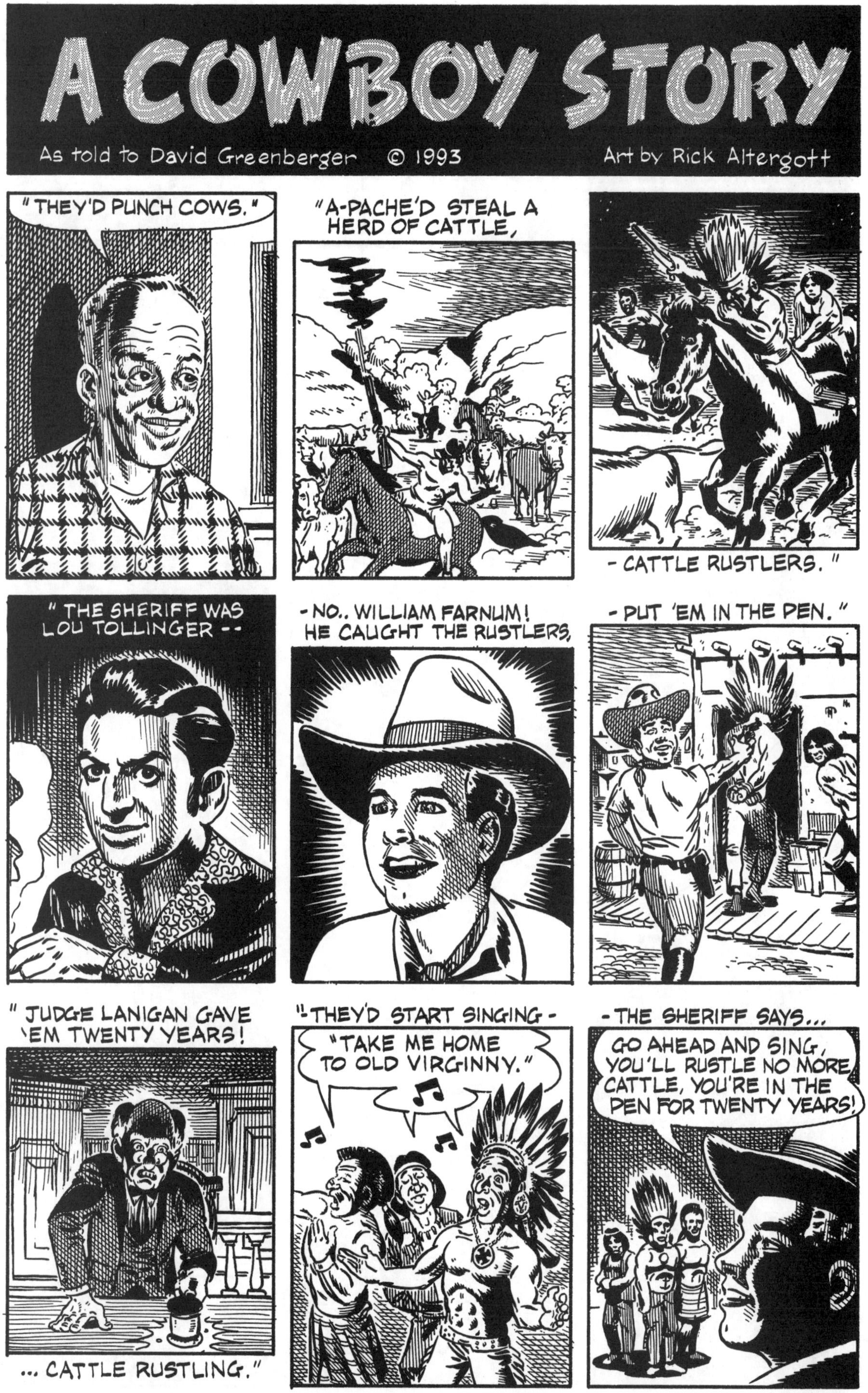
A COWBOY STORY
As told to David Greenberger © 1993
Art by Rick Altergott
"THEY'D PUNCH COWS."
"A-PACHE'D STEAL A HERD OF CATTLE,
- CATTLE RUSTLERS."
"THE SHERIFF WAS LOU TOLLINGER --
- NO.. WILLIAM FARNUM! HE CAUGHT THE RUSTLERS,
- PUT 'EM IN THE PEN."
"JUDGE LANIGAN GAVE 'EM TWENTY YEARS!
... CATTLE RUSTLING."
"- THEY'D START SINGING -
"TAKE ME HOME TO OLD VIRGINNY."
- THE SHERIFF SAYS...
GO AHEAD AND SING, YOU'LL RUSTLE NO MORE CATTLE, YOU'RE IN THE PEN FOR TWENTY YEARS!

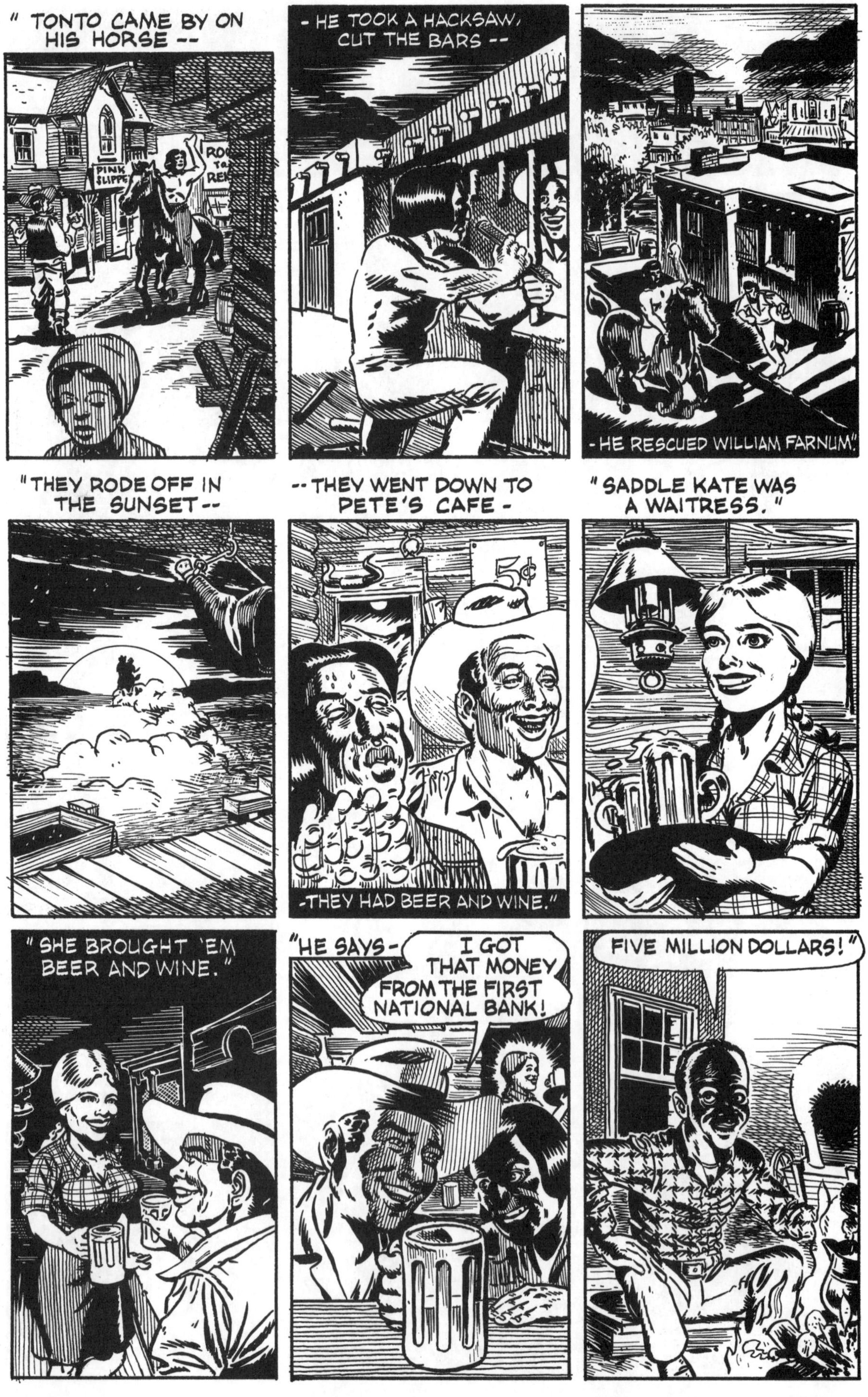
" TONTO CAME BY ON HIS HORSE --
PINK SLIPPE
- HE TOOK A HACKSAW, CUT THE BARS --
- HE RESCUED WILLIAM FARNUM."
"THEY RODE OFF IN THE SUNSET --
-- THEY WENT DOWN TO PETE'S CAFE -
5¢
-THEY HAD BEER AND WINE."
" SADDLE KATE WAS A WAITRESS. "
" SHE BROUGHT 'EM BEER AND WINE. "
"HE SAYS -
I GOT THAT MONEY FROM THE FIRST NATIONAL BANK!
FIVE MILLION DOLLARS!"

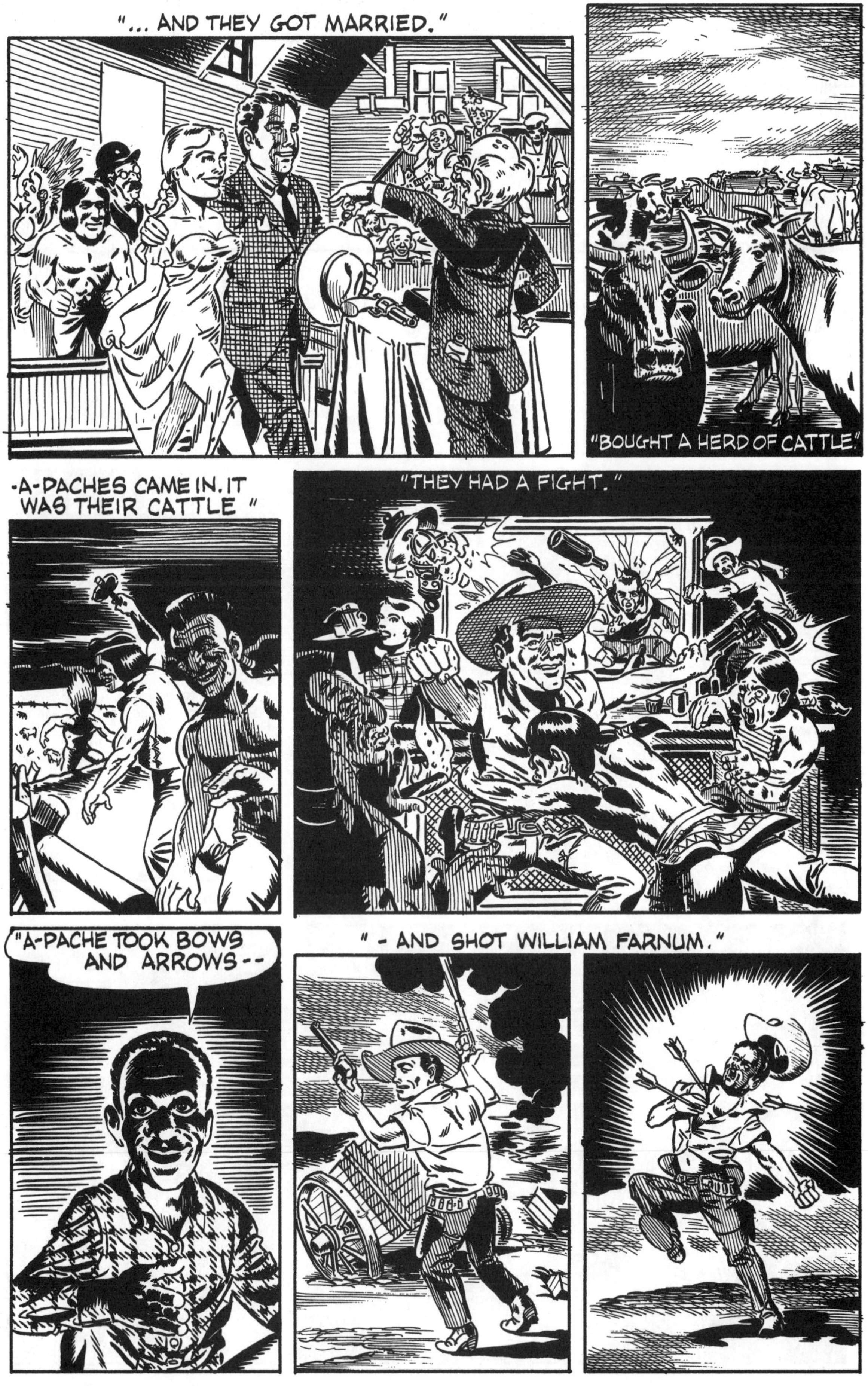
"... AND THEY GOT MARRIED."
"BOUGHT A HERD OF CATTLE."
-A-PACHES CAME IN. IT WAS THEIR CATTLE "
"THEY HAD A FIGHT."
"A-PACHE TOOK BOWS AND ARROWS --
" - AND SHOT WILLIAM FARNUM."

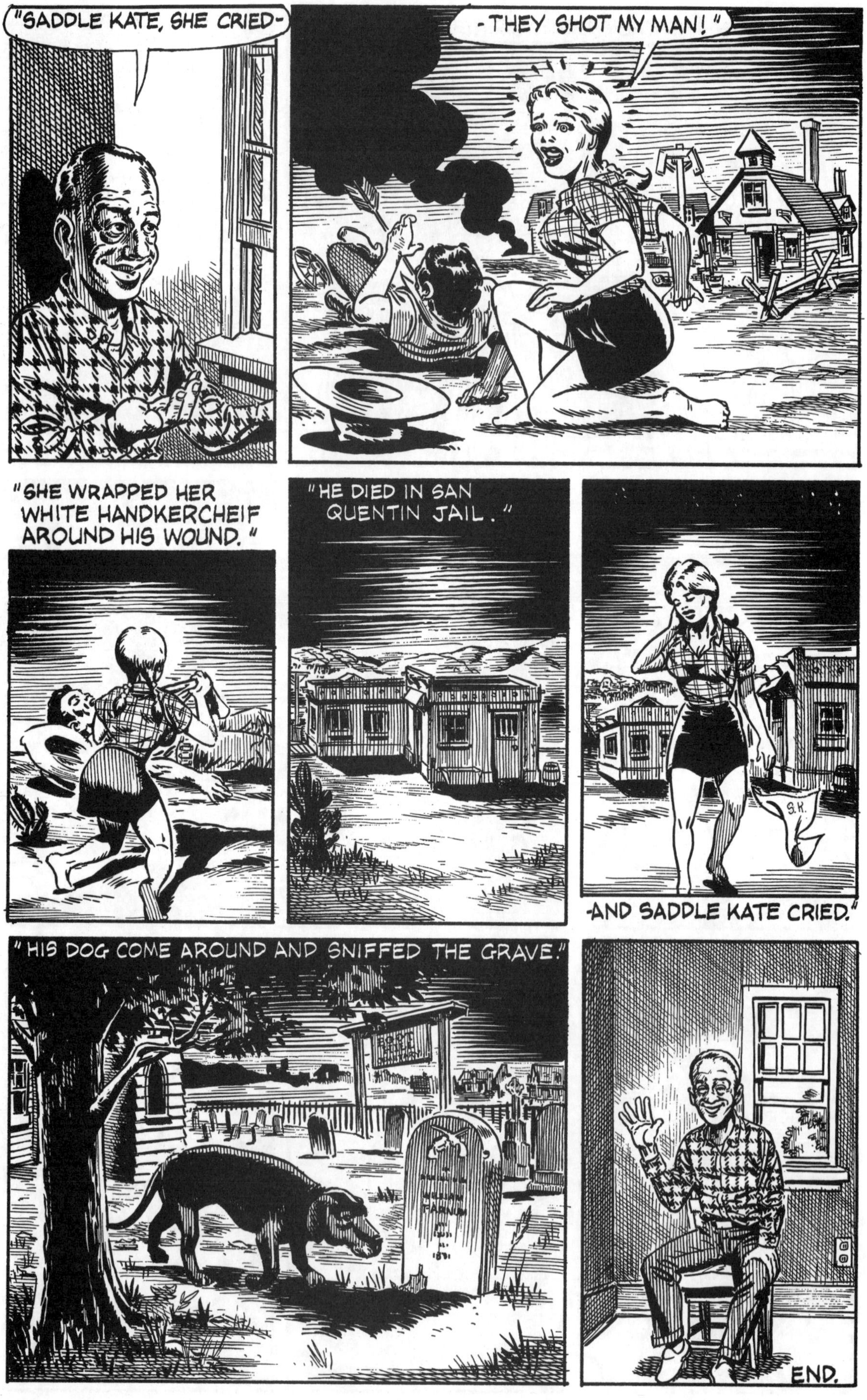

"SADDLE KATE, SHE CRIED-
-THEY SHOT MY MAN!"
"SHE WRAPPED HER WHITE HANDKERCHEIF AROUND HIS WOUND."
"HE DIED IN SAN QUENTIN JAIL."
S.K.
-AND SADDLE KATE CRIED."
"HIS DOG COME AROUND AND SNIFFED THE GRAVE."
END.

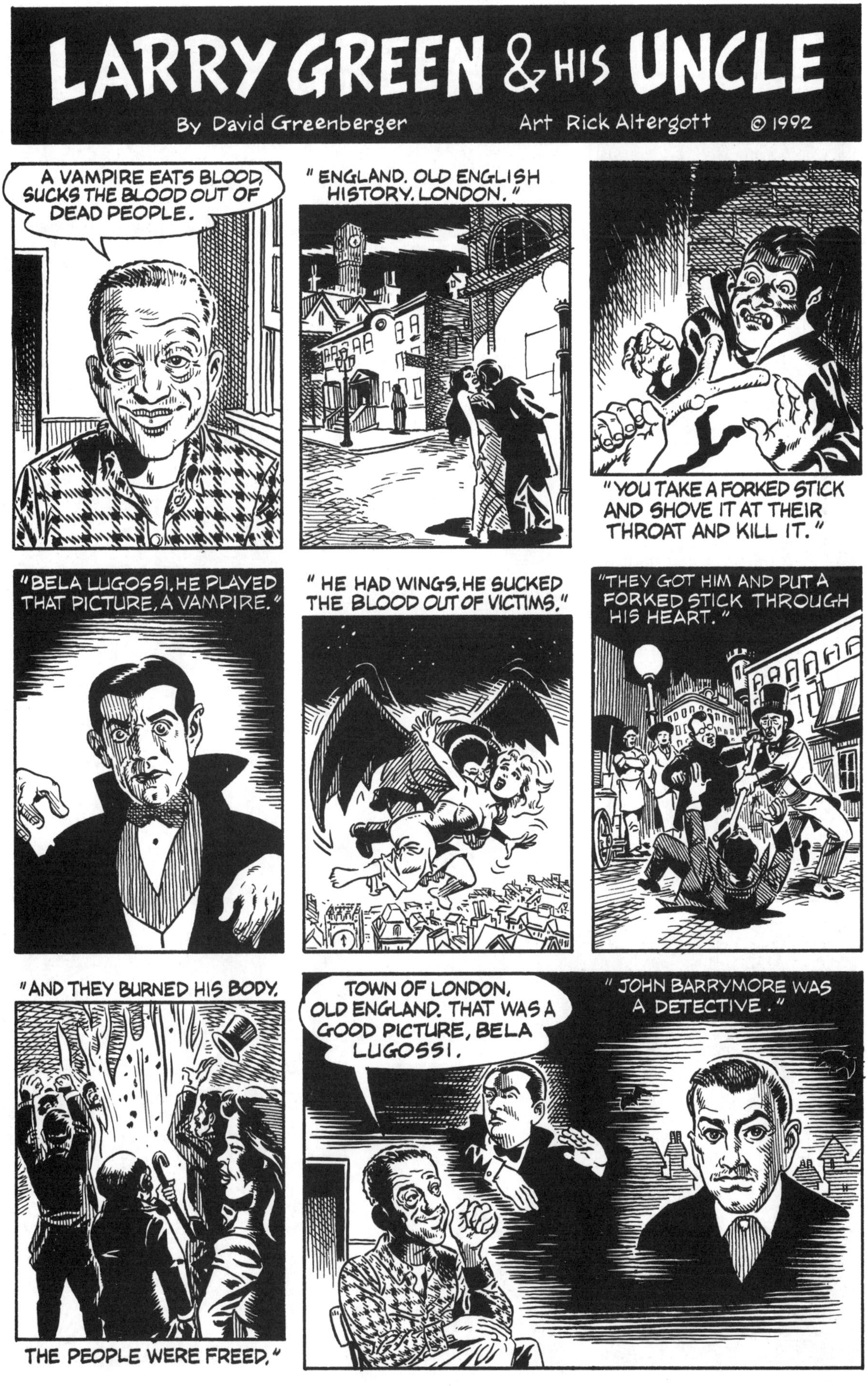
LARRY GREEN & HIS UNCLE
By David Greenberger
Art Rick Altergott
© 1992
A VAMPIRE EATS BLOOD, SUCKS THE BLOOD OUT OF DEAD PEOPLE.
" ENGLAND. OLD ENGLISH HISTORY. LONDON. "
"YOU TAKE A FORKED STICK AND SHOVE IT AT THEIR THROAT AND KILL IT."
"BELA LUGOSSI. HE PLAYED THAT PICTURE, A VAMPIRE."
" HE HAD WINGS. HE SUCKED THE BLOOD OUT OF VICTIMS."
"THEY GOT HIM AND PUT A FORKED STICK THROUGH HIS HEART."
"AND THEY BURNED HIS BODY.
THE PEOPLE WERE FREED."
TOWN OF LONDON, OLD ENGLAND. THAT WAS A GOOD PICTURE, BELA LUGOSSI.
" JOHN BARRYMORE WAS A DETECTIVE."

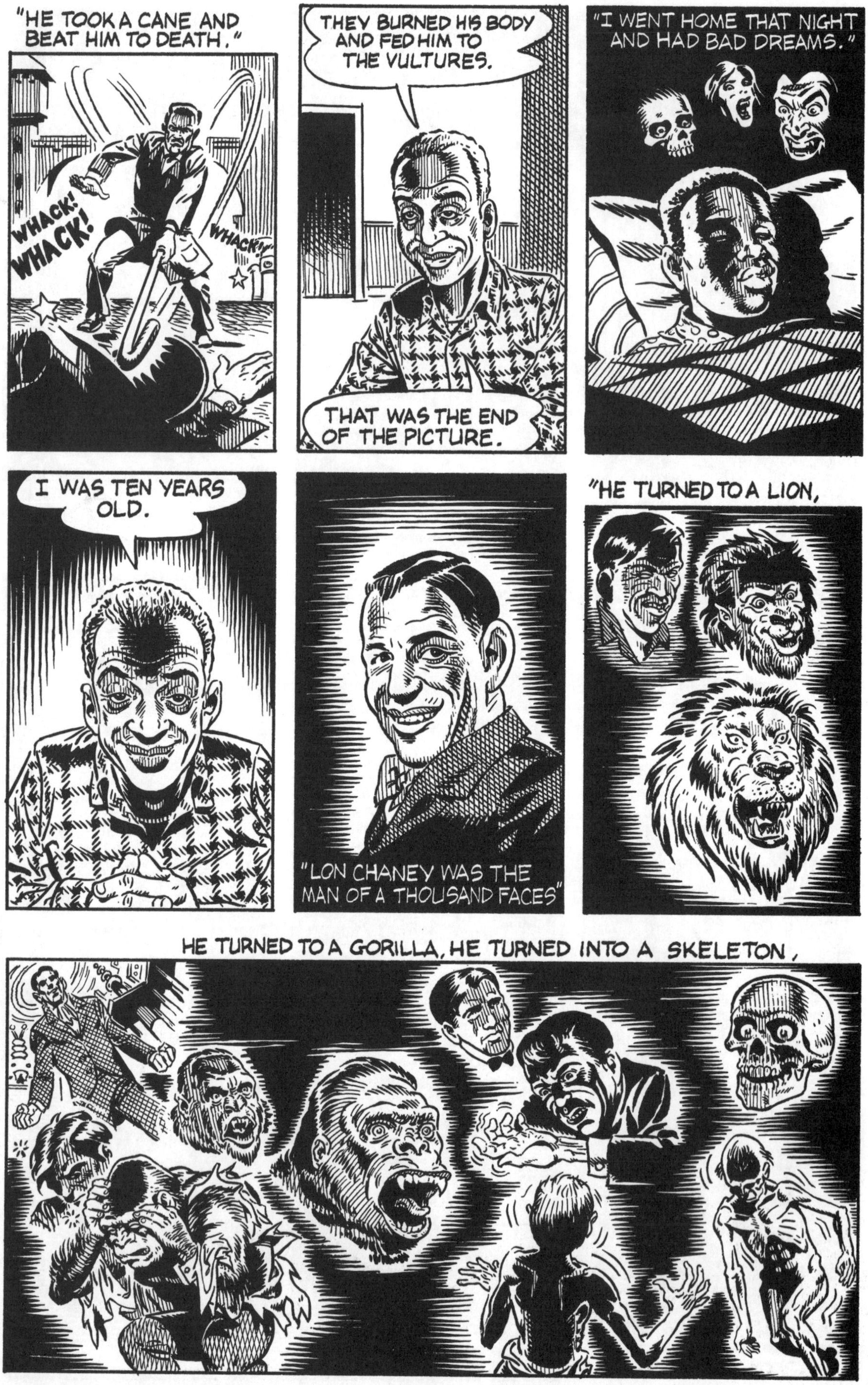
"HE TOOK A CANE AND BEAT HIM TO DEATH."
WHACK! WHACK!
WHACK!
THEY BURNED HIS BODY AND FED HIM TO THE VULTURES.
THAT WAS THE END OF THE PICTURE.
"I WENT HOME THAT NIGHT AND HAD BAD DREAMS."
I WAS TEN YEARS OLD.
"LON CHANEY WAS THE MAN OF A THOUSAND FACES"
"HE TURNED TO A LION,
HE TURNED TO A GORILLA, HE TURNED INTO A SKELETON,

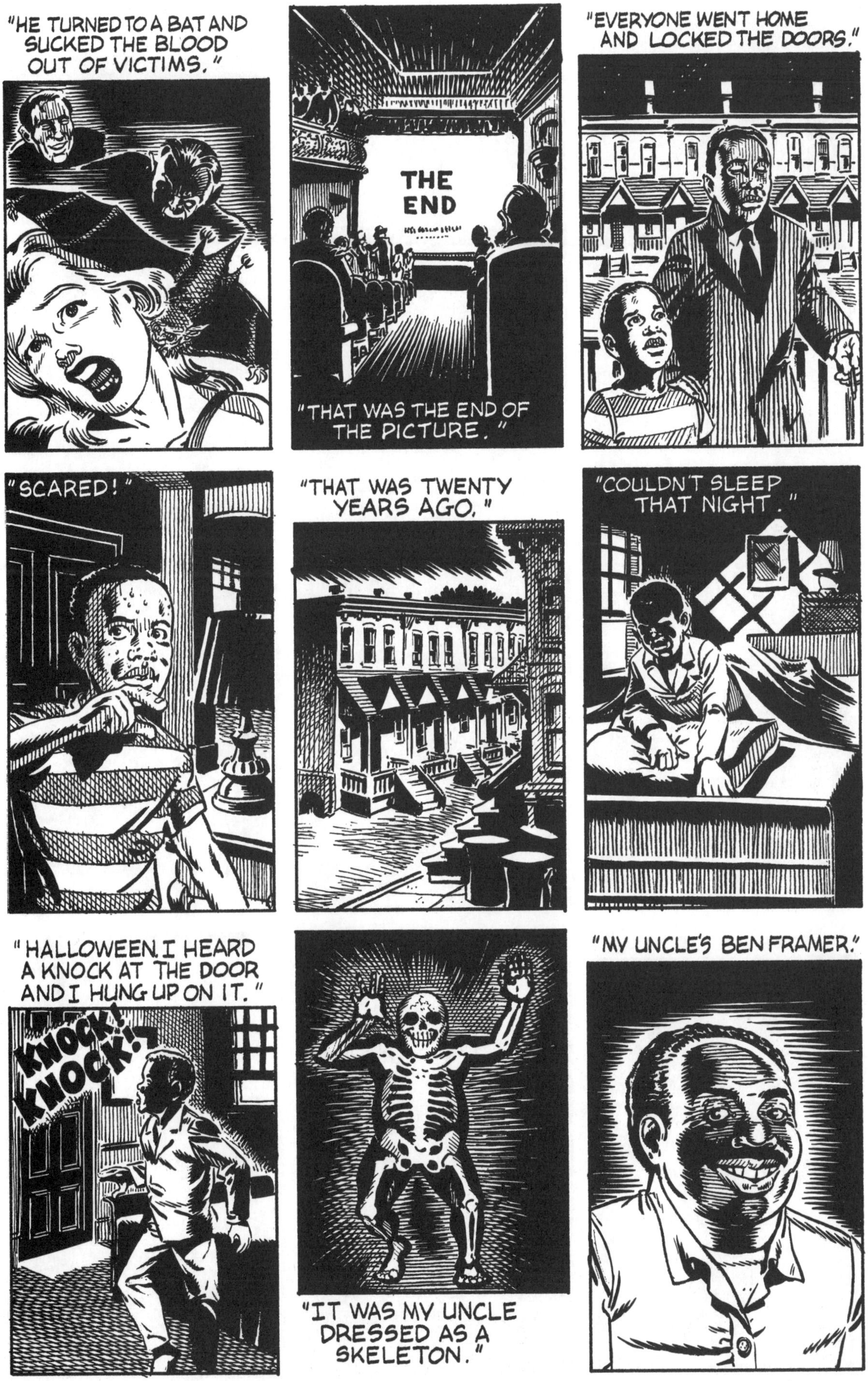
"HE TURNED TO A BAT AND SUCKED THE BLOOD OUT OF VICTIMS."
THE END
"THAT WAS THE END OF THE PICTURE."
"EVERYONE WENT HOME AND LOCKED THE DOORS."
"SCARED!"
"THAT WAS TWENTY YEARS AGO."
"COULDN'T SLEEP THAT NIGHT."
"HALLOWEEN. I HEARD A KNOCK AT THE DOOR AND I HUNG UP ON IT."
KNOCK! KNOCK!
"IT WAS MY UNCLE DRESSED AS A SKELETON."
"MY UNCLE'S BEN FRAMER."

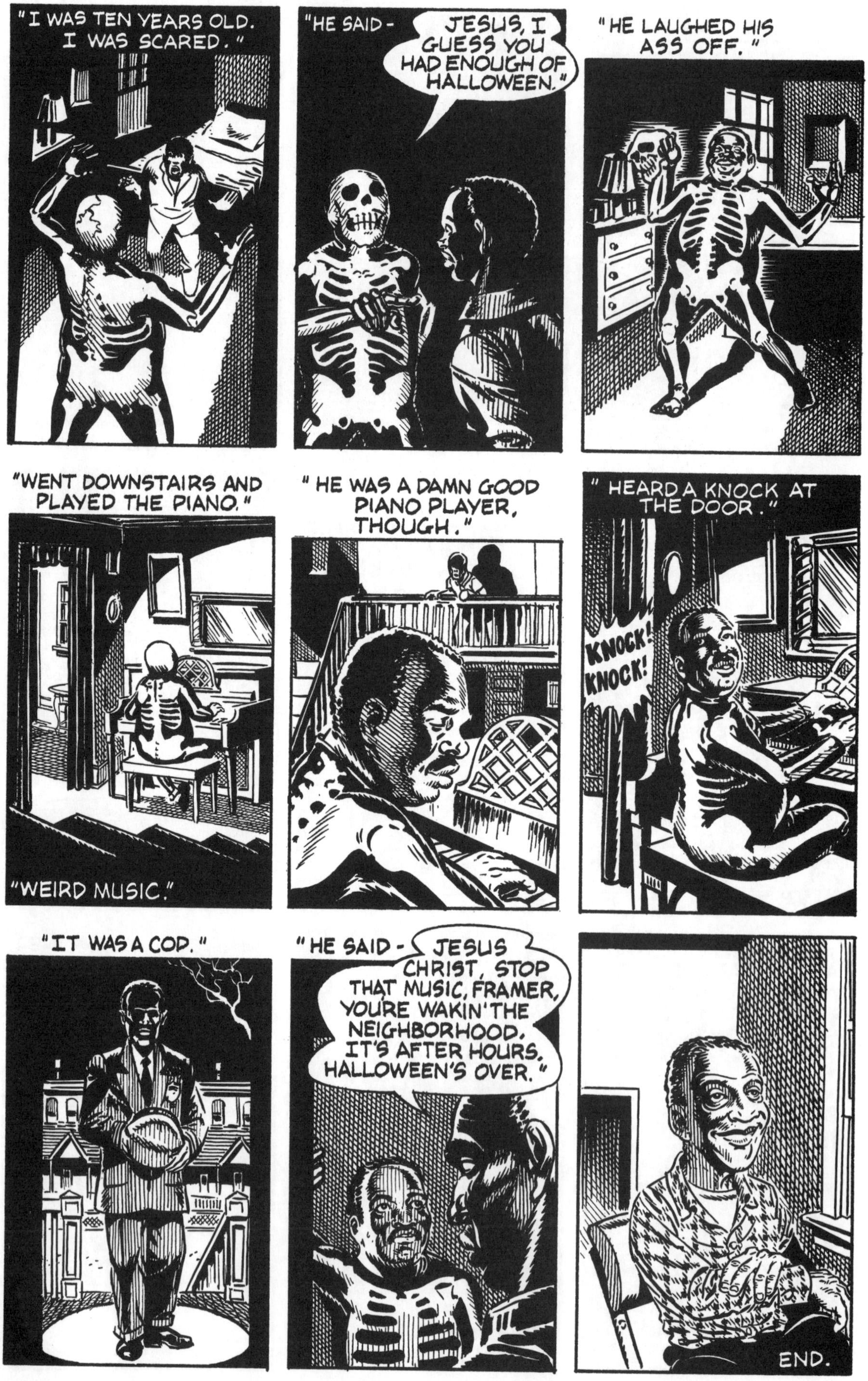
"I WAS TEN YEARS OLD. I WAS SCARED."
"HE SAID -
JESUS, I GUESS YOU HAD ENOUGH OF HALLOWEEN."
"HE LAUGHED HIS ASS OFF."
"WENT DOWNSTAIRS AND PLAYED THE PIANO."
"WEIRD MUSIC."
"HE WAS A DAMN GOOD PIANO PLAYER, THOUGH."
"HEARD A KNOCK AT THE DOOR."
KNOCK! KNOCK!
"IT WAS A COP."
"HE SAID -
JESUS CHRIST, STOP THAT MUSIC, FRAMER, YOURE WAKIN' THE NEIGHBORHOOD. IT'S AFTER HOURS. HALLOWEEN'S OVER."
END.

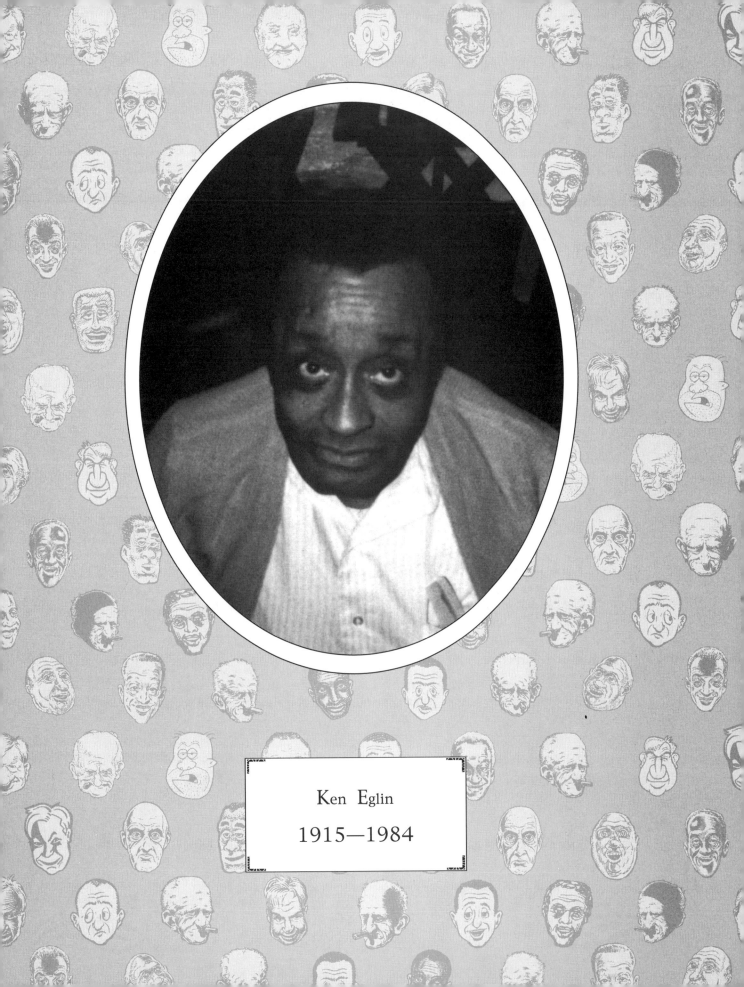

Ken Eglin

1915—1984

I may be lyin' in my bed or sittin' in my wheelchair, but I've got my opinion of what I feel, in my heart.

◆

You can't pull the eyes over mama, mama knows everything. That's what they're here for.

◆

Mars will probably be a state someday.

◆

I've always been against lettuce for a long, long time — even before I lost my teeth.

◆

You ever hear that saying, "Elephants never forget"? Well it's a lot of shit! Elephants forget the same as everyone else.

◆

There's two words I don't know how to spell: job and work. Run — I know how to spell that! (*laughs*) And the cops know it!

◆

You ever seen a mackerel fish when it's cooked? I hate it. I've got to get five blocks away from it. I don't like no fish, period. No. My mother would send my brother to the fish market, but not me. I'd take a walk down by the Charles River and stay by myself.

◆

Don't you be wearin' a tie in front of me! Of course, if you go to some clubs you have to wear one, but you can wear a bow and pull it right off — except in front of a lady.

◆

It took Elrey Presley to wake up the United States.

◆

I always say "so long," I never say "goodbye." Why? I'll see you again.

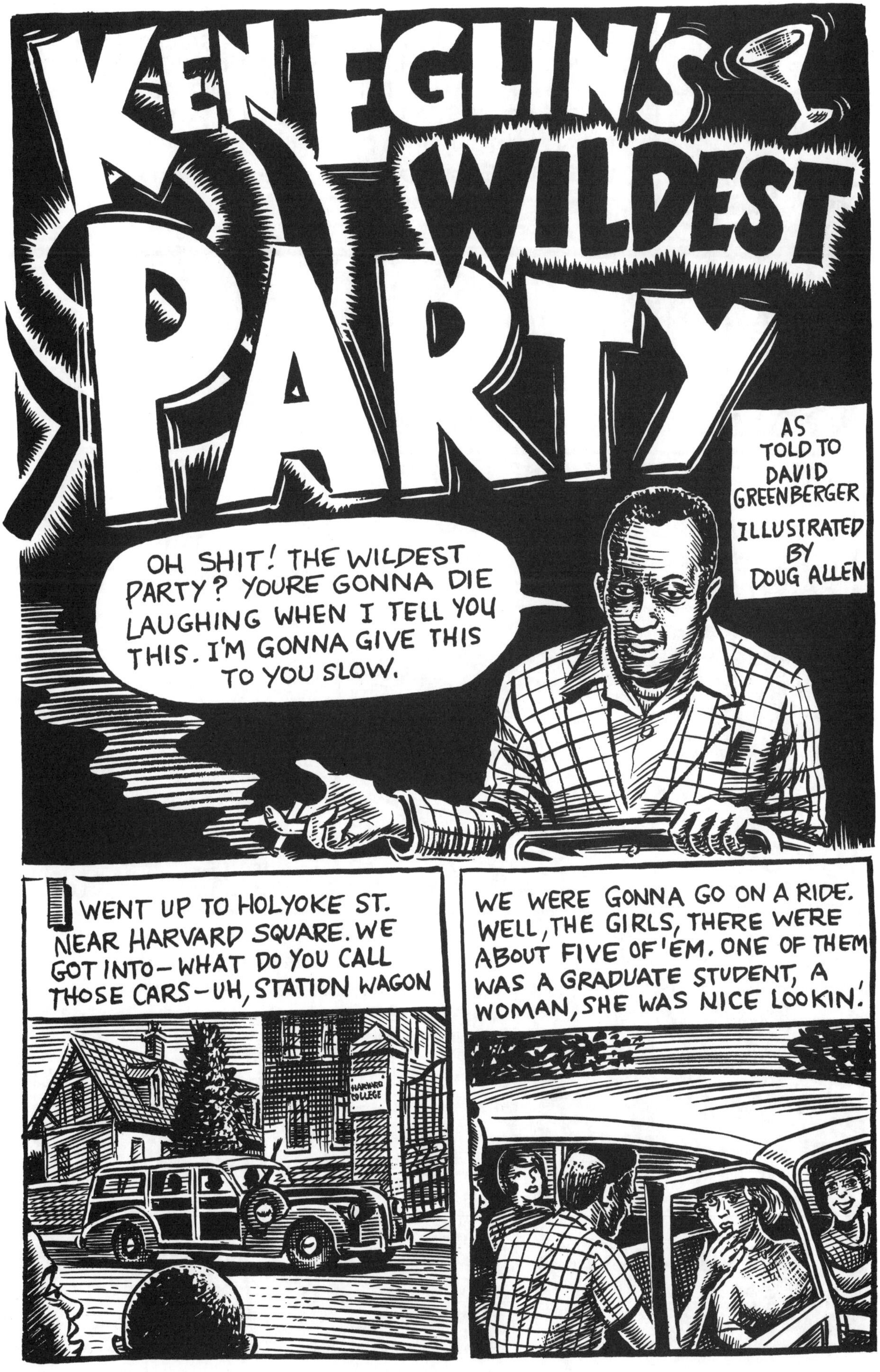
KEN EGLIN'S WILDEST PARTY
AS TOLD TO DAVID GREENBERGER
ILLUSTRATED BY DOUG ALLEN
OH SHIT! THE WILDEST PARTY? YOURE GONNA DIE LAUGHING WHEN I TELL YOU THIS. I'M GONNA GIVE THIS TO YOU SLOW.
I WENT UP TO HOLYOKE ST. NEAR HARVARD SQUARE. WE GOT INTO- WHAT DO YOU CALL THOSE CARS-UH, STATION WAGON
HARVARD COLLEGE
WE WERE GONNA GO ON A RIDE. WELL, THE GIRLS, THERE WERE ABOUT FIVE OF 'EM. ONE OF THEM WAS A GRADUATE STUDENT, A WOMAN, SHE WAS NICE LOOKIN'.

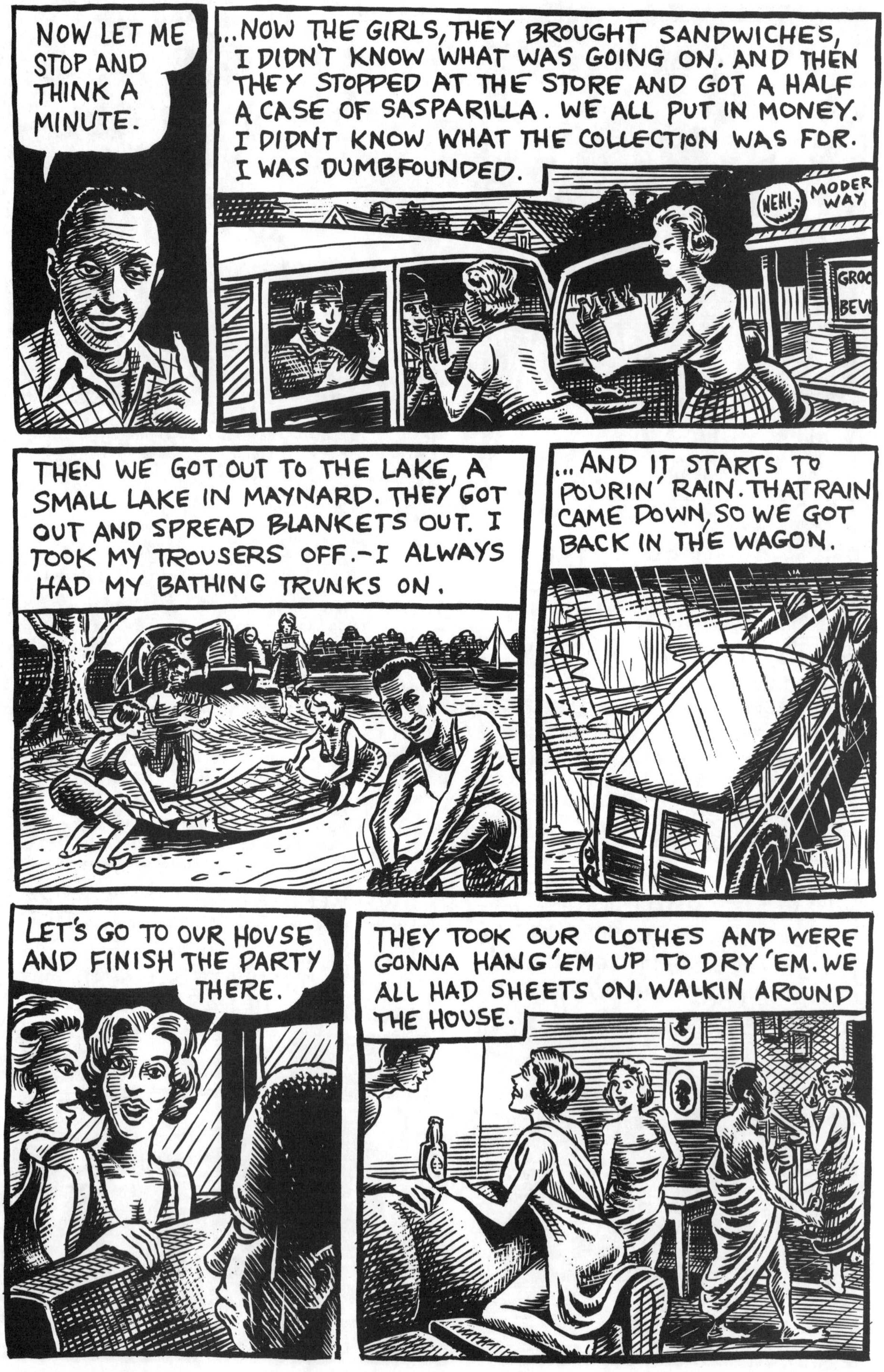
NOW LET ME STOP AND THINK A MINUTE.
...NOW THE GIRLS, THEY BROUGHT SANDWICHES, I DIDN'T KNOW WHAT WAS GOING ON. AND THEN THEY STOPPED AT THE STORE AND GOT A HALF A CASE OF SASPARILLA. WE ALL PUT IN MONEY. I DIDN'T KNOW WHAT THE COLLECTION WAS FOR. I WAS DUMBFOUNDED.
NEHI
MODER WAY
GROC
BEV
THEN WE GOT OUT TO THE LAKE, A SMALL LAKE IN MAYNARD. THEY GOT OUT AND SPREAD BLANKETS OUT. I TOOK MY TROUSERS OFF.–I ALWAYS HAD MY BATHING TRUNKS ON.
...AND IT STARTS TO POURIN' RAIN. THAT RAIN CAME DOWN, SO WE GOT BACK IN THE WAGON.
LET'S GO TO OUR HOUSE AND FINISH THE PARTY THERE.
THEY TOOK OUR CLOTHES AND WERE GONNA HANG'EM UP TO DRY 'EM. WE ALL HAD SHEETS ON. WALKIN AROUND THE HOUSE.

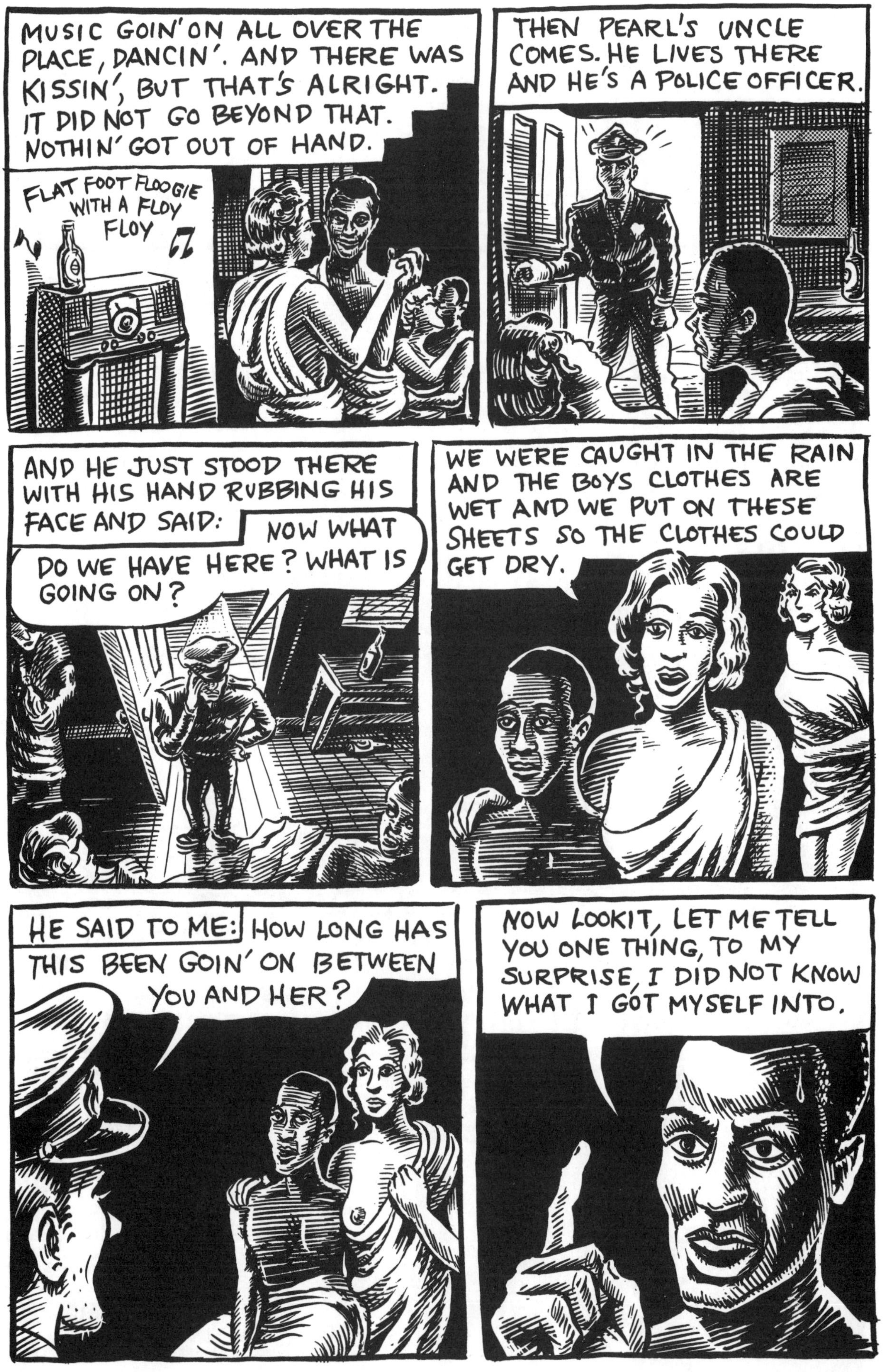
MUSIC GOIN' ON ALL OVER THE PLACE, DANCIN'. AND THERE WAS KISSIN', BUT THAT'S ALRIGHT. IT DID NOT GO BEYOND THAT. NOTHIN' GOT OUT OF HAND.
FLAT FOOT FLOOGIE WITH A FLOY FLOY
THEN PEARL'S UNCLE COMES. HE LIVES THERE AND HE'S A POLICE OFFICER.
AND HE JUST STOOD THERE WITH HIS HAND RUBBING HIS FACE AND SAID:
NOW WHAT DO WE HAVE HERE? WHAT IS GOING ON?
WE WERE CAUGHT IN THE RAIN AND THE BOYS CLOTHES ARE WET AND WE PUT ON THESE SHEETS SO THE CLOTHES COULD GET DRY.
HE SAID TO ME:
HOW LONG HAS THIS BEEN GOIN' ON BETWEEN YOU AND HER?
NOW LOOKIT, LET ME TELL YOU ONE THING, TO MY SURPRISE, I DID NOT KNOW WHAT I GOT MYSELF INTO.

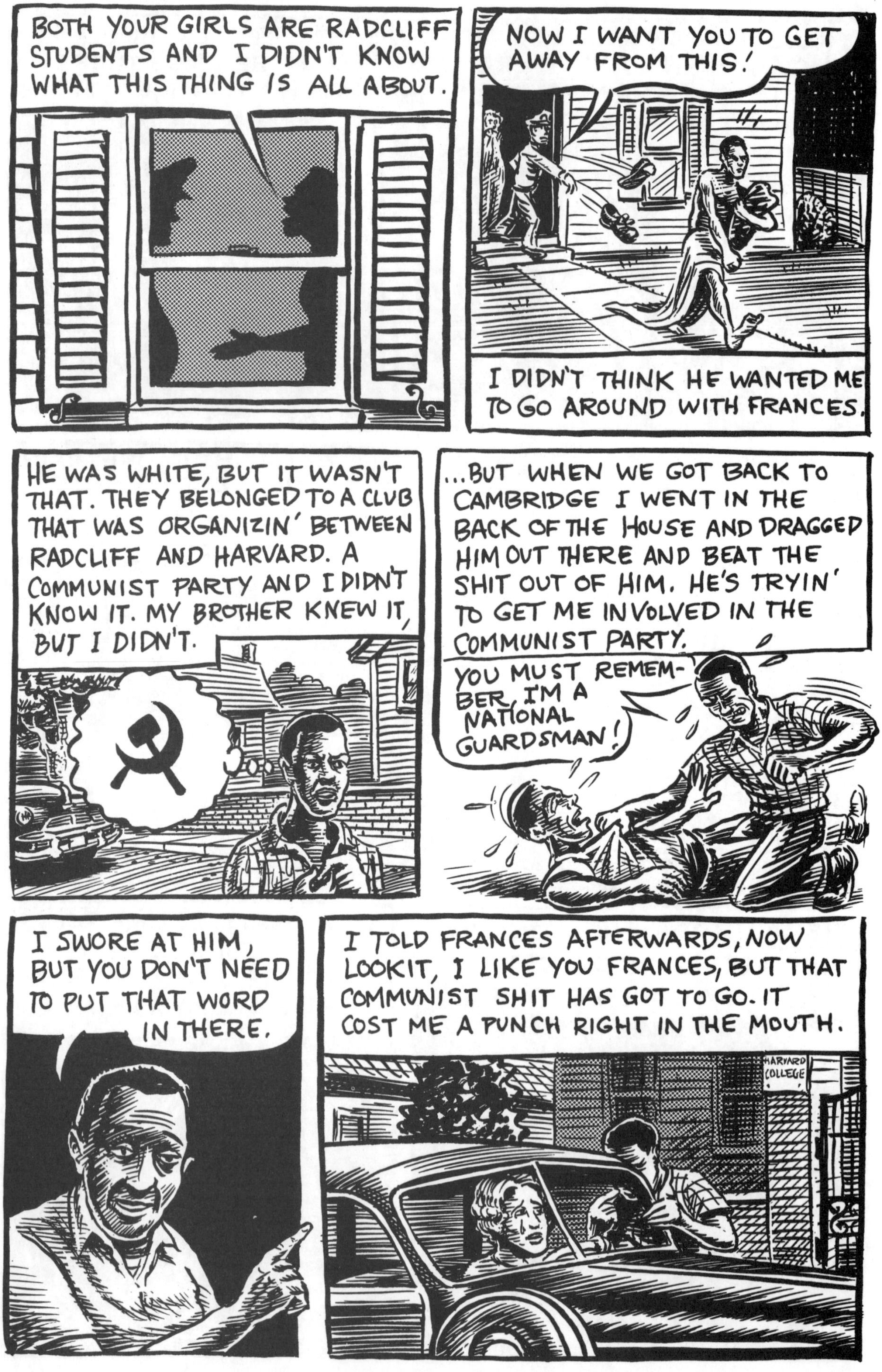
BOTH YOUR GIRLS ARE RADCLIFF STUDENTS AND I DIDN'T KNOW WHAT THIS THING IS ALL ABOUT.
NOW I WANT YOU TO GET AWAY FROM THIS!
I DIDN'T THINK HE WANTED ME TO GO AROUND WITH FRANCES.
HE WAS WHITE, BUT IT WASN'T THAT. THEY BELONGED TO A CLUB THAT WAS ORGANIZIN' BETWEEN RADCLIFF AND HARVARD. A COMMUNIST PARTY AND I DIDN'T KNOW IT. MY BROTHER KNEW IT, BUT I DIDN'T.
...BUT WHEN WE GOT BACK TO CAMBRIDGE I WENT IN THE BACK OF THE HOUSE AND DRAGGED HIM OUT THERE AND BEAT THE SHIT OUT OF HIM. HE'S TRYIN' TO GET ME INVOLVED IN THE COMMUNIST PARTY.
YOU MUST REMEMBER, I'M A NATIONAL GUARDSMAN!
I SWORE AT HIM, BUT YOU DON'T NEED TO PUT THAT WORD IN THERE.
I TOLD FRANCES AFTERWARDS, NOW LOOKIT, I LIKE YOU FRANCES, BUT THAT COMMUNIST SHIT HAS GOT TO GO. IT COST ME A PUNCH RIGHT IN THE MOUTH.
HARVARD COLLEGE

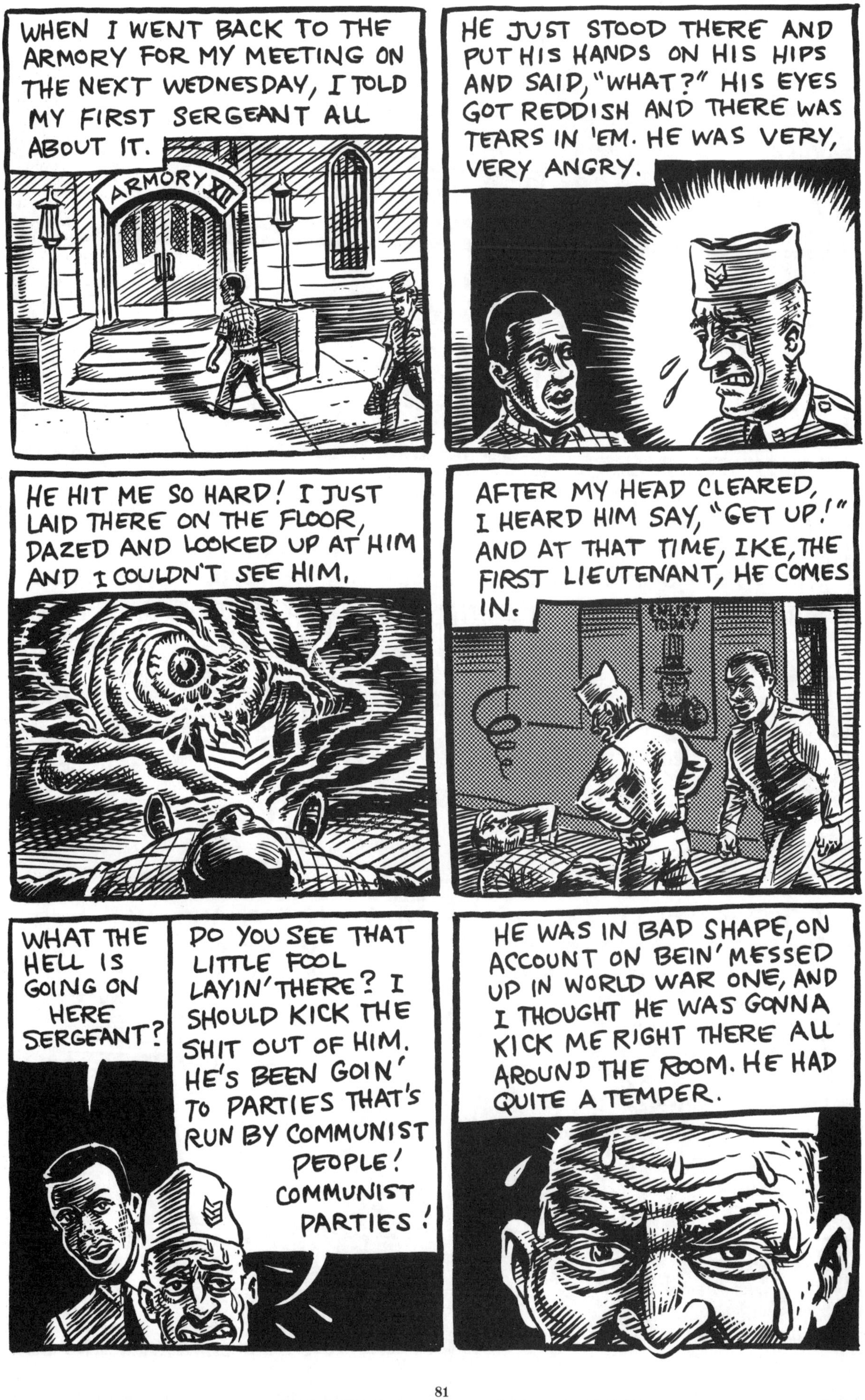
WHEN I WENT BACK TO THE ARMORY FOR MY MEETING ON THE NEXT WEDNESDAY, I TOLD MY FIRST SERGEANT ALL ABOUT IT.
ARMORY XII
HE JUST STOOD THERE AND PUT HIS HANDS ON HIS HIPS AND SAID, "WHAT?" HIS EYES GOT REDDISH AND THERE WAS TEARS IN 'EM. HE WAS VERY, VERY ANGRY.
HE HIT ME SO HARD! I JUST LAID THERE ON THE FLOOR, DAZED AND LOOKED UP AT HIM AND I COULDN'T SEE HIM.
AFTER MY HEAD CLEARED, I HEARD HIM SAY, "GET UP!" AND AT THAT TIME, IKE, THE FIRST LIEUTENANT, HE COMES IN.
WHAT THE HELL IS GOING ON HERE SERGEANT?
DO YOU SEE THAT LITTLE FOOL LAYIN' THERE? I SHOULD KICK THE SHIT OUT OF HIM. HE'S BEEN GOIN' TO PARTIES THAT'S RUN BY COMMUNIST PEOPLE! COMMUNIST PARTIES!
HE WAS IN BAD SHAPE, ON ACCOUNT ON BEIN' MESSED UP IN WORLD WAR ONE, AND I THOUGHT HE WAS GONNA KICK ME RIGHT THERE ALL AROUND THE ROOM. HE HAD QUITE A TEMPER.

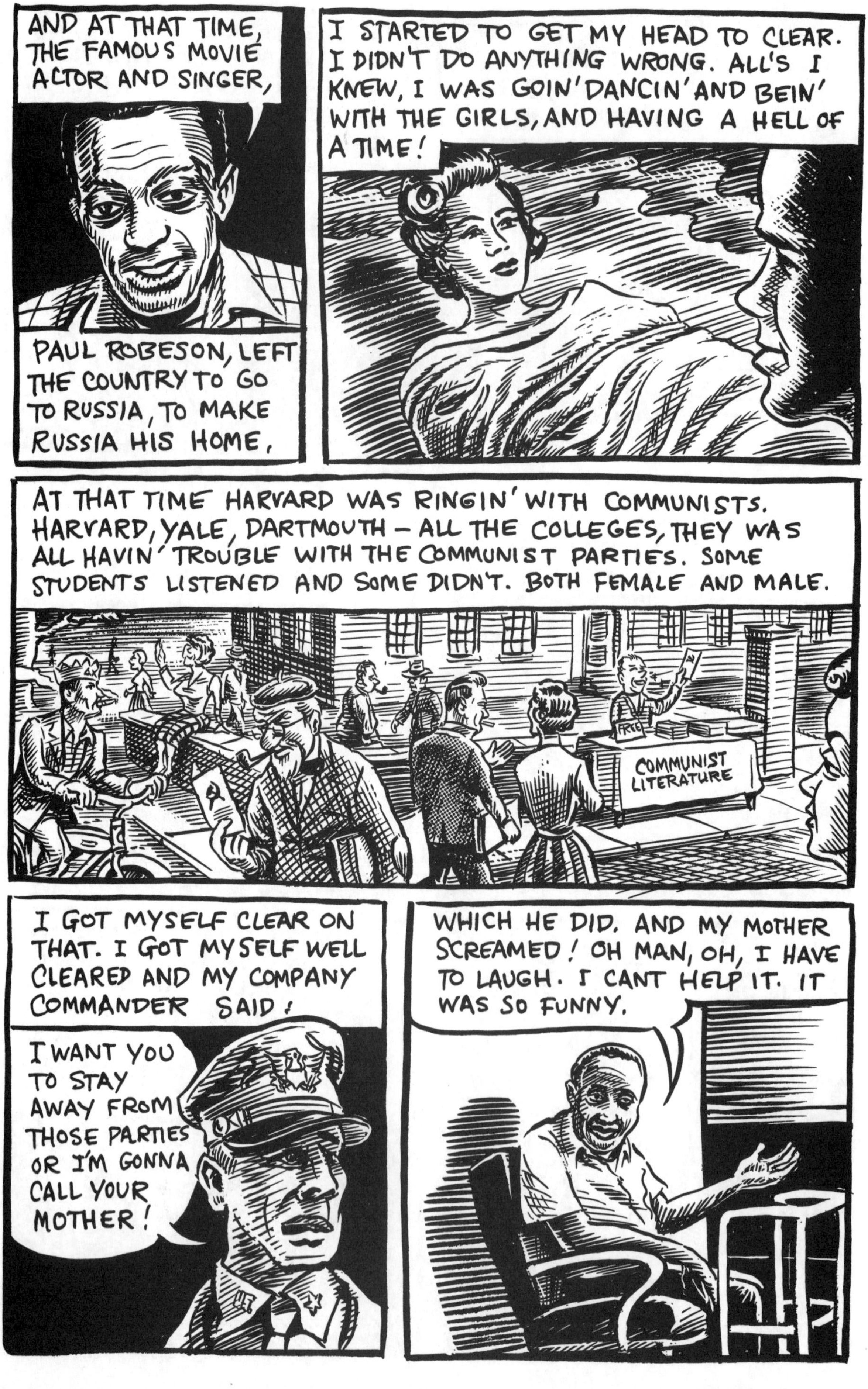
AND AT THAT TIME, THE FAMOUS MOVIE ACTOR AND SINGER,
PAUL ROBESON, LEFT THE COUNTRY TO GO TO RUSSIA, TO MAKE RUSSIA HIS HOME,
I STARTED TO GET MY HEAD TO CLEAR. I DIDN'T DO ANYTHING WRONG. ALL'S I KNEW, I WAS GOIN' DANCIN' AND BEIN' WITH THE GIRLS, AND HAVING A HELL OF A TIME!
AT THAT TIME HARVARD WAS RINGIN' WITH COMMUNISTS. HARVARD, YALE, DARTMOUTH – ALL THE COLLEGES, THEY WAS ALL HAVIN' TROUBLE WITH THE COMMUNIST PARTIES. SOME STUDENTS LISTENED AND SOME DIDN'T. BOTH FEMALE AND MALE.
FREE
COMMUNIST LITERATURE
I GOT MYSELF CLEAR ON THAT. I GOT MYSELF WELL CLEARED AND MY COMPANY COMMANDER SAID:
I WANT YOU TO STAY AWAY FROM THOSE PARTIES OR I'M GONNA CALL YOUR MOTHER!
WHICH HE DID. AND MY MOTHER SCREAMED! OH MAN, OH, I HAVE TO LAUGH. I CANT HELP IT. IT WAS SO FUNNY.

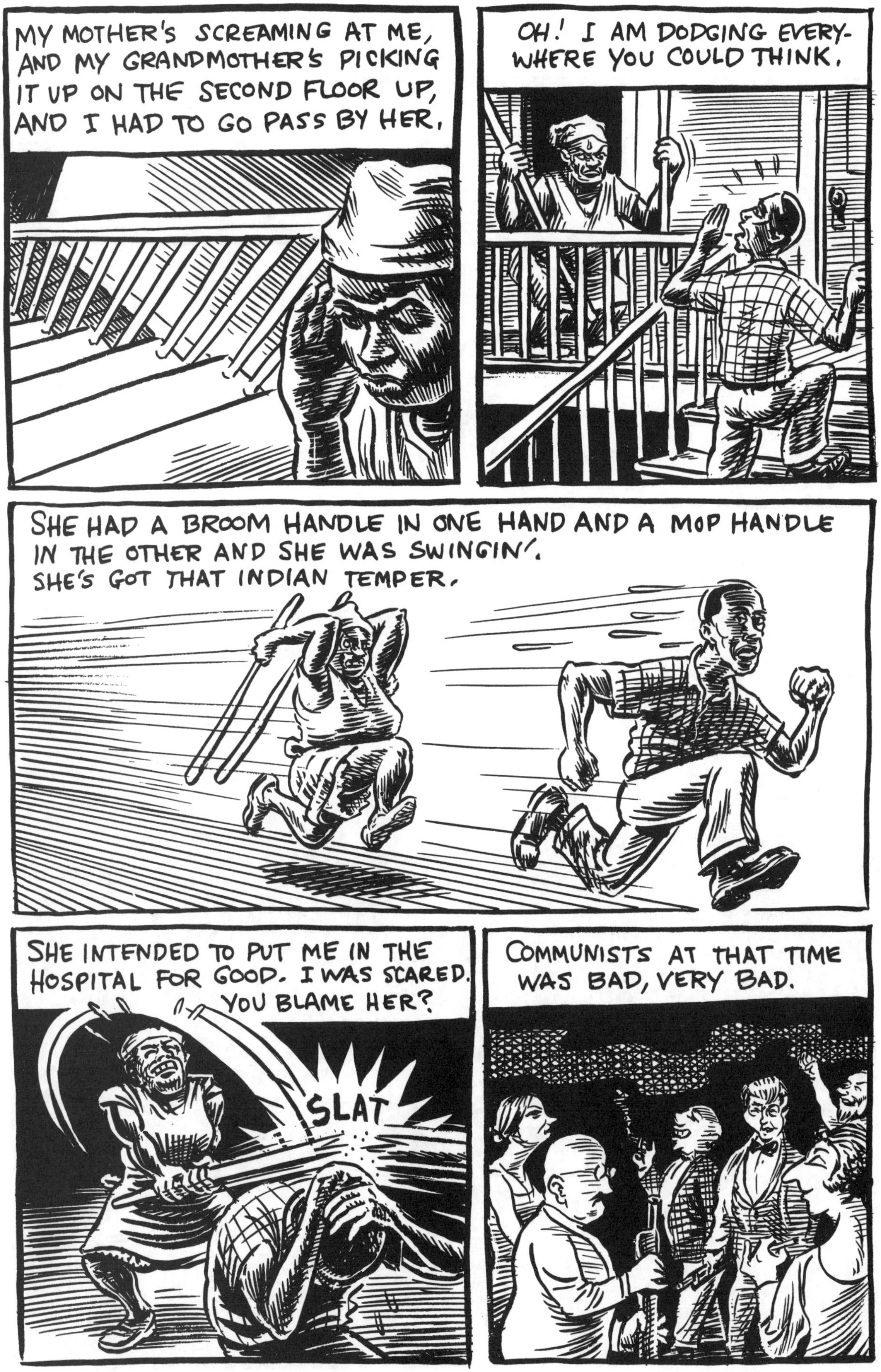
MY MOTHER'S SCREAMING AT ME, AND MY GRANDMOTHER'S PICKING IT UP ON THE SECOND FLOOR UP, AND I HAD TO GO PASS BY HER.
OH! I AM DODGING EVERY-WHERE YOU COULD THINK.
SHE HAD A BROOM HANDLE IN ONE HAND AND A MOP HANDLE IN THE OTHER AND SHE WAS SWINGIN'. SHE'S GOT THAT INDIAN TEMPER.
SHE INTENDED TO PUT ME IN THE HOSPITAL FOR GOOD. I WAS SCARED. YOU BLAME HER?
SLAT
COMMUNISTS AT THAT TIME WAS BAD, VERY BAD.

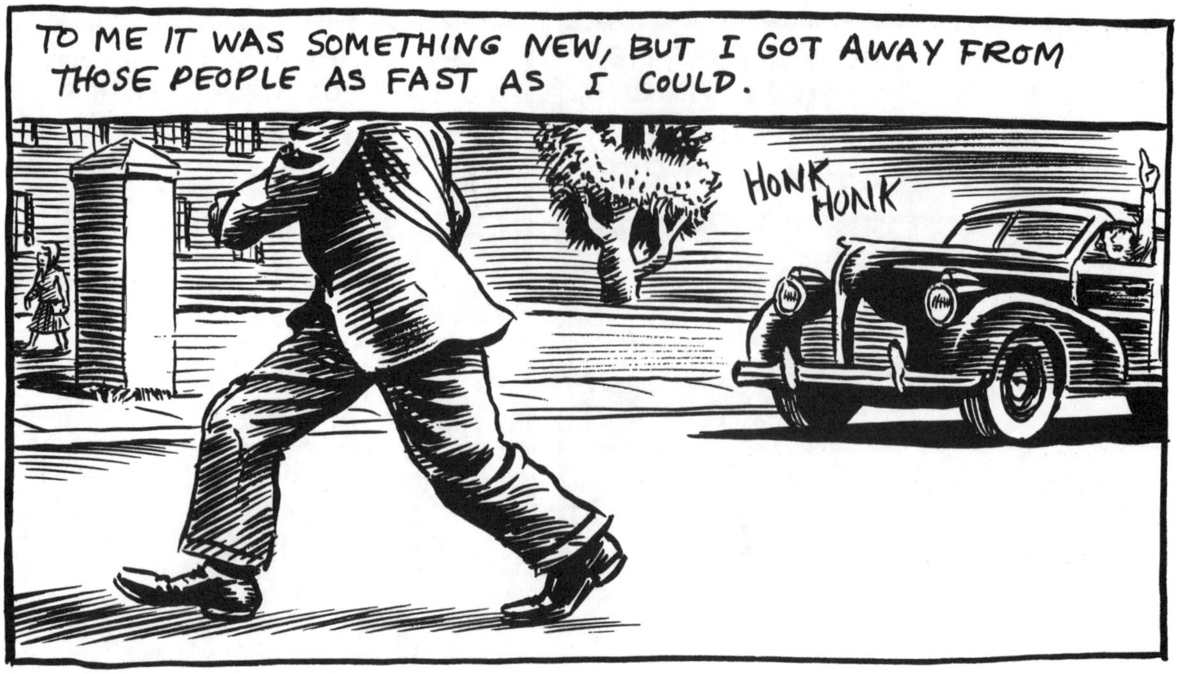
TO ME IT WAS SOMETHING NEW, BUT I GOT AWAY FROM THOSE PEOPLE AS FAST AS I COULD.
HONK HONK

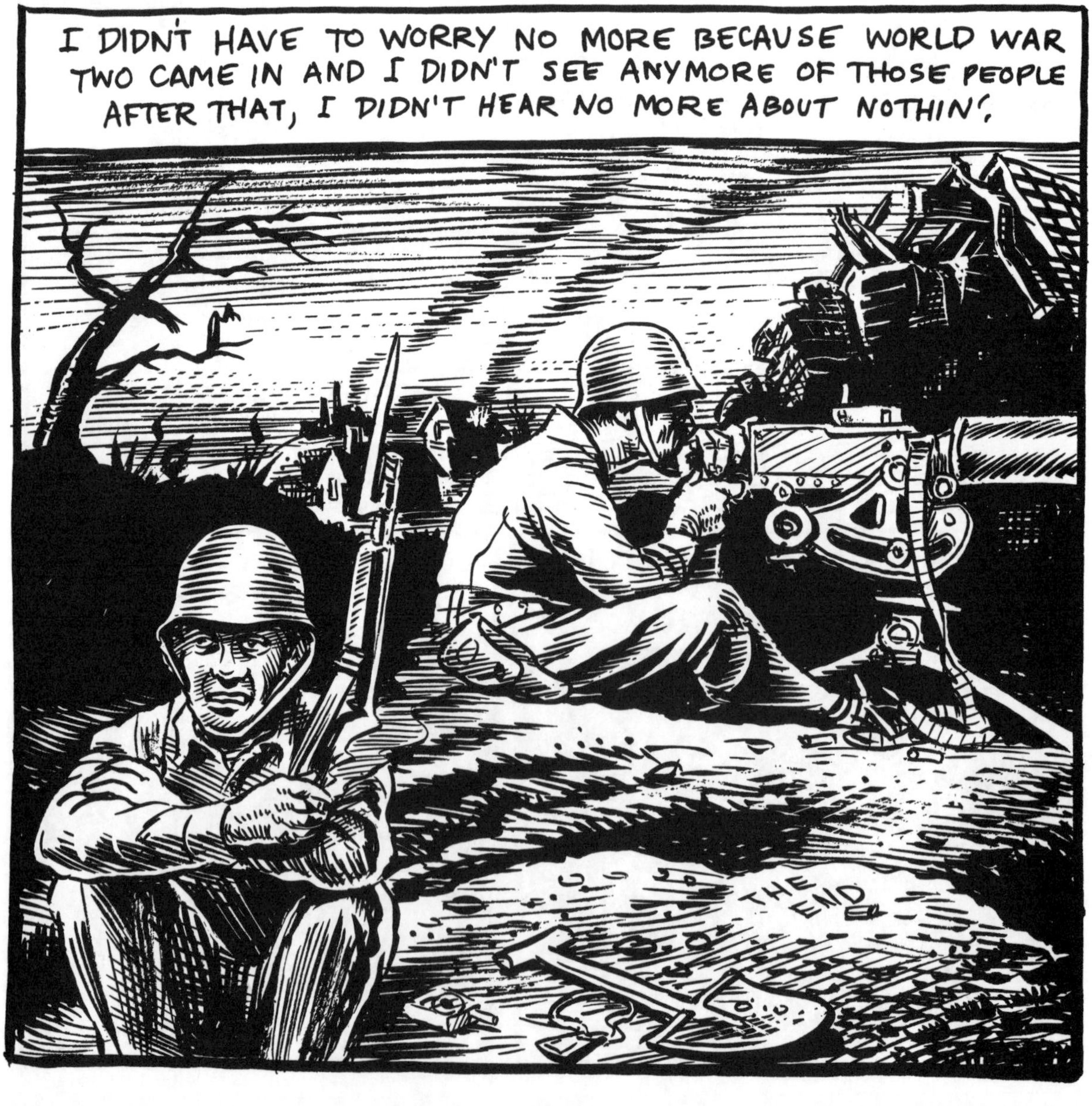
I DIDN'T HAVE TO WORRY NO MORE BECAUSE WORLD WAR TWO CAME IN AND I DIDN'T SEE ANYMORE OF THOSE PEOPLE AFTER THAT, I DIDN'T HEAR NO MORE ABOUT NOTHIN'.
THE END

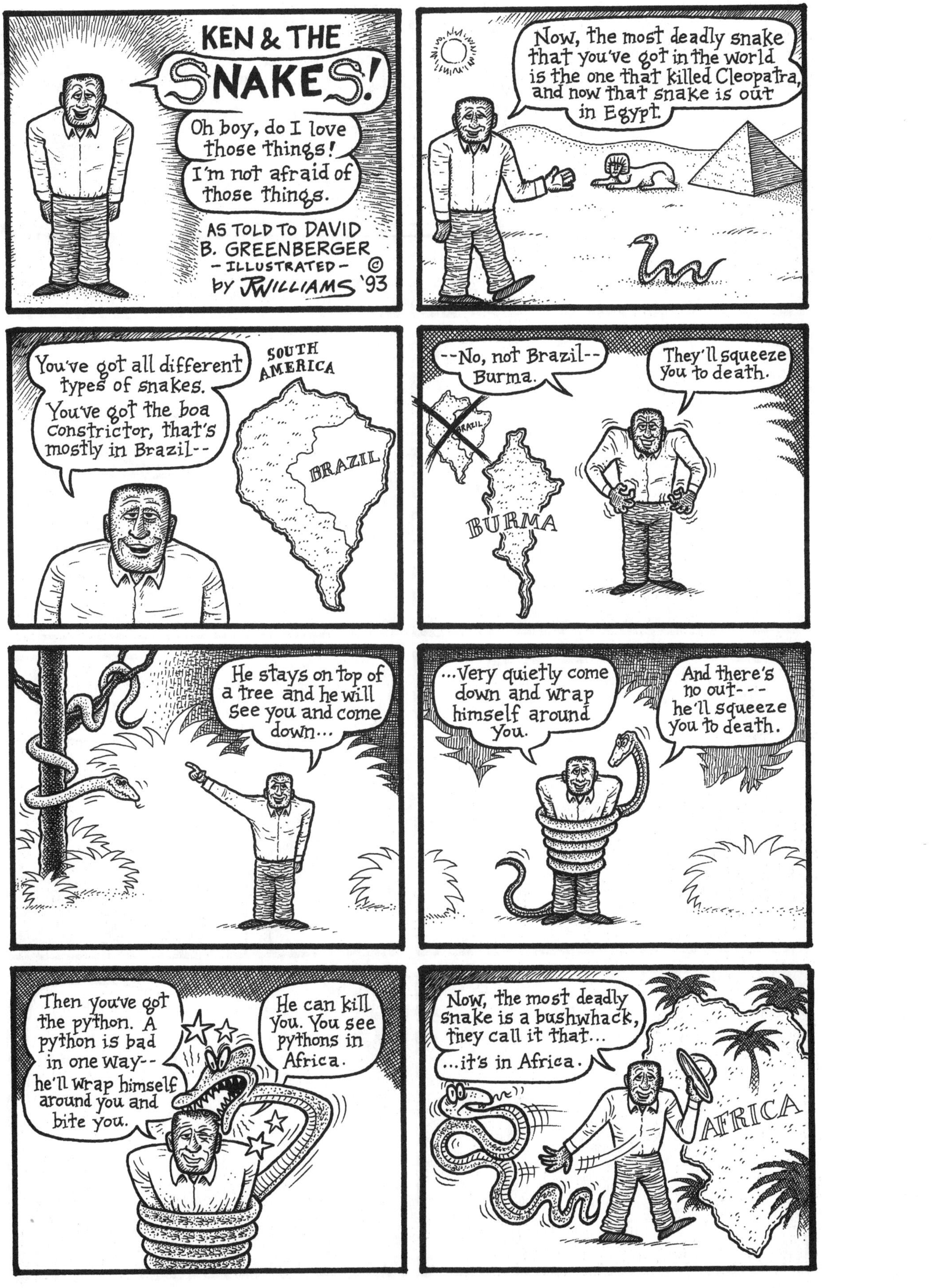
KEN & THE SNAKES!
Oh boy, do I love those things! I'm not afraid of those things.
AS TOLD TO DAVID B. GREENBERGER
-ILLUSTRATED- by JWILLIAMS ©'93
Now, the most deadly snake that you've got in the world is the one that killed Cleopatra, and now that snake is out in Egypt.
You've got all different types of snakes. You've got the boa constrictor, that's mostly in Brazil--
SOUTH AMERICA
BRAZIL
--No, not Brazil-- Burma.
They'll squeeze you to death.
BRAZIL
BURMA
He stays on top of a tree and he will see you and come down...
...Very quietly come down and wrap himself around you.
And there's no out--- he'll squeeze you to death.
Then you've got the python. A python is bad in one way-- he'll wrap himself around you and bite you.
He can kill you. You see pythons in Africa.
Now, the most deadly snake is a bushwhack, they call it that...
...it's in Africa.
AFRICA

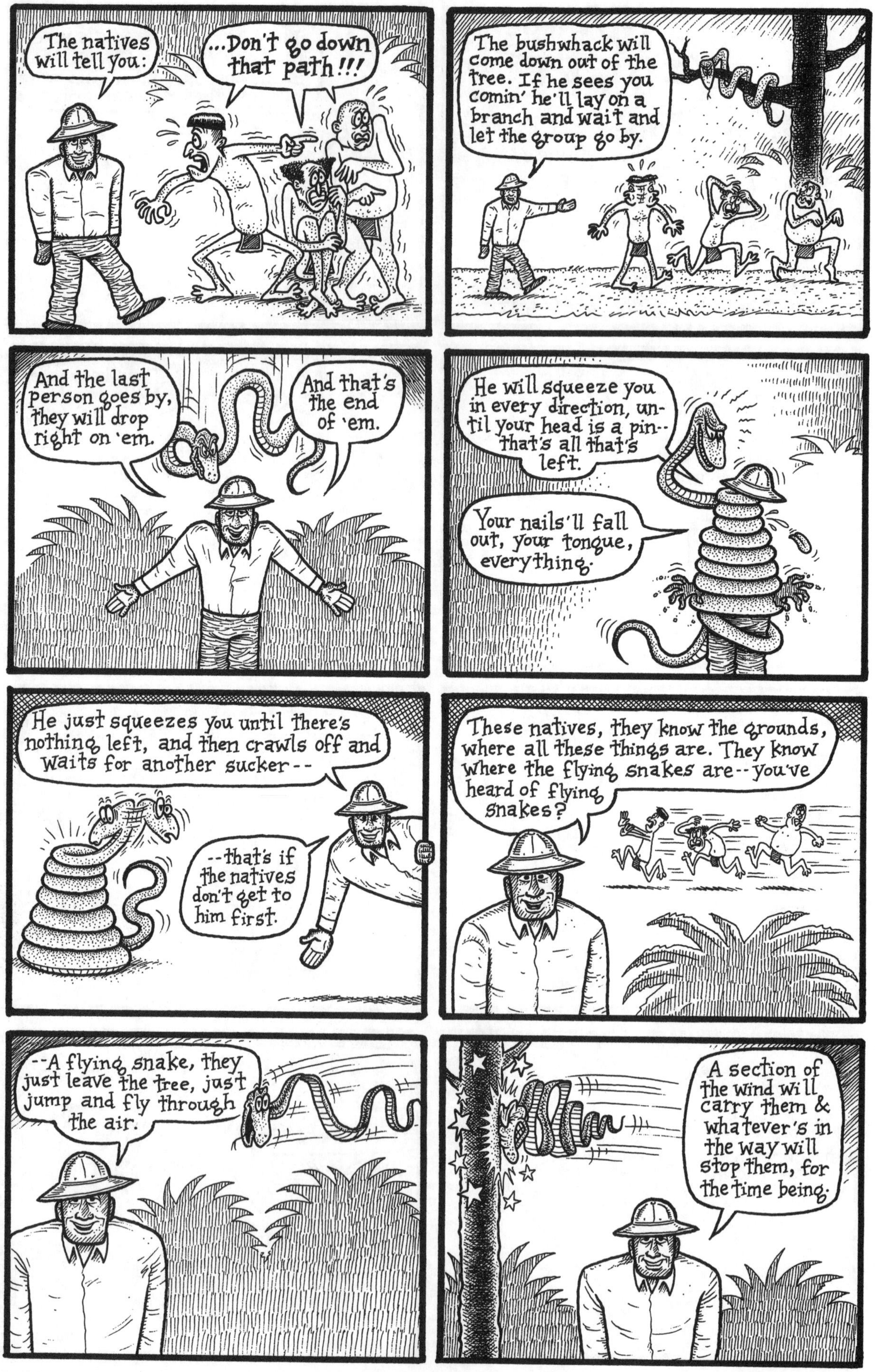
The natives will tell you:
...Don't go down that path!!!
The bushwhack will come down out of the tree. If he sees you comin' he'll lay on a branch and wait and let the group go by.
And the last person goes by, they will drop right on 'em.
And that's the end of 'em.
He will squeeze you in every direction, until your head is a pin-- that's all that's left.
Your nails'll fall out, your tongue, everything.
He just squeezes you until there's nothing left, and then crawls off and waits for another sucker--
--that's if the natives don't get to him first.
These natives, they know the grounds, where all these things are. They know where the flying snakes are--you've heard of flying snakes?
--A flying snake, they just leave the tree, just jump and fly through the air.
A section of the wind will carry them & whatever's in the way will stop them, for the time being.

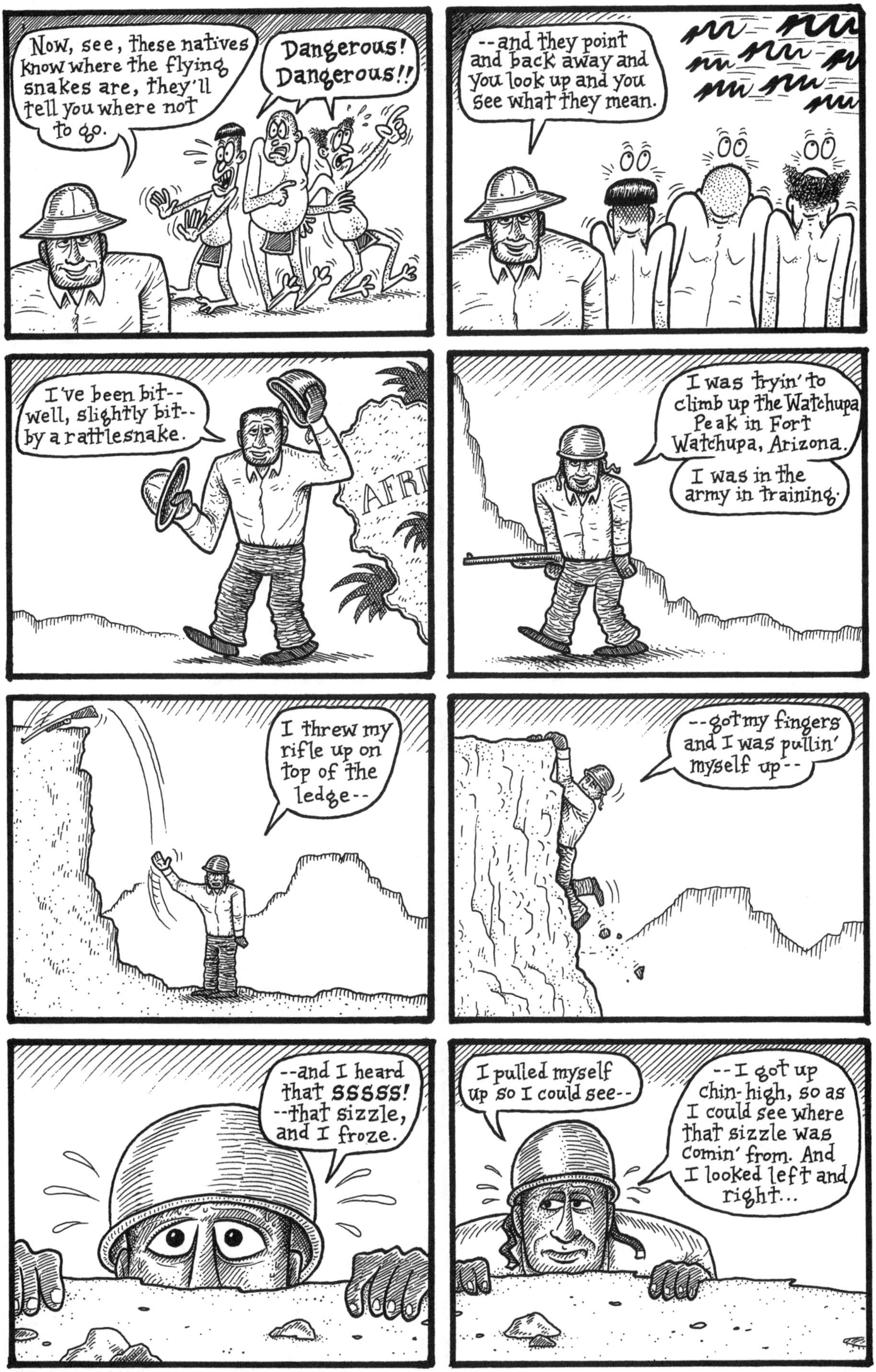
Now, see, these natives know where the flying snakes are, they'll tell you where not to go.
Dangerous! Dangerous!!
--and they point and back away and you look up and you see what they mean.
I've been bit--well, slightly bit--by a rattlesnake.
AFRI
I was tryin' to climb up the Watchupa Peak in Fort Watchupa, Arizona.
I was in the army in training.
I threw my rifle up on top of the ledge--
--got my fingers and I was pullin' myself up--
--and I heard that SSSSS! --that sizzle, and I froze.
I pulled myself up so I could see--
--I got up chin-high, so as I could see where that sizzle was comin' from. And I looked left and right...

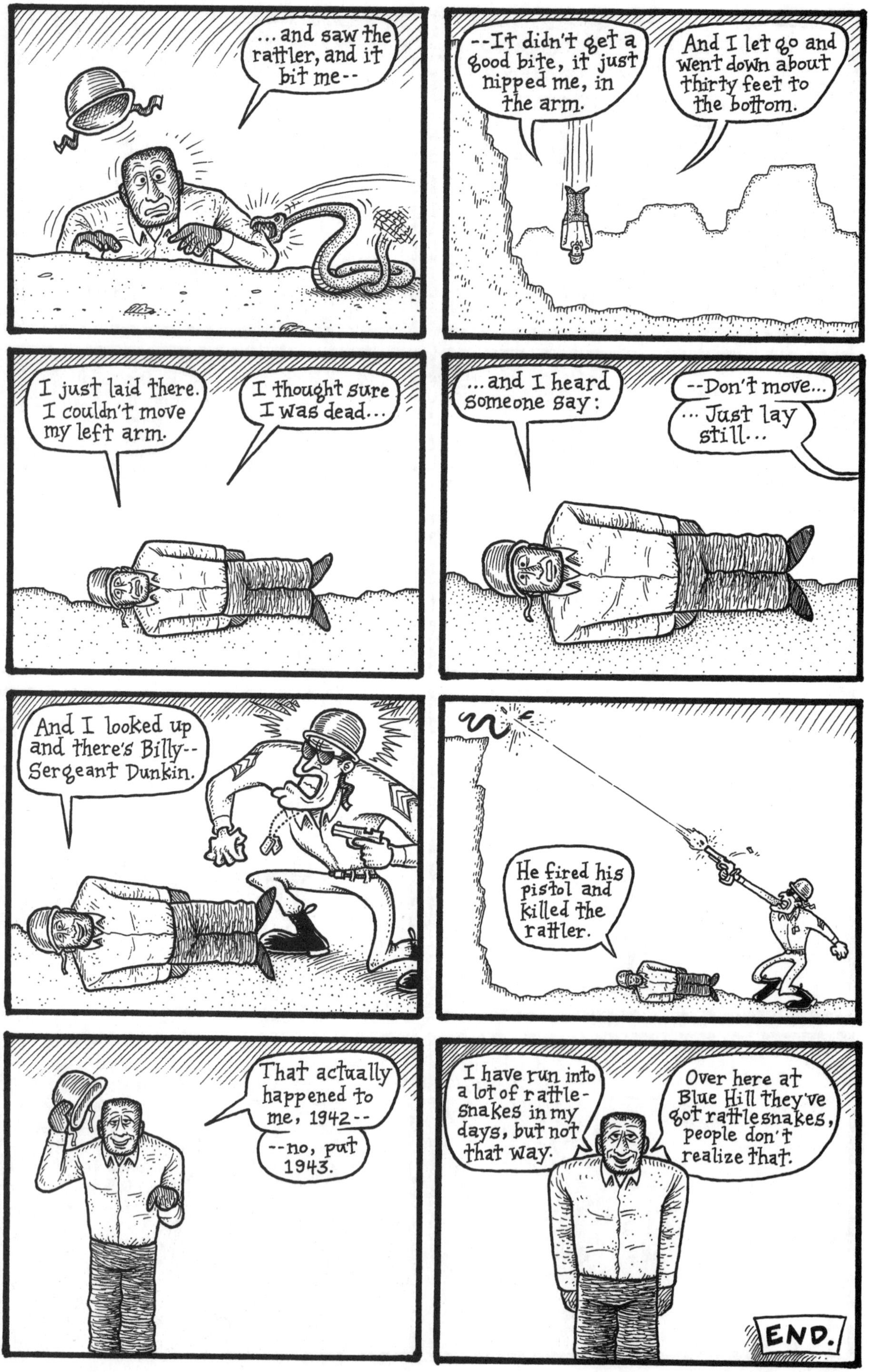
...and saw the rattler, and it bit me--
--It didn't get a good bite, it just nipped me, in the arm.
And I let go and went down about thirty feet to the bottom.
I just laid there. I couldn't move my left arm.
I thought sure I was dead...
...and I heard someone say:
--Don't move...
...Just lay still...
And I looked up and there's Billy--Sergeant Dunkin.
He fired his pistol and killed the rattler.
That actually happened to me, 1942--
--no, put 1943.
I have run into a lot of rattle-snakes in my days, but not that way.
Over here at Blue Hill they've got rattlesnakes, people don't realize that.
END.

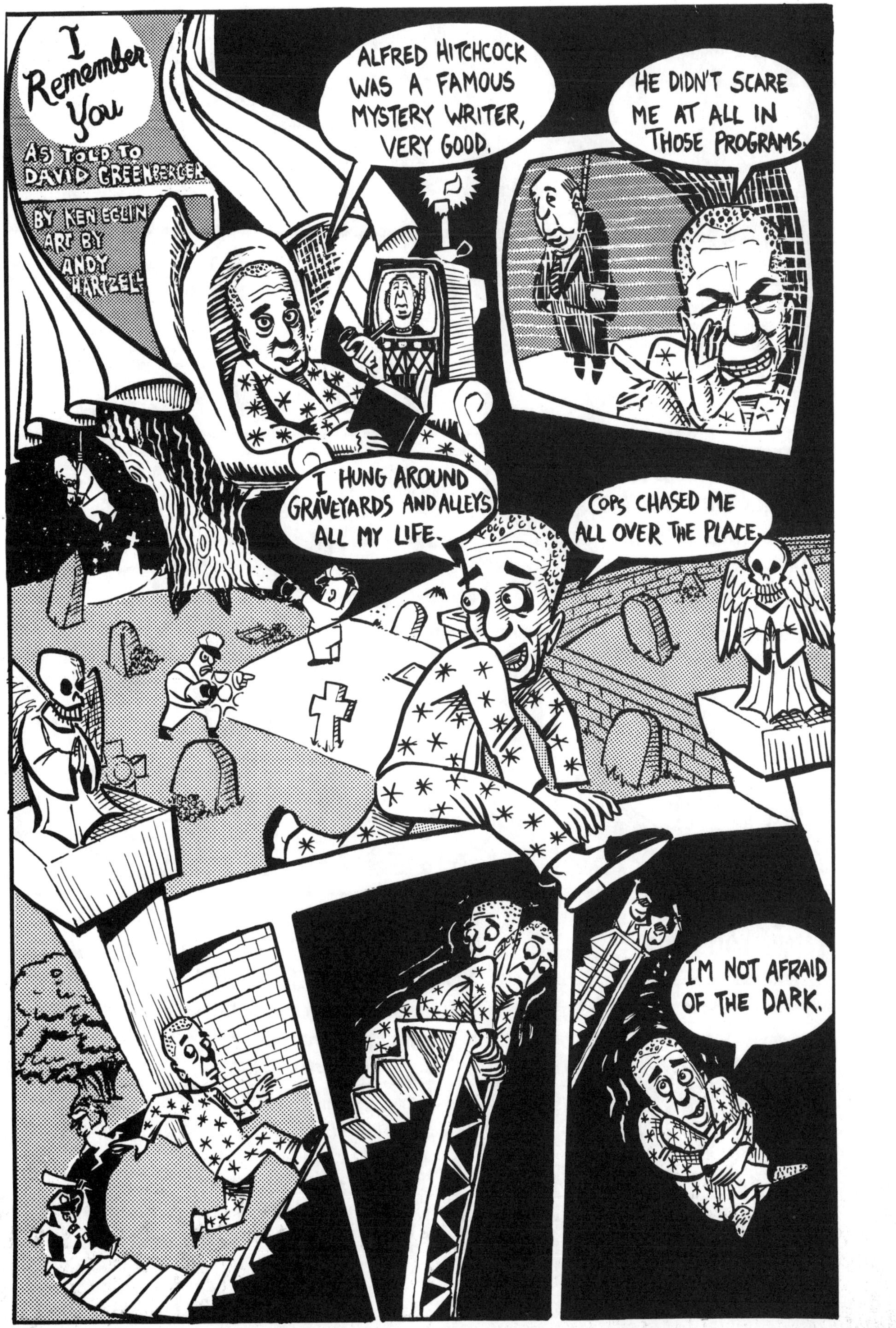
I Remember You
AS TOLD TO DAVID GREENBERGER
BY KEN EGLIN
ART BY ANDY HARTZELL
ALFRED HITCHCOCK WAS A FAMOUS MYSTERY WRITER, VERY GOOD.
HE DIDN'T SCARE ME AT ALL IN THOSE PROGRAMS.
I HUNG AROUND GRAVEYARDS AND ALLEYS ALL MY LIFE.
COPS CHASED ME ALL OVER THE PLACE.
I'M NOT AFRAID OF THE DARK.

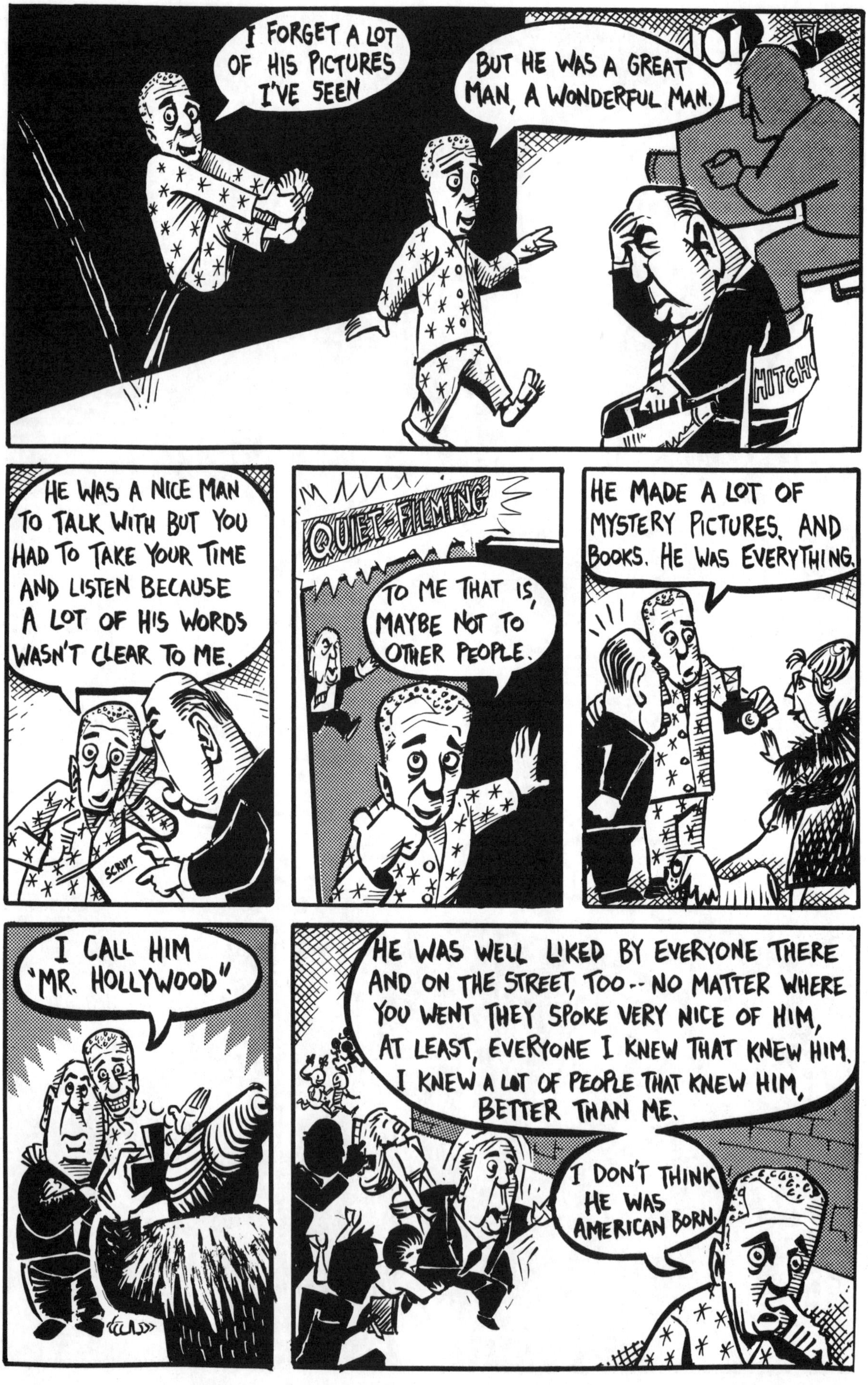
I FORGET A LOT OF HIS PICTURES I'VE SEEN
BUT HE WAS A GREAT MAN, A WONDERFUL MAN.
HITCH
HE WAS A NICE MAN TO TALK WITH BUT YOU HAD TO TAKE YOUR TIME AND LISTEN BECAUSE A LOT OF HIS WORDS WASN'T CLEAR TO ME.
SCRIPT
QUIET-FILMING
TO ME THAT IS, MAYBE NOT TO OTHER PEOPLE.
HE MADE A LOT OF MYSTERY PICTURES. AND BOOKS. HE WAS EVERYTHING.
I CALL HIM "MR. HOLLYWOOD".
HE WAS WELL LIKED BY EVERYONE THERE AND ON THE STREET, TOO-- NO MATTER WHERE YOU WENT THEY SPOKE VERY NICE OF HIM, AT LEAST, EVERYONE I KNEW THAT KNEW HIM. I KNEW A LOT OF PEOPLE THAT KNEW HIM, BETTER THAN ME.
I DON'T THINK HE WAS AMERICAN BORN.

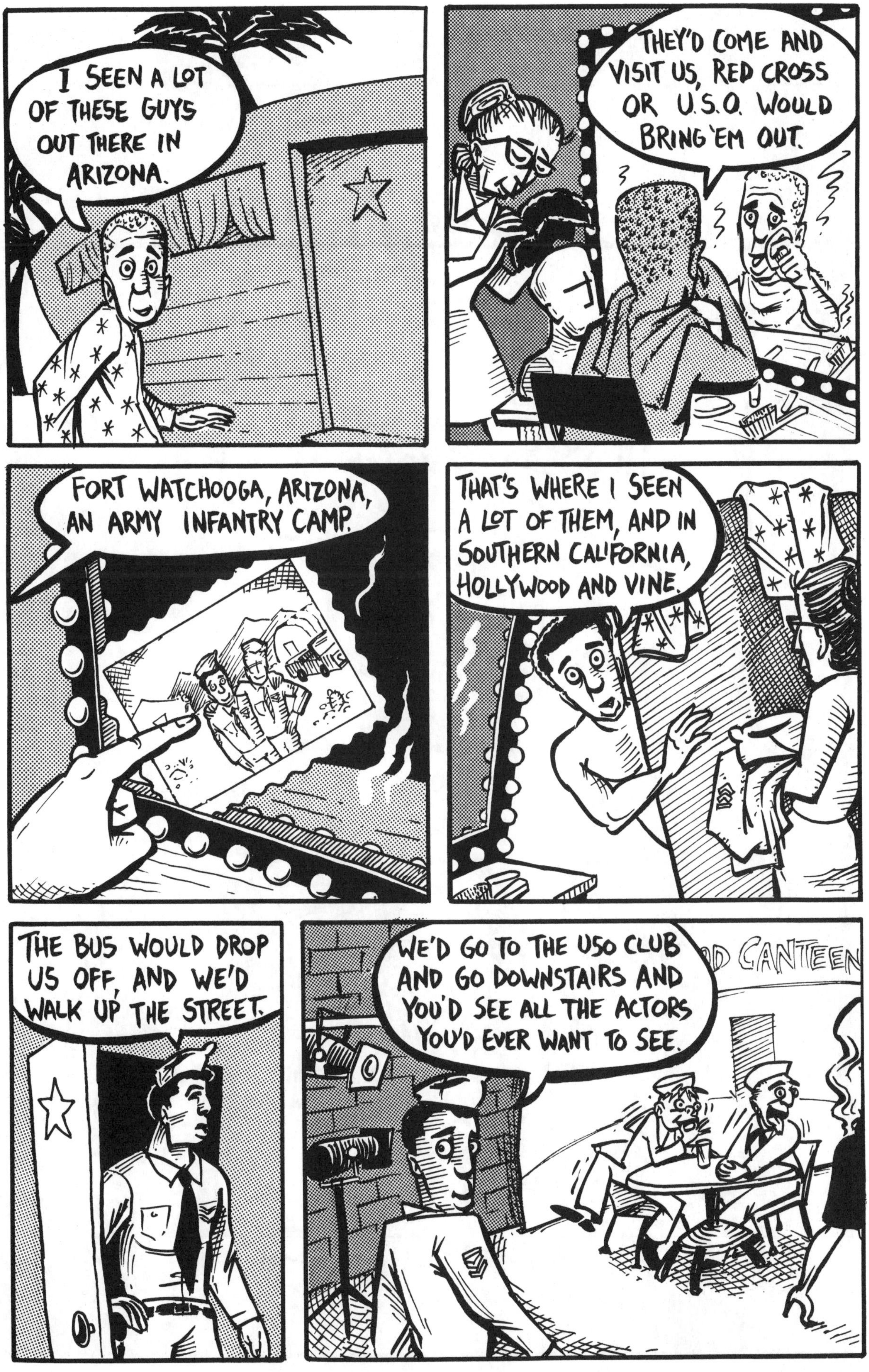
I SEEN A LOT OF THESE GUYS OUT THERE IN ARIZONA.
THEY'D COME AND VISIT US, RED CROSS OR U.S.O. WOULD BRING 'EM OUT.
FORT WATCHOOGA, ARIZONA, AN ARMY INFANTRY CAMP.
THAT'S WHERE I SEEN A LOT OF THEM, AND IN SOUTHERN CALIFORNIA, HOLLYWOOD AND VINE.
THE BUS WOULD DROP US OFF, AND WE'D WALK UP THE STREET.
WE'D GO TO THE USO CLUB AND GO DOWNSTAIRS AND YOU'D SEE ALL THE ACTORS YOU'D EVER WANT TO SEE.
OD CANTEEN

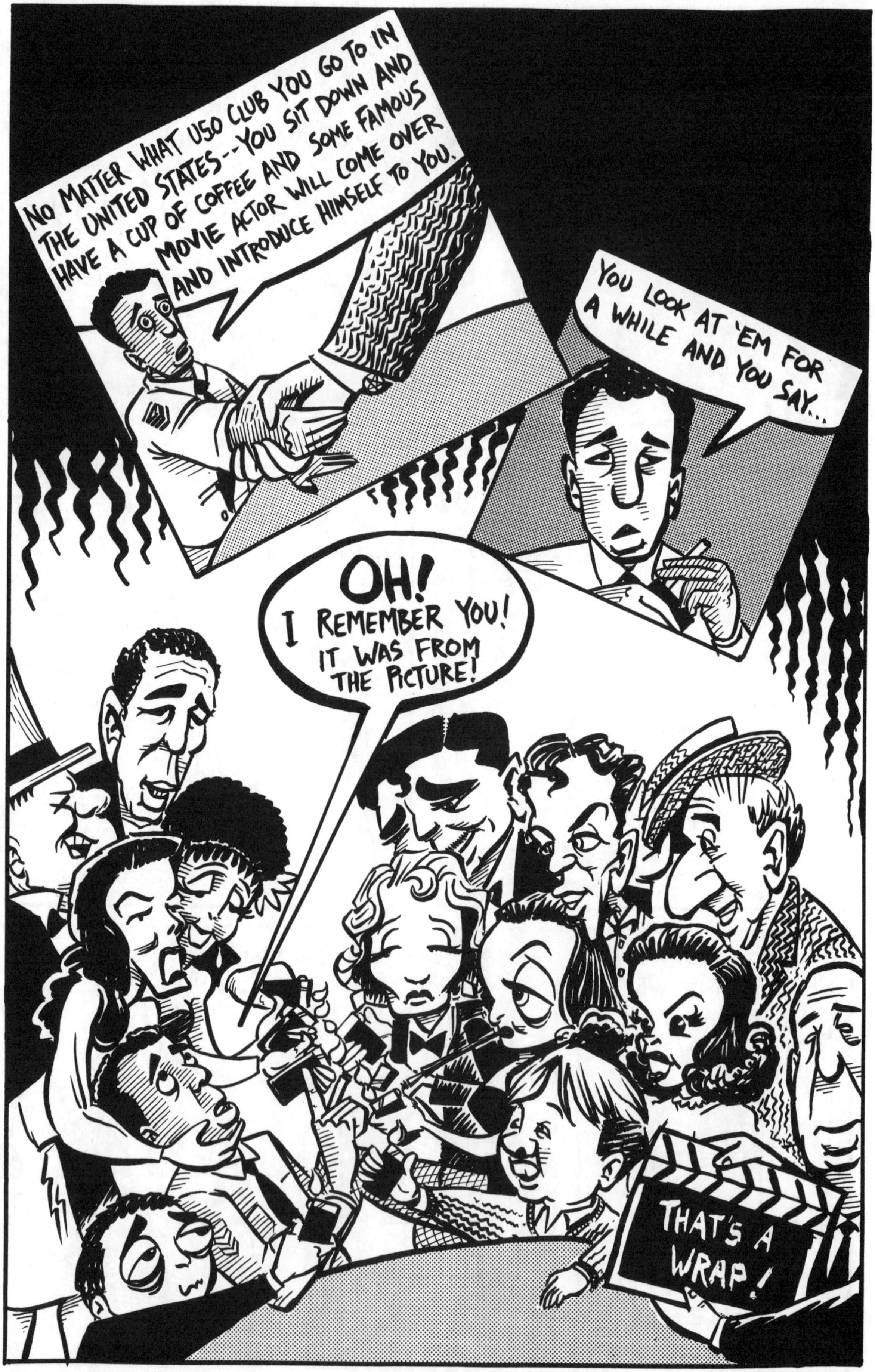
NO MATTER WHAT USO CLUB YOU GO TO IN THE UNITED STATES--YOU SIT DOWN AND HAVE A CUP OF COFFEE AND SOME FAMOUS MOVIE ACTOR WILL COME OVER AND INTRODUCE HIMSELF TO YOU.
YOU LOOK AT 'EM FOR A WHILE AND YOU SAY...
OH! I REMEMBER YOU! IT WAS FROM THE PICTURE!
THAT'S A WRAP!

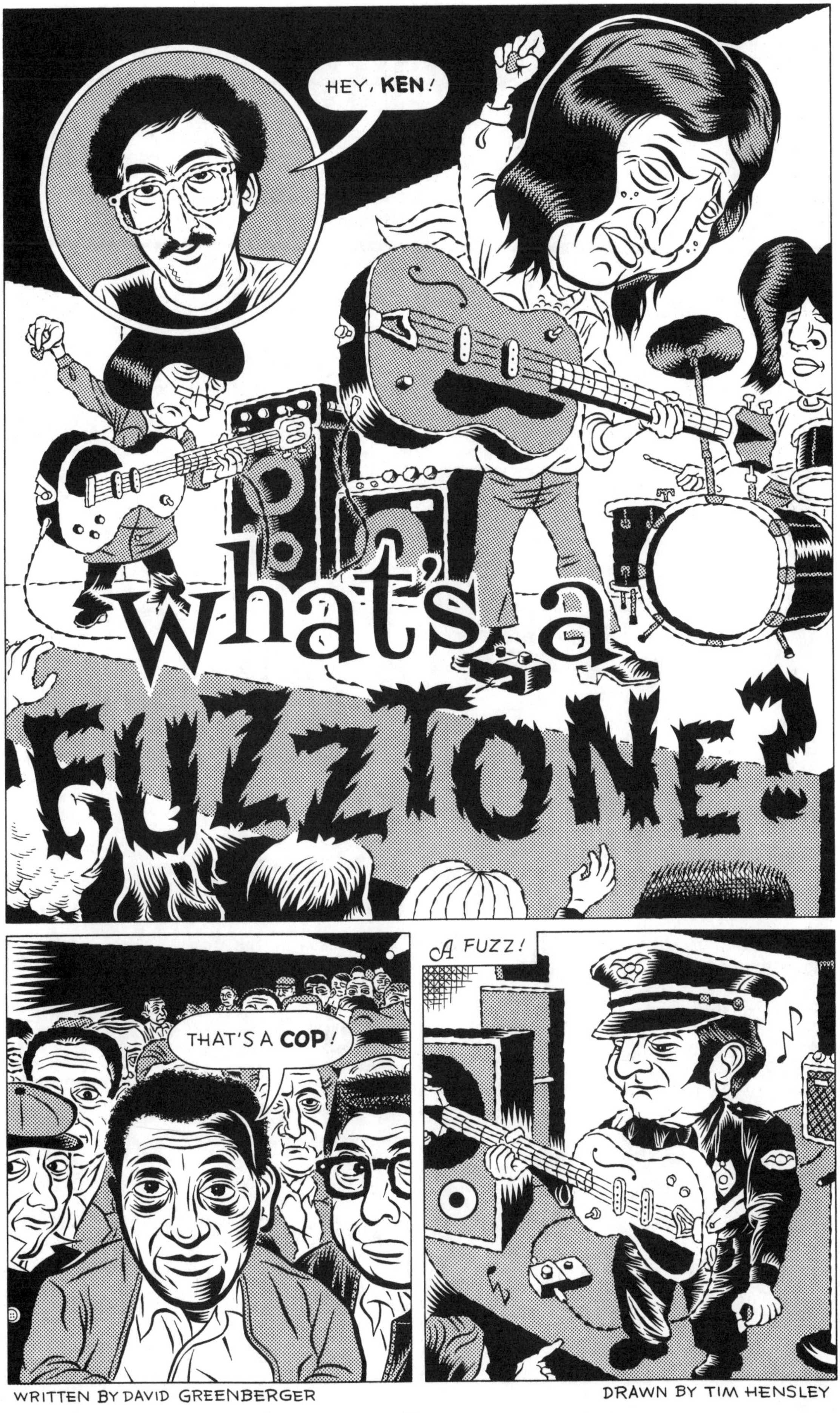
HEY, KEN!
what's a FUZZTONE?
THAT'S A COP!
A FUZZ!
WRITTEN BY DAVID GREENBERGER
DRAWN BY TIM HENSLEY

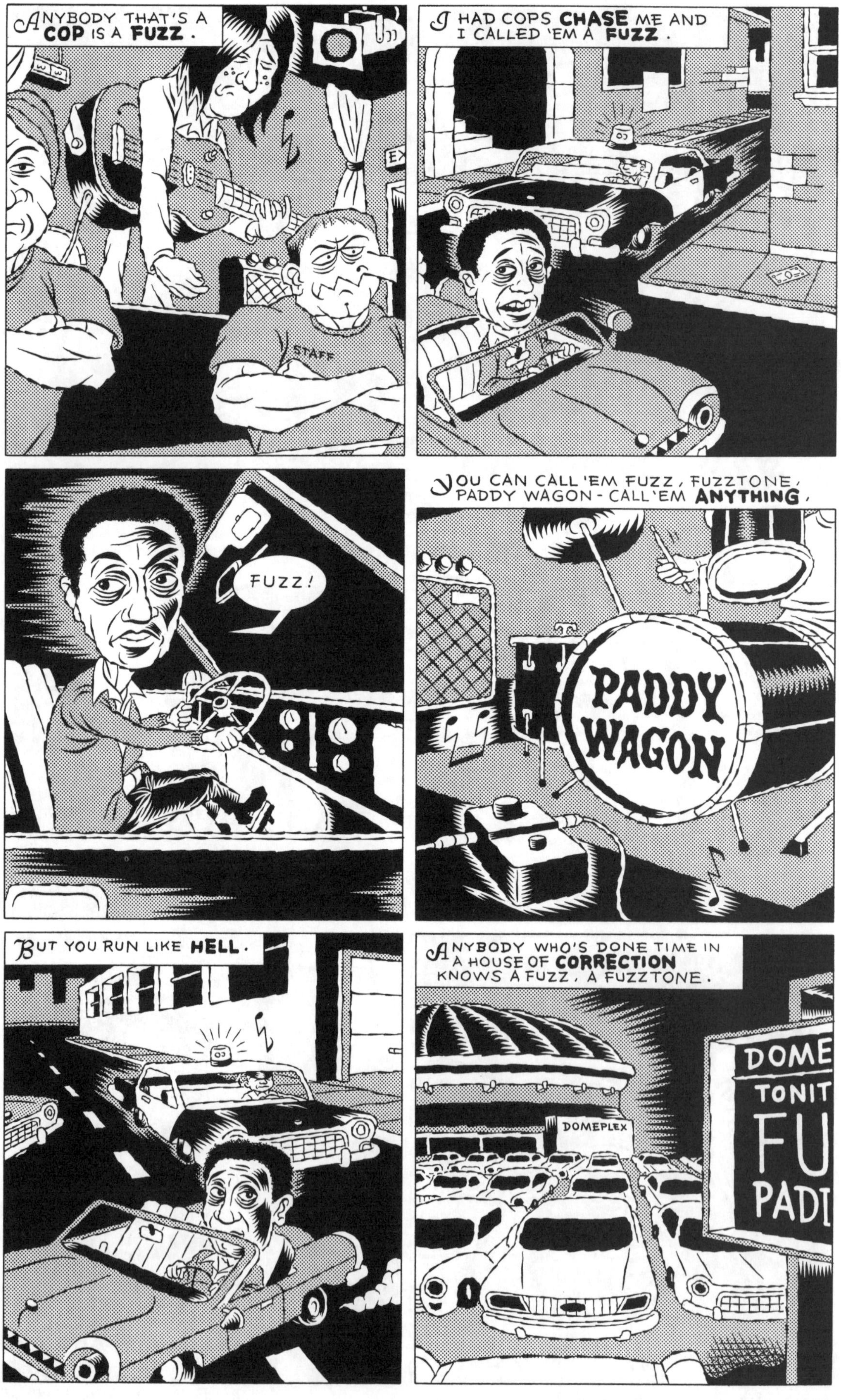

ANYBODY THAT'S A COP IS A FUZZ.
STAFF
I HAD COPS CHASE ME AND I CALLED 'EM A FUZZ.
FUZZ!
YOU CAN CALL 'EM FUZZ, FUZZTONE, PADDY WAGON - CALL 'EM ANYTHING,
PADDY WAGON
BUT YOU RUN LIKE HELL.
ANYBODY WHO'S DONE TIME IN A HOUSE OF CORRECTION KNOWS A FUZZ, A FUZZTONE.
DOMEPLEX
DOME
TONIT
FU
PADI

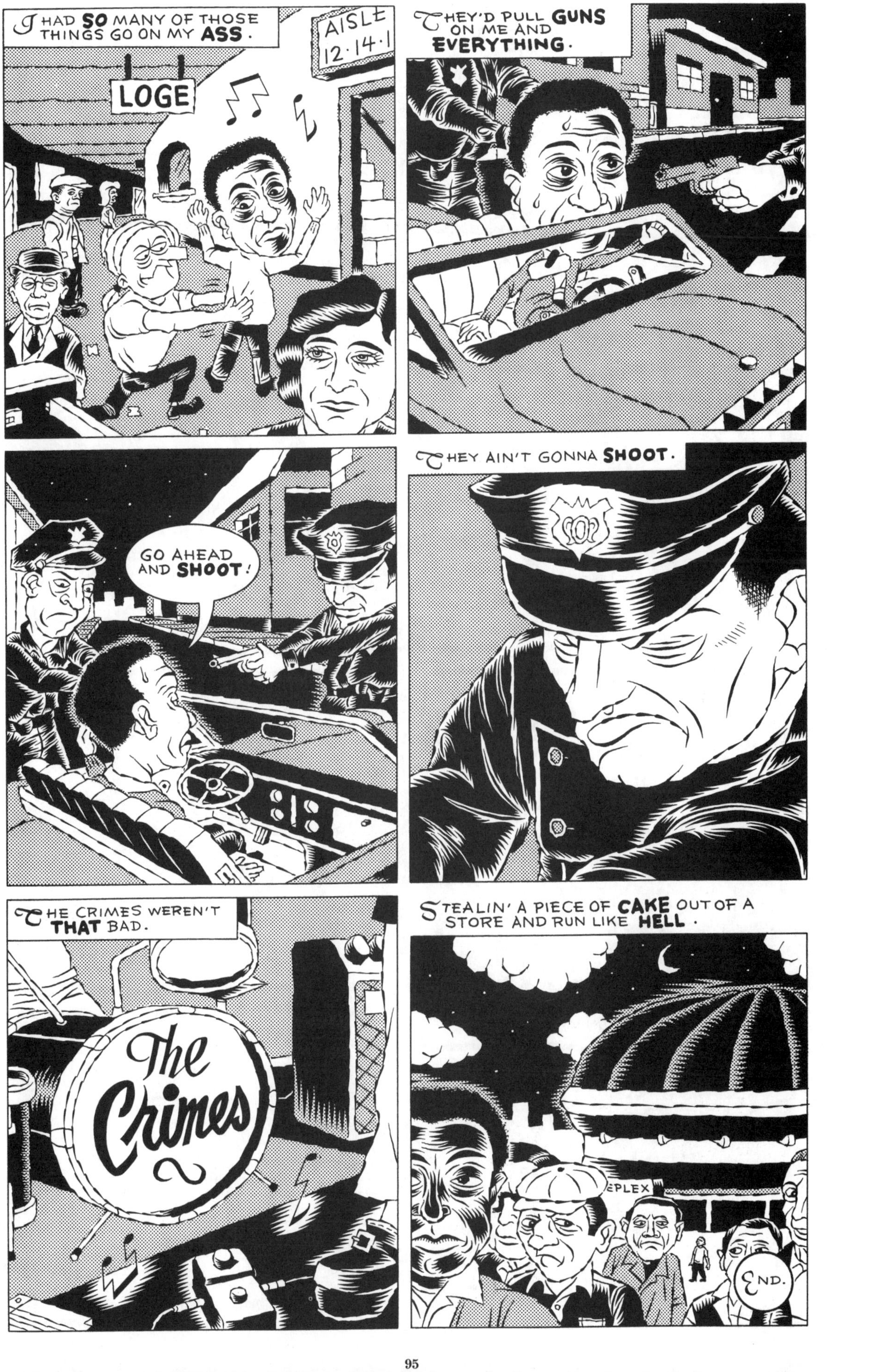
I HAD SO MANY OF THOSE THINGS GO ON MY ASS.
AISLE 12·14·1
LOGE
THEY'D PULL GUNS ON ME AND EVERYTHING.
GO AHEAD AND SHOOT!
THEY AIN'T GONNA SHOOT.
THE CRIMES WEREN'T THAT BAD.
The Crimes
STEALIN' A PIECE OF CAKE OUT OF A STORE AND RUN LIKE HELL.
EPLEX
END.

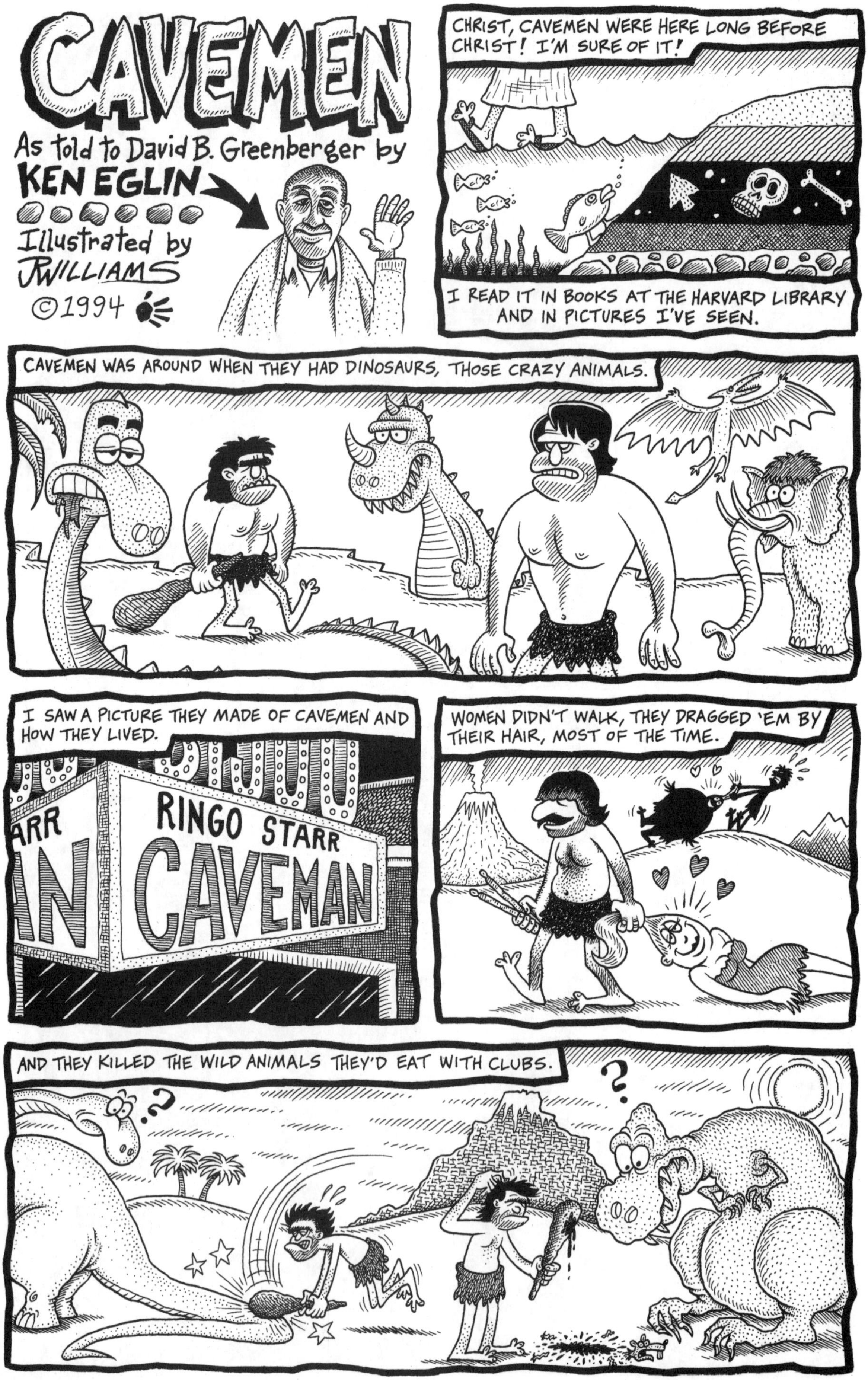
CAVEMEN
As told to David B. Greenberger by
KEN EGLIN
Illustrated by
J WILLIAMS
©1994
CHRIST, CAVEMEN WERE HERE LONG BEFORE CHRIST! I'M SURE OF IT!
I READ IT IN BOOKS AT THE HARVARD LIBRARY AND IN PICTURES I'VE SEEN.
CAVEMEN WAS AROUND WHEN THEY HAD DINOSAURS, THOSE CRAZY ANIMALS.
I SAW A PICTURE THEY MADE OF CAVEMEN AND HOW THEY LIVED.
RINGO STARR
CAVEMAN
ARR
AN
WOMEN DIDN'T WALK, THEY DRAGGED 'EM BY THEIR HAIR, MOST OF THE TIME.
AND THEY KILLED THE WILD ANIMALS THEY'D EAT WITH CLUBS.
?
?

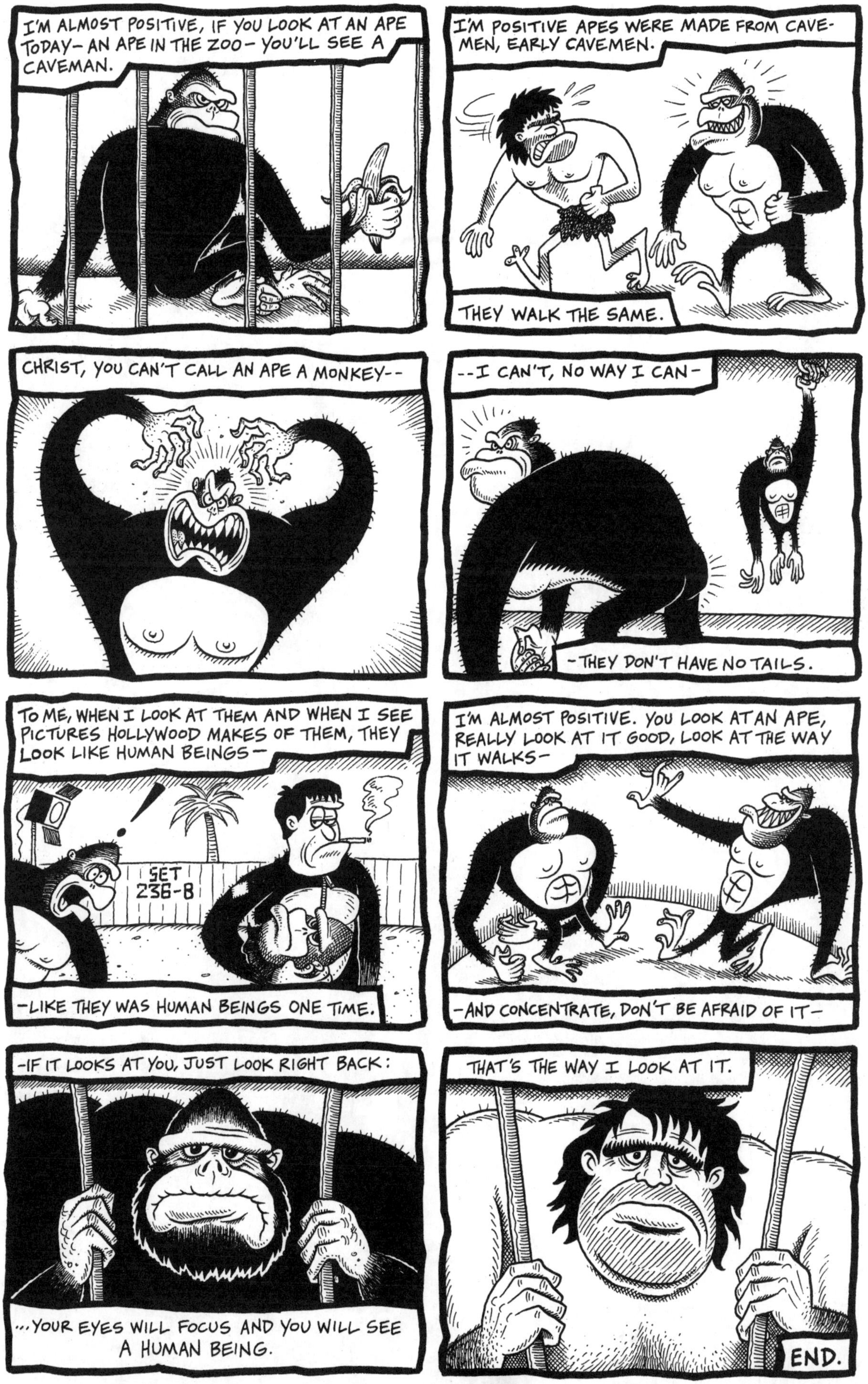
I'M ALMOST POSITIVE, IF YOU LOOK AT AN APE TODAY— AN APE IN THE ZOO— YOU'LL SEE A CAVEMAN.
I'M POSITIVE APES WERE MADE FROM CAVE-MEN, EARLY CAVEMEN.
THEY WALK THE SAME.
CHRIST, YOU CAN'T CALL AN APE A MONKEY--
--I CAN'T, NO WAY I CAN—
—THEY DON'T HAVE NO TAILS.
TO ME, WHEN I LOOK AT THEM AND WHEN I SEE PICTURES HOLLYWOOD MAKES OF THEM, THEY LOOK LIKE HUMAN BEINGS—
SET 236-B
—LIKE THEY WAS HUMAN BEINGS ONE TIME.
I'M ALMOST POSITIVE. YOU LOOK AT AN APE, REALLY LOOK AT IT GOOD, LOOK AT THE WAY IT WALKS—
—AND CONCENTRATE, DON'T BE AFRAID OF IT—
—IF IT LOOKS AT YOU, JUST LOOK RIGHT BACK:
...YOUR EYES WILL FOCUS AND YOU WILL SEE A HUMAN BEING.
THAT'S THE WAY I LOOK AT IT.
END.

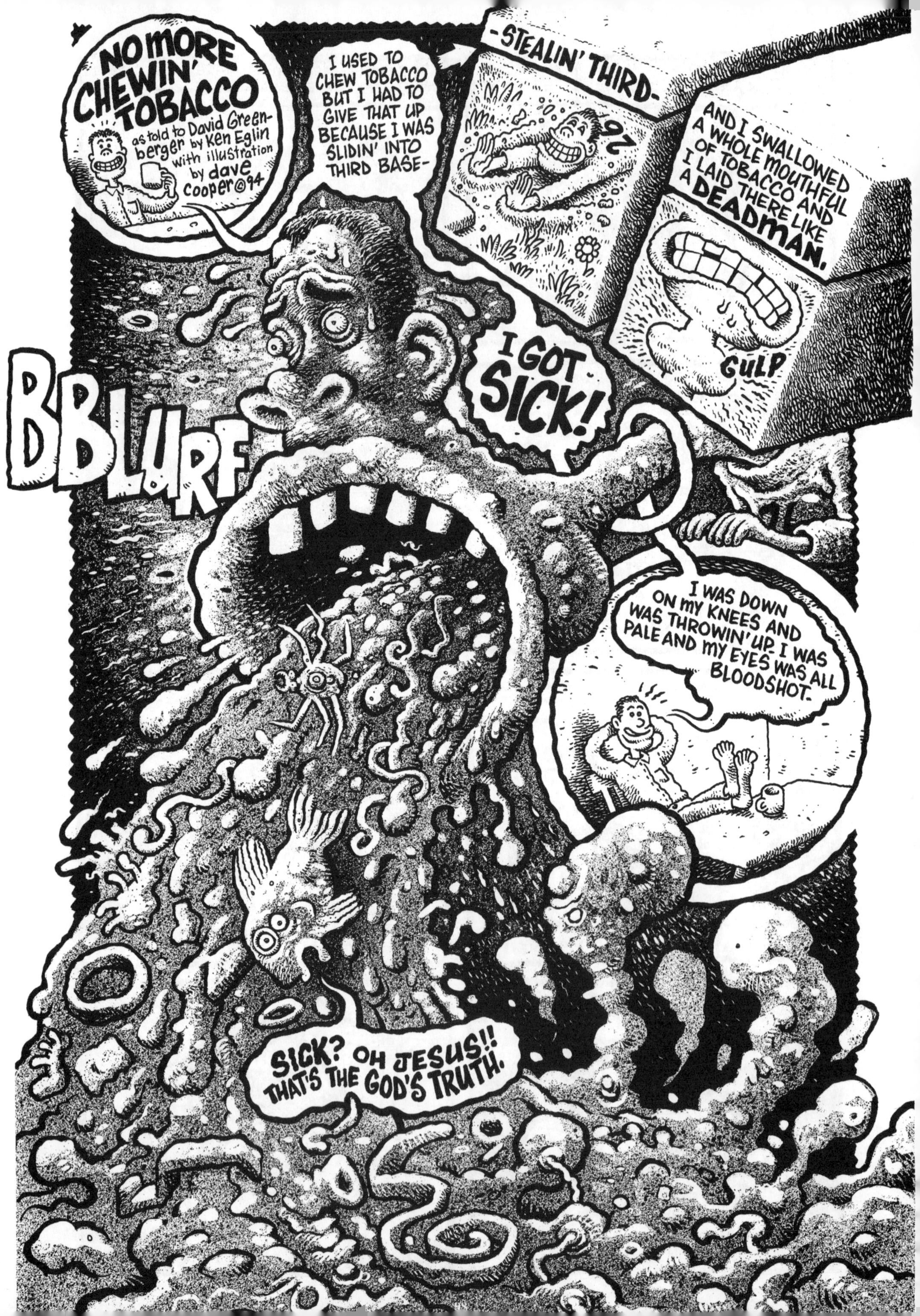
NO MORE CHEWIN' TOBACCO
as told to David Greenberger by Ken Eglin with illustration by dave cooper ©94
I USED TO CHEW TOBACCO BUT I HAD TO GIVE THAT UP BECAUSE I WAS SLIDIN' INTO THIRD BASE-
-STEALIN' THIRD-
AND I SWALLOWED A WHOLE MOUTHFUL OF TOBACCO AND I LAID THERE LIKE A DEADMAN.
GULP
I GOT SICK!
BBLURF!
I WAS DOWN ON MY KNEES AND WAS THROWIN' UP. I WAS PALE AND MY EYES WAS ALL BLOODSHOT.
SICK? OH JESUS!! THAT'S THE GOD'S TRUTH.

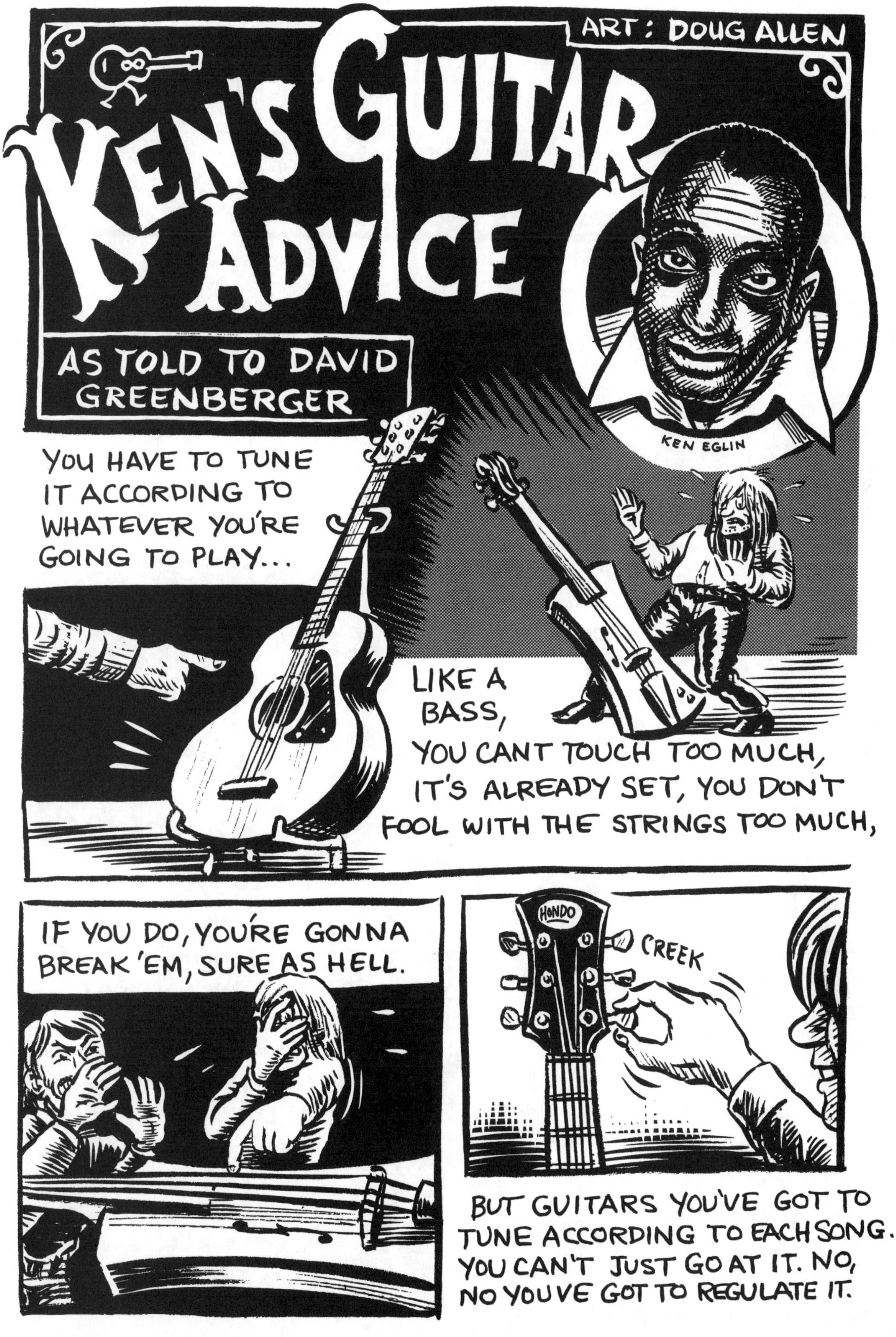
ART: DOUG ALLEN
KEN'S GUITAR ADVICE
AS TOLD TO DAVID GREENBERGER
KEN EGLIN
YOU HAVE TO TUNE IT ACCORDING TO WHATEVER YOU'RE GOING TO PLAY...
LIKE A BASS, YOU CANT TOUCH TOO MUCH, IT'S ALREADY SET, YOU DON'T FOOL WITH THE STRINGS TOO MUCH,
IF YOU DO, YOU'RE GONNA BREAK 'EM, SURE AS HELL.
HONDO
CREEK
BUT GUITARS YOU'VE GOT TO TUNE ACCORDING TO EACH SONG. YOU CAN'T JUST GO AT IT. NO, NO YOU'VE GOT TO REGULATE IT.

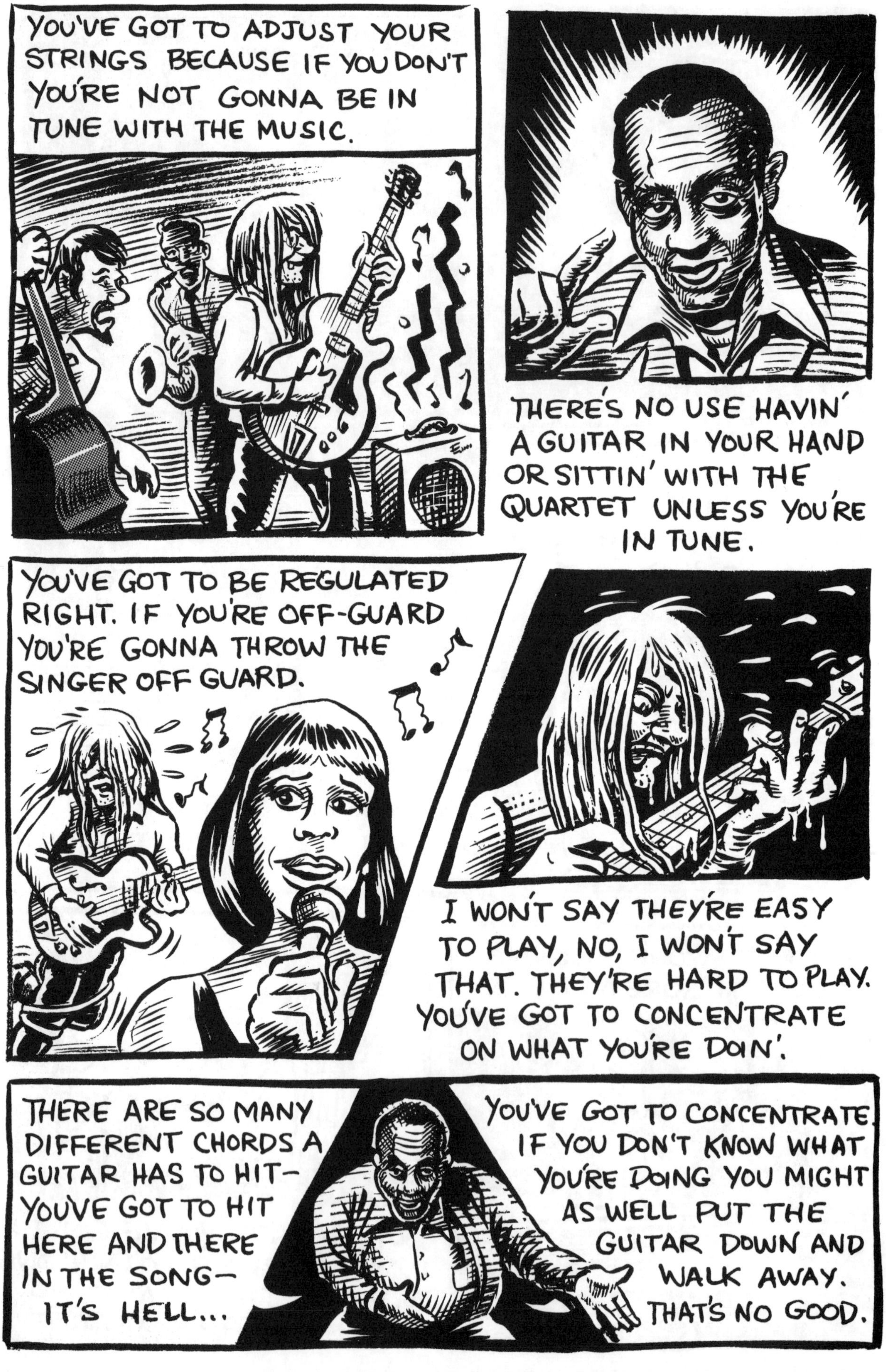
YOU'VE GOT TO ADJUST YOUR STRINGS BECAUSE IF YOU DON'T YOU'RE NOT GONNA BE IN TUNE WITH THE MUSIC.
THERE'S NO USE HAVIN' A GUITAR IN YOUR HAND OR SITTIN' WITH THE QUARTET UNLESS YOU'RE IN TUNE.
YOU'VE GOT TO BE REGULATED RIGHT. IF YOU'RE OFF-GUARD YOU'RE GONNA THROW THE SINGER OFF GUARD.
I WON'T SAY THEY'RE EASY TO PLAY, NO, I WON'T SAY THAT. THEY'RE HARD TO PLAY. YOU'VE GOT TO CONCENTRATE ON WHAT YOU'RE DOIN'.
THERE ARE SO MANY DIFFERENT CHORDS A GUITAR HAS TO HIT- YOU'VE GOT TO HIT HERE AND THERE IN THE SONG- IT'S HELL...
YOU'VE GOT TO CONCENTRATE. IF YOU DON'T KNOW WHAT YOU'RE DOING YOU MIGHT AS WELL PUT THE GUITAR DOWN AND WALK AWAY. THAT'S NO GOOD.

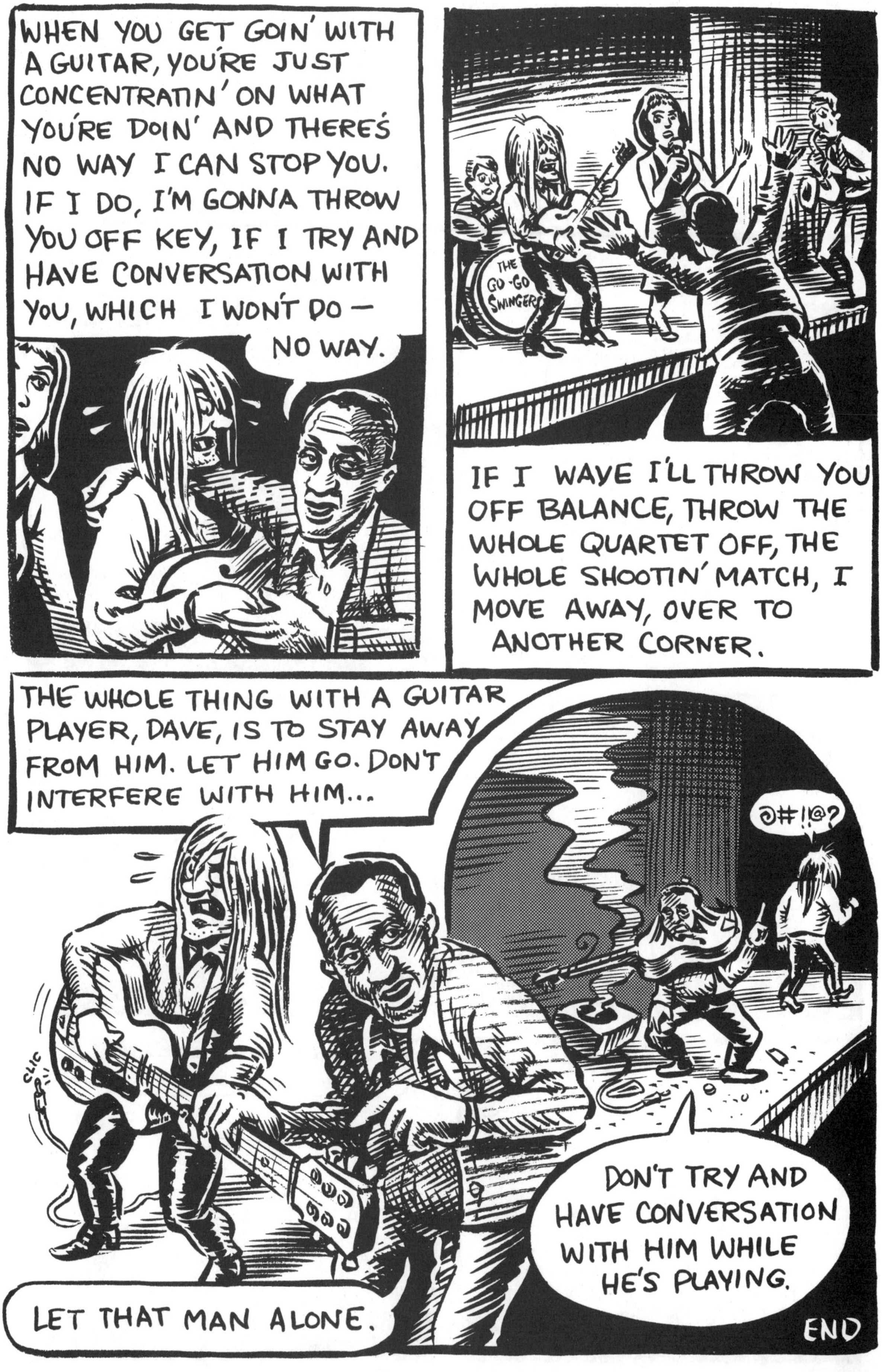
WHEN YOU GET GOIN' WITH A GUITAR, YOU'RE JUST CONCENTRATIN' ON WHAT YOU'RE DOIN' AND THERE'S NO WAY I CAN STOP YOU. IF I DO, I'M GONNA THROW YOU OFF KEY, IF I TRY AND HAVE CONVERSATION WITH YOU, WHICH I WON'T DO —
NO WAY.
THE GO-GO SWINGERS
IF I WAVE I'LL THROW YOU OFF BALANCE, THROW THE WHOLE QUARTET OFF, THE WHOLE SHOOTIN' MATCH, I MOVE AWAY, OVER TO ANOTHER CORNER.
THE WHOLE THING WITH A GUITAR PLAYER, DAVE, IS TO STAY AWAY FROM HIM. LET HIM GO. DON'T INTERFERE WITH HIM...
@#!!@?
CLIC
DON'T TRY AND HAVE CONVERSATION WITH HIM WHILE HE'S PLAYING.
LET THAT MAN ALONE.
END

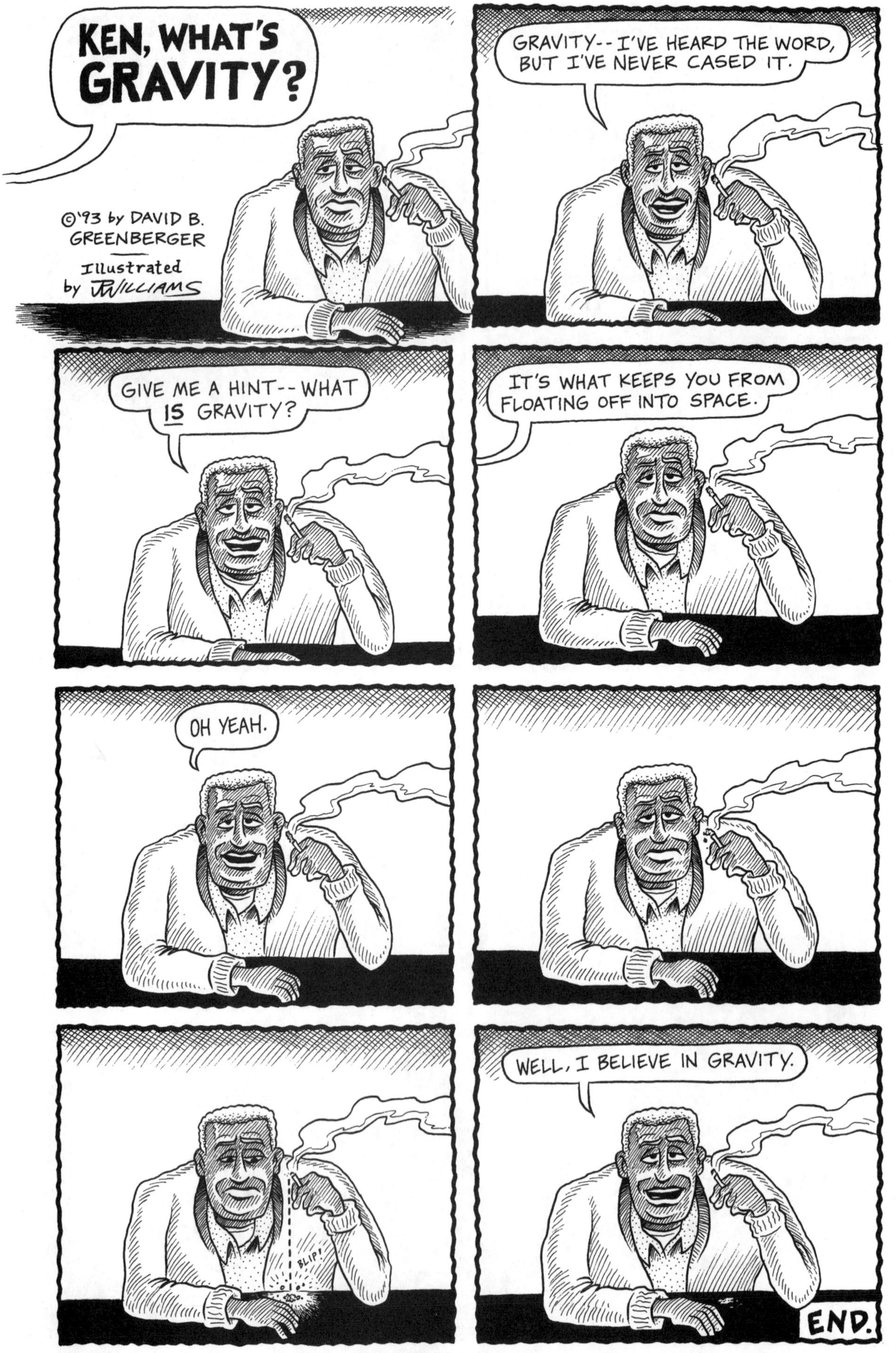

KEN, WHAT'S GRAVITY?
©'93 by DAVID B. GREENBERGER
Illustrated by J. WILLIAMS
GRAVITY-- I'VE HEARD THE WORD, BUT I'VE NEVER CASED IT.
GIVE ME A HINT-- WHAT IS GRAVITY?
IT'S WHAT KEEPS YOU FROM FLOATING OFF INTO SPACE.
OH YEAH.
BLIP!
WELL, I BELIEVE IN GRAVITY.
END.

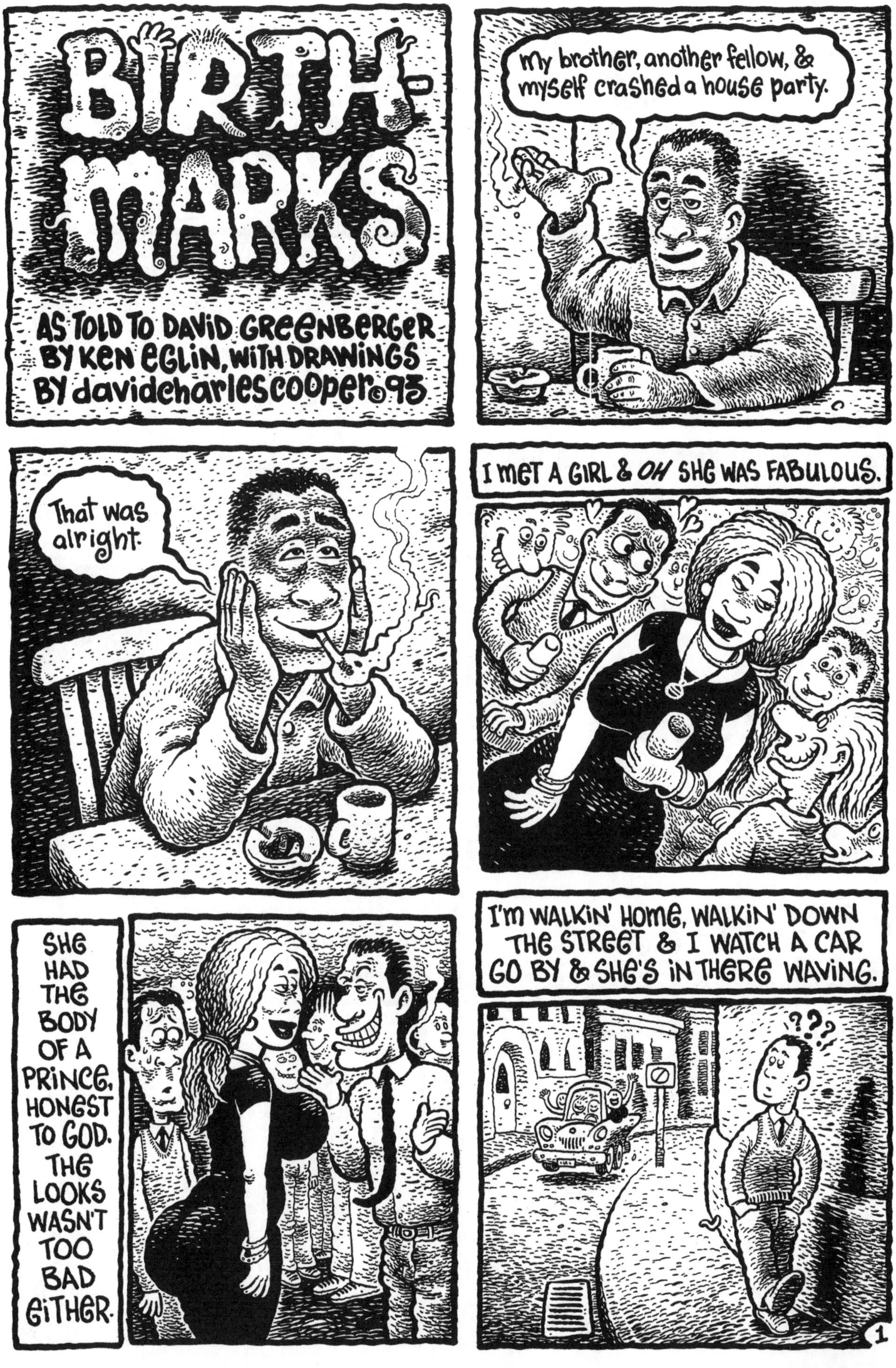
BIRTH-MARKS
AS TOLD TO DAVID GREENBERGER BY KEN EGLIN, WITH DRAWINGS BY davidcharlescooper © 93
My brother, another fellow, & myself crashed a house party.
That was alright.
I MET A GIRL & OH SHE WAS FABULOUS.
SHE HAD THE BODY OF A PRINCE. HONEST TO GOD. THE LOOKS WASN'T TOO BAD EITHER.
I'M WALKIN' HOME, WALKIN' DOWN THE STREET & I WATCH A CAR GO BY & SHE'S IN THERE WAVING.
???
1

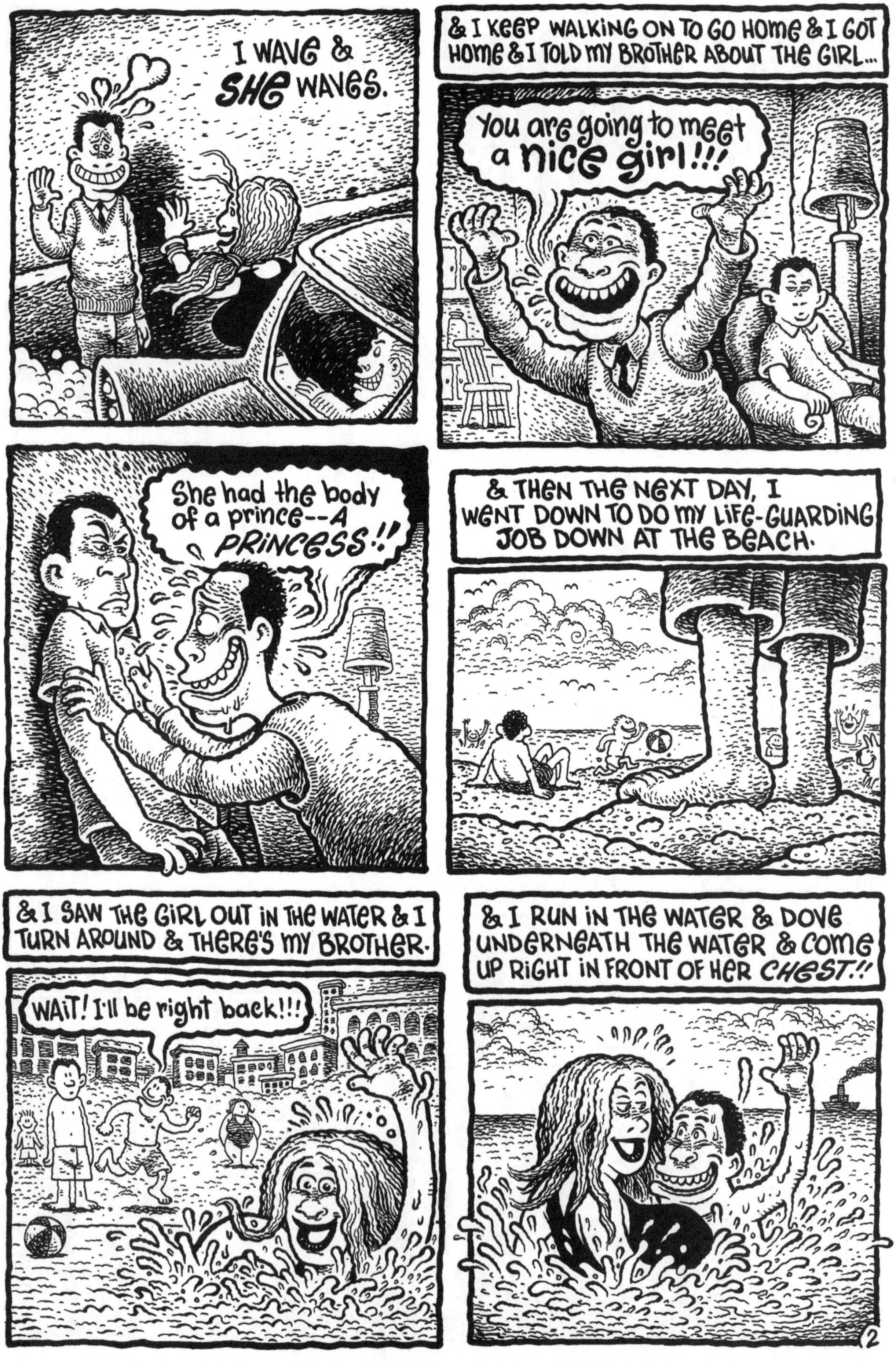
I WAVE &
SHE WAVES.
& I KEEP WALKING ON TO GO HOME & I GOT HOME & I TOLD MY BROTHER ABOUT THE GIRL...
You are going to meet a nice girl!!!
She had the body of a prince--A PRINCESS!!
& THEN THE NEXT DAY, I WENT DOWN TO DO MY LIFE-GUARDING JOB DOWN AT THE BEACH.
& I SAW THE GIRL OUT IN THE WATER & I TURN AROUND & THERE'S MY BROTHER.
WAIT! I'll be right back!!!
& I RUN IN THE WATER & DOVE UNDERNEATH THE WATER & COME UP RIGHT IN FRONT OF HER CHEST!!
2

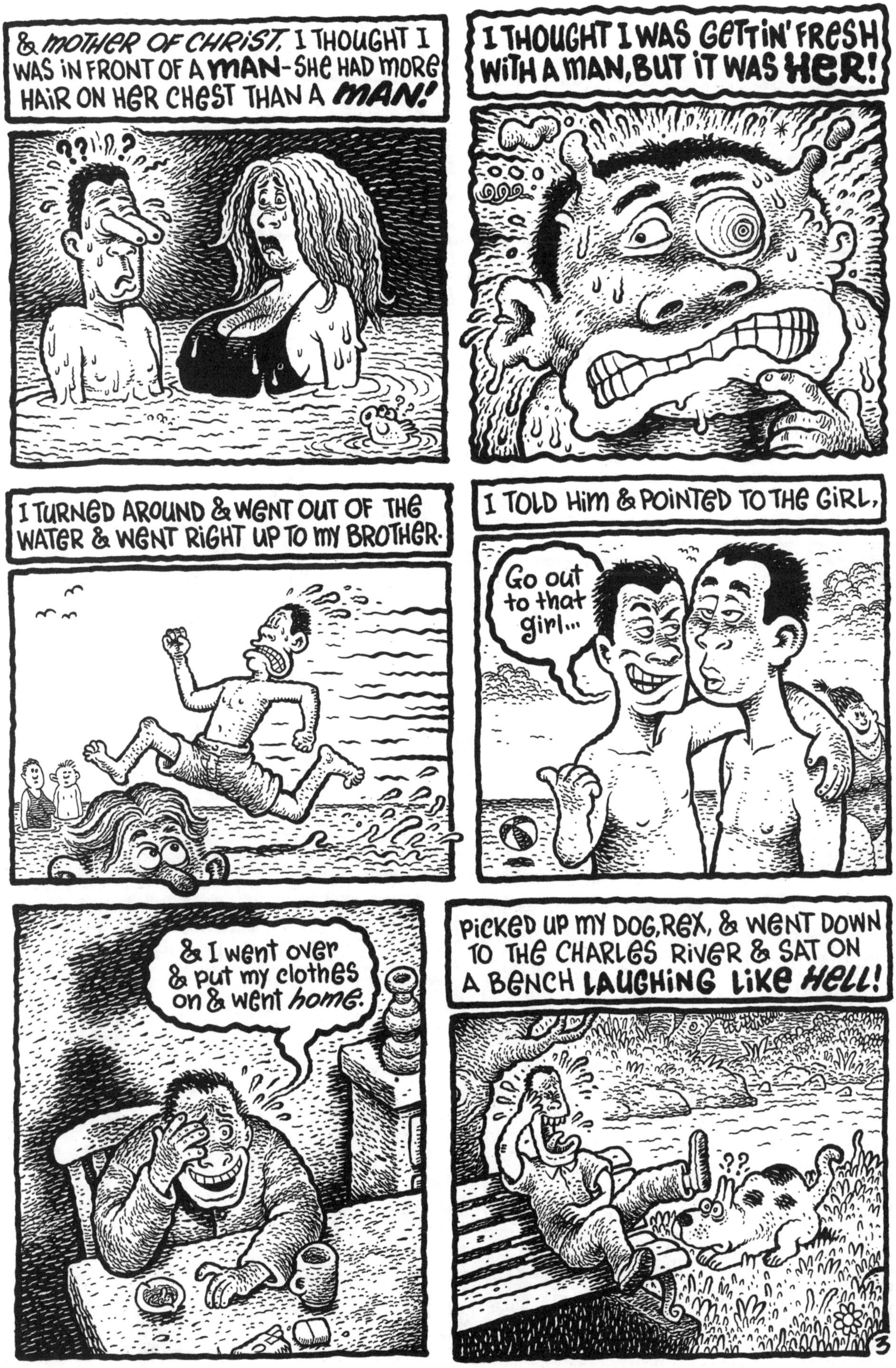
& MOTHER OF CHRIST, I THOUGHT I WAS IN FRONT OF A MAN - SHE HAD MORE HAIR ON HER CHEST THAN A MAN!
I THOUGHT I WAS GETTIN' FRESH WITH A MAN, BUT IT WAS HER!
I TURNED AROUND & WENT OUT OF THE WATER & WENT RIGHT UP TO MY BROTHER.
I TOLD HIM & POINTED TO THE GIRL,
Go out to that girl...
& I went over & put my clothes on & went home.
PICKED UP MY DOG, REX, & WENT DOWN TO THE CHARLES RIVER & SAT ON A BENCH LAUGHING LIKE HELL!
3

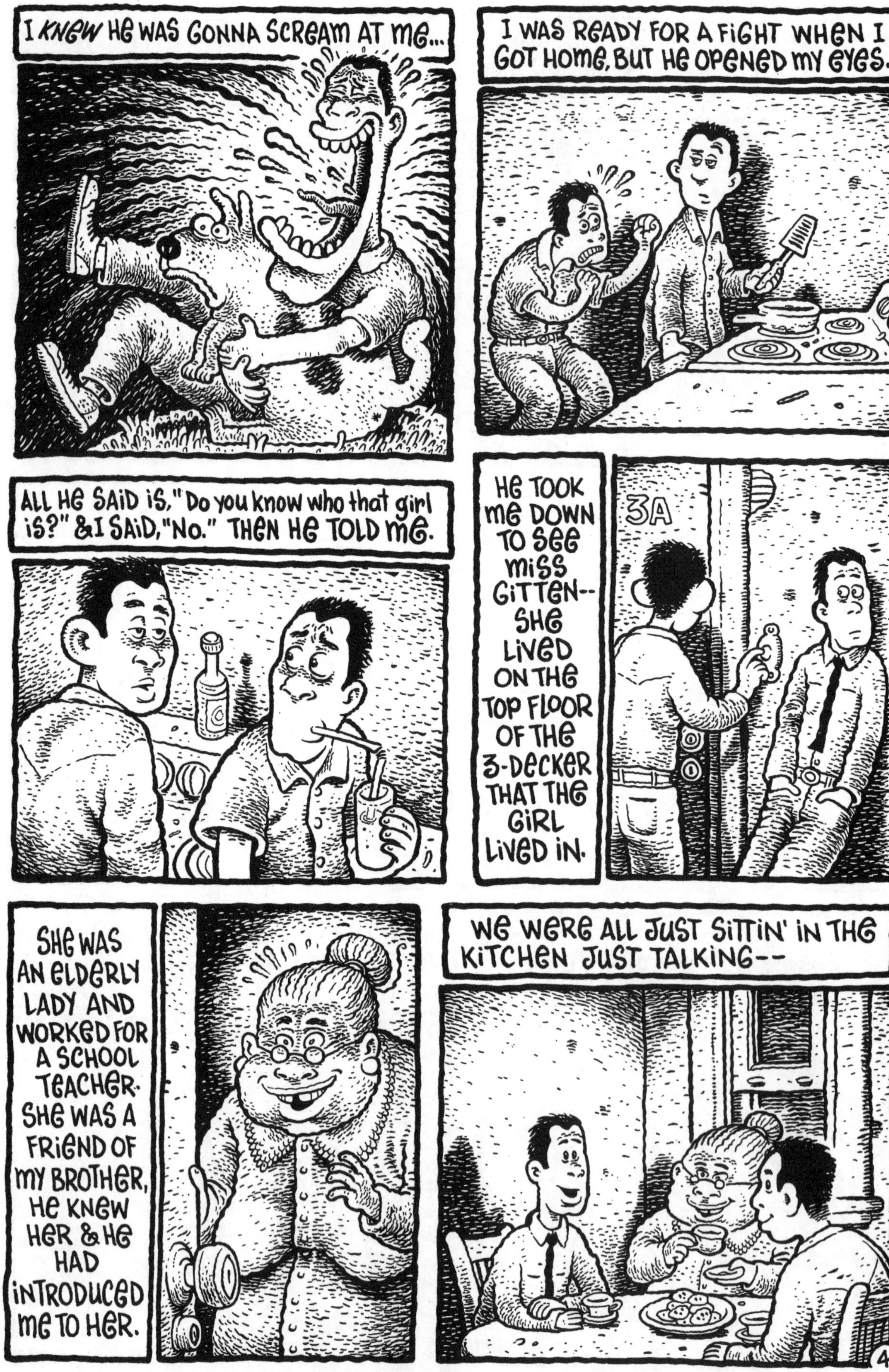
I *KNEW* HE WAS GONNA SCREAM AT ME...
I WAS READY FOR A FIGHT WHEN I GOT HOME, BUT HE OPENED MY EYES.
ALL HE SAID IS, "Do you know who that girl is?" & I SAID, "No." THEN HE TOLD ME.
HE TOOK ME DOWN TO SEE MISS GITTEN-- SHE LIVED ON THE TOP FLOOR OF THE 3-DECKER THAT THE GIRL LIVED IN.
3A
SHE WAS AN ELDERLY LADY AND WORKED FOR A SCHOOL TEACHER. SHE WAS A FRIEND OF MY BROTHER, HE KNEW HER & HE HAD INTRODUCED ME TO HER.
WE WERE ALL JUST SITTIN' IN THE KITCHEN JUST TALKING--
4

SHE'D TALK ABOUT HER WORK & SUCH— & A KNOCK COME ON THE DOOR.

KNOCK KNOCK

SO I WENT OVER TO ANSWER THE DOOR & THERE WAS THE GIRL, **RUTH**, TO MY SURPRISE.

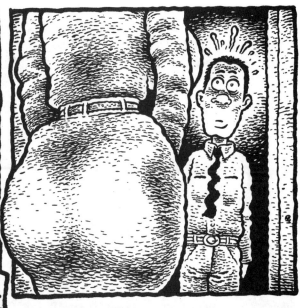

I DIDN'T KNOW SHE LIVED IN THAT HOUSE. HER MOTHER OWNED THE 3-DECKER.

3A

& OH SHE LOOKED LOVELY, ALL DRESSED UP & ALL MADE UP.

BUT ALL I COULD SEE WAS THAT **HAIRY** CHEST!!

HHHAWHA WHAW

5

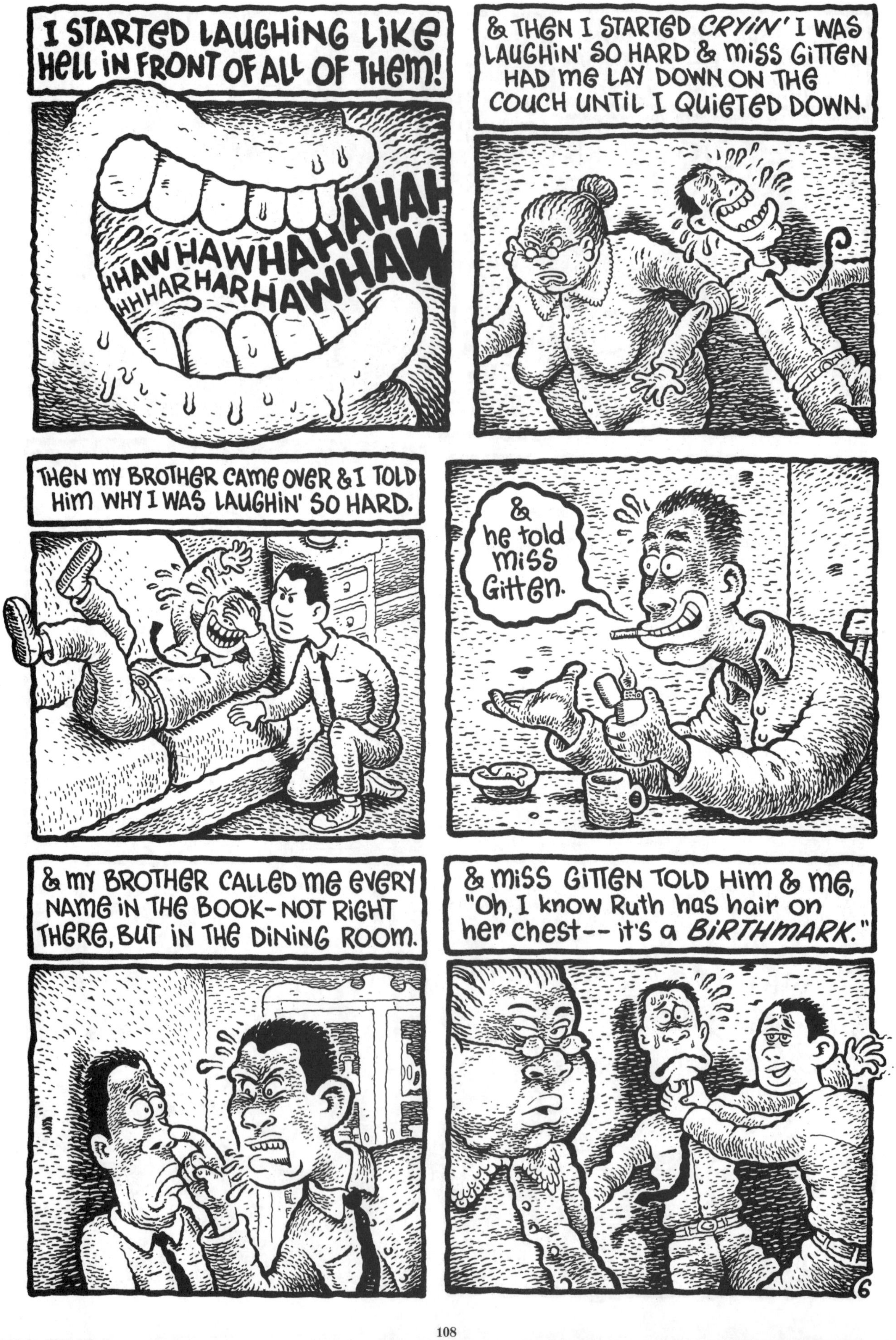
I STARTED LAUGHING LIKE HELL IN FRONT OF ALL OF THEM!
HHAW HAW HAW HAHAHAH HHHAR HAR HAR HAWHAW
& THEN I STARTED CRYIN' I WAS LAUGHIN' SO HARD & MISS GITTEN HAD ME LAY DOWN ON THE COUCH UNTIL I QUIETED DOWN.
THEN MY BROTHER CAME OVER & I TOLD HIM WHY I WAS LAUGHIN' SO HARD.
& he told miss Gitten.
& MY BROTHER CALLED ME EVERY NAME IN THE BOOK- NOT RIGHT THERE, BUT IN THE DINING ROOM.
& MISS GITTEN TOLD HIM & ME, "Oh, I know Ruth has hair on her chest-- it's a BIRTHMARK."
6

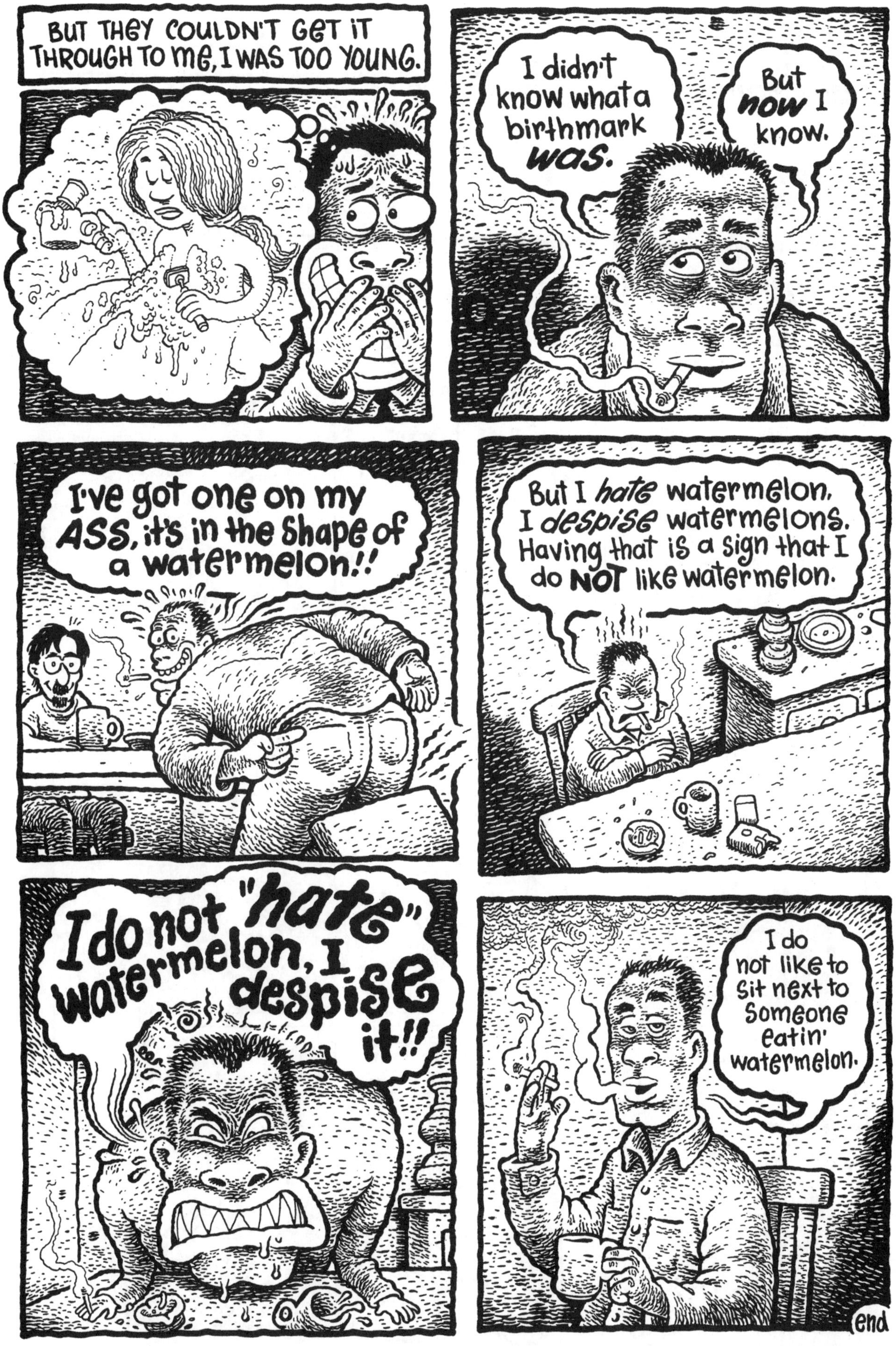
BUT THEY COULDN'T GET IT THROUGH TO ME, I WAS TOO YOUNG.
I didn't know what a birthmark *was*.
But *now* I know.
I've got one on my *ASS*, it's in the shape of a watermelon!!
But I *hate* watermelon, I *despise* watermelons. Having that is a sign that I do **NOT** like watermelon.
I do not "hate" watermelon, I despise it!!
I do not like to sit next to someone eatin' watermelon.
end

KEN'S CORNER

Ken Eglin's reviews of records, etc. As told to David Greenberger, Illustrated by Wayno

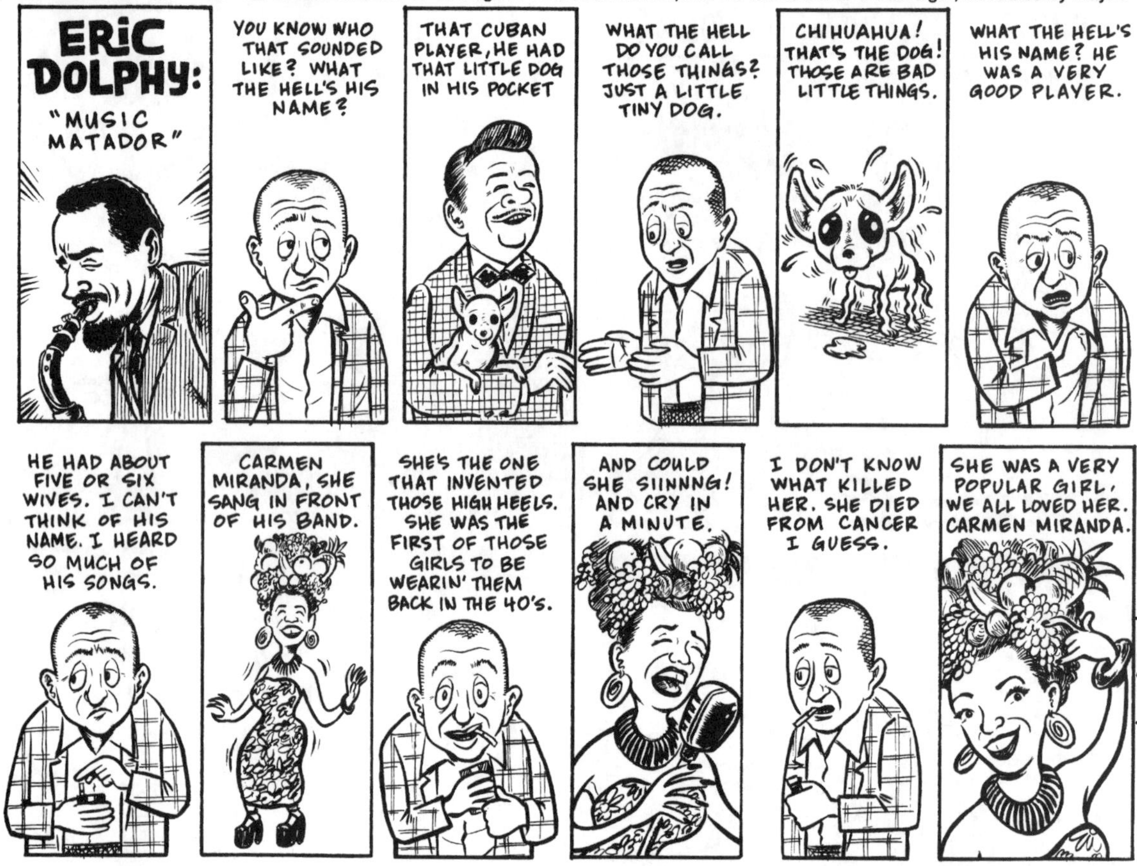
ERIC DOLPHY:
"MUSIC MATADOR"
YOU KNOW WHO THAT SOUNDED LIKE? WHAT THE HELL'S HIS NAME?
THAT CUBAN PLAYER, HE HAD THAT LITTLE DOG IN HIS POCKET
WHAT THE HELL DO YOU CALL THOSE THINGS? JUST A LITTLE TINY DOG.
CHIHUAHUA! THAT'S THE DOG! THOSE ARE BAD LITTLE THINGS.
WHAT THE HELL'S HIS NAME? HE WAS A VERY GOOD PLAYER.
HE HAD ABOUT FIVE OR SIX WIVES. I CAN'T THINK OF HIS NAME. I HEARD SO MUCH OF HIS SONGS.
CARMEN MIRANDA, SHE SANG IN FRONT OF HIS BAND.
SHE'S THE ONE THAT INVENTED THOSE HIGH HEELS. SHE WAS THE FIRST OF THOSE GIRLS TO BE WEARIN' THEM BACK IN THE 40'S.
AND COULD SHE SIINNNG! AND CRY IN A MINUTE.
I DON'T KNOW WHAT KILLED HER. SHE DIED FROM CANCER I GUESS.
SHE WAS A VERY POPULAR GIRL, WE ALL LOVED HER. CARMEN MIRANDA.
Wayno ©94

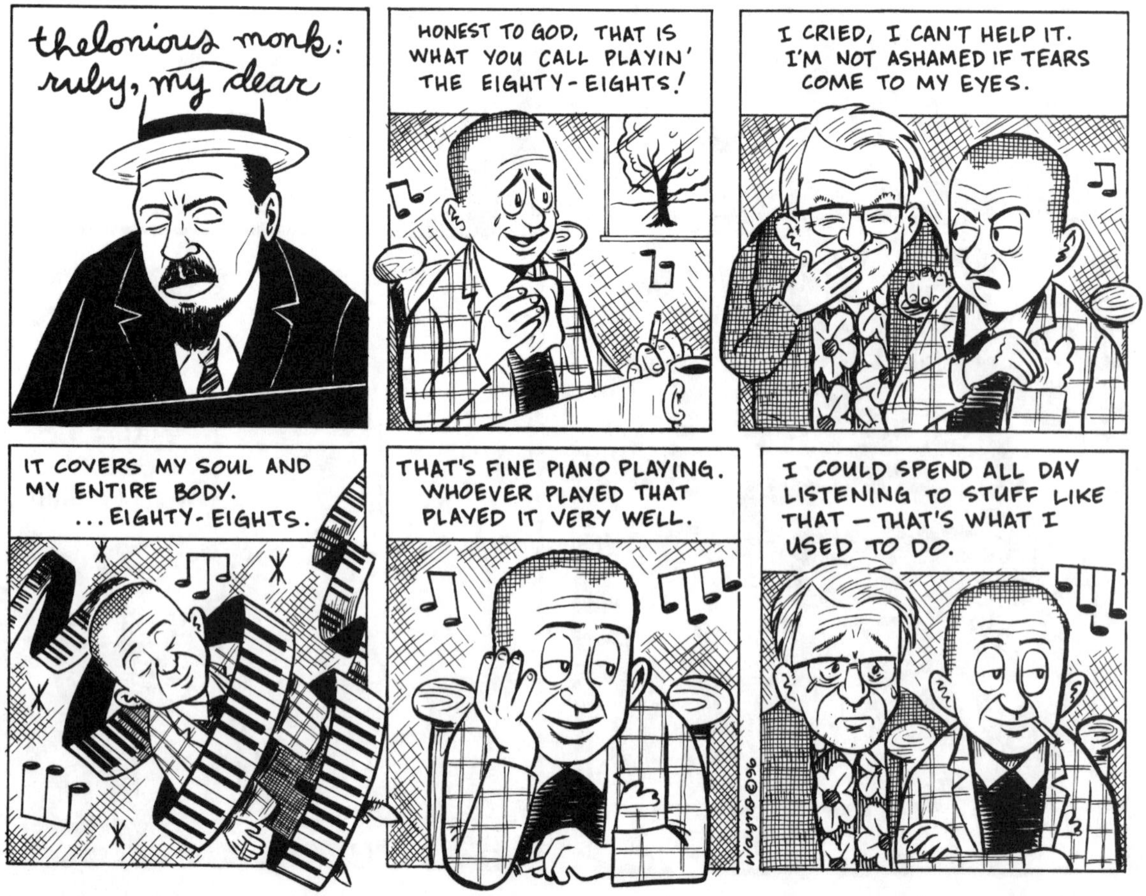
thelonious monk: ruby, my dear
HONEST TO GOD, THAT IS WHAT YOU CALL PLAYIN' THE EIGHTY-EIGHTS!
I CRIED, I CAN'T HELP IT. I'M NOT ASHAMED IF TEARS COME TO MY EYES.
IT COVERS MY SOUL AND MY ENTIRE BODY. ...EIGHTY-EIGHTS.
THAT'S FINE PIANO PLAYING. WHOEVER PLAYED THAT PLAYED IT VERY WELL.
I COULD SPEND ALL DAY LISTENING TO STUFF LIKE THAT — THAT'S WHAT I USED TO DO.
Wayno ©96

Abe Surgecoff

1920—

Shoes is in the Bible. Read the Bible in the library, and it came out that you're not supposed to have any sneakers on, just plain shoes. And not torn stockings.

◆

Frankenstein was a man. He used a mask on his face. This guy had no doubts, and he liked to kill people. He didn't like to live too long in his old age. So the people after a while would dislike him. He himself made a couple masks to kill people for their existence. And well, he was a man that had no fear for people. But when he was in that cage — if you want to call it that — well, they used to feed him, and he sat down and invented medicine. Medicine for disrupting the face and hands. He used to make this medicine so he could disrobe some person, and to disfigure himself.

◆

I used to play banjo in the service and they made me cut it out. I can't play it now. I played it pretty good, but I lost touch with it. I couldn't play it anymore when I came out of the service.

◆

Gravity is oxygen that it takes and eliminates the air and you can't breathe. Gravity also, you can't live without gravity, you have to have gravity. Gravity is another thing that you cannot get around, gravity is not to move around, your oxygen is worn out. And another thing, you can't hold anything in your hand or the gravity would be forced to take it away and you're a dead guy if property comes down, down on the ground.

◆

These boys like hot coffee — give 'em hot coffee and they'll be your friend. These guys wait for hot coffee in the morning.

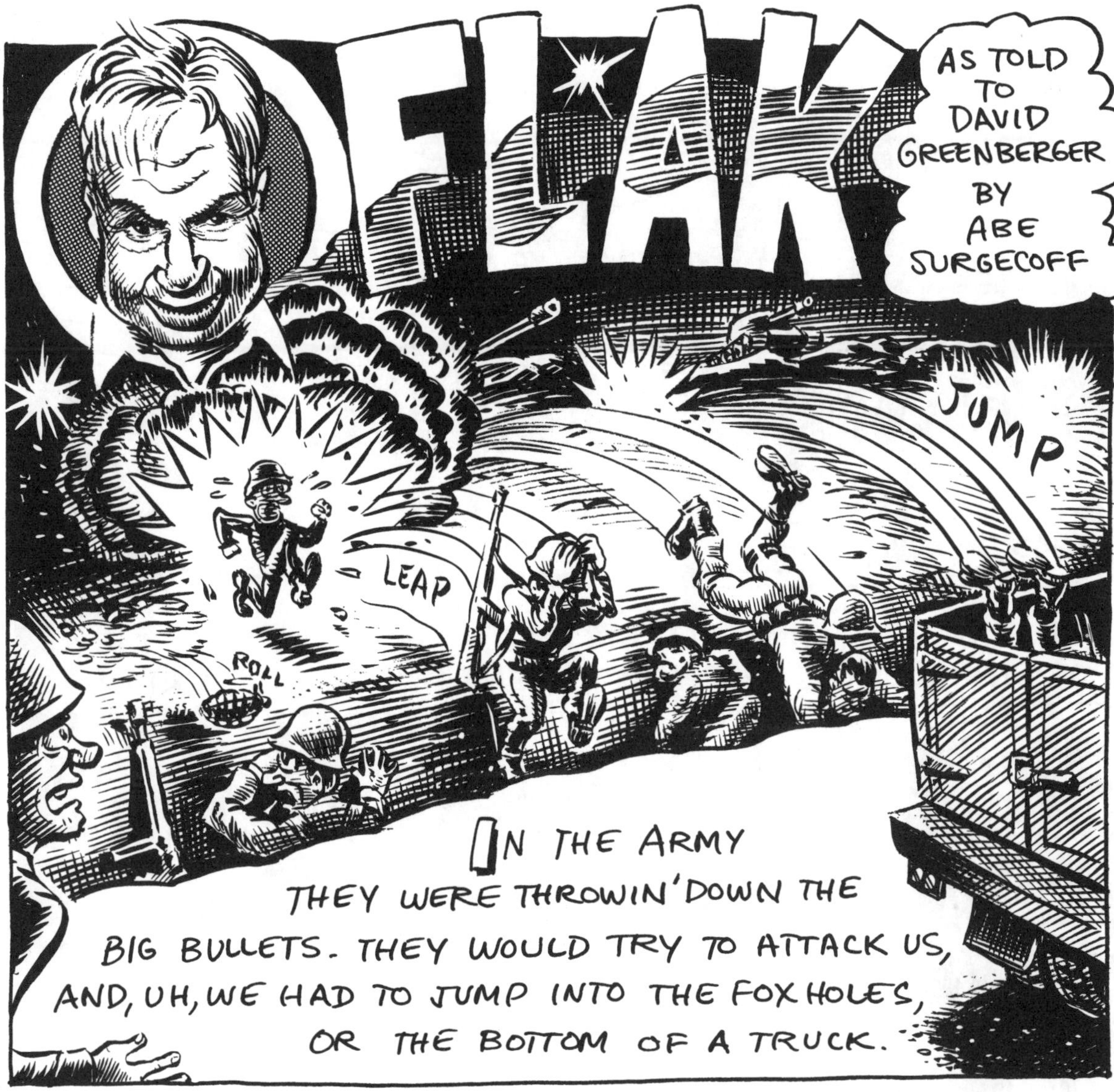
FLAK
AS TOLD TO DAVID GREENBERGER BY ABE SURGECOFF
JUMP
LEAP
ROLL
IN THE ARMY THEY WERE THROWIN' DOWN THE BIG BULLETS. THEY WOULD TRY TO ATTACK US, AND, UH, WE HAD TO JUMP INTO THE FOX HOLES, OR THE BOTTOM OF A TRUCK.

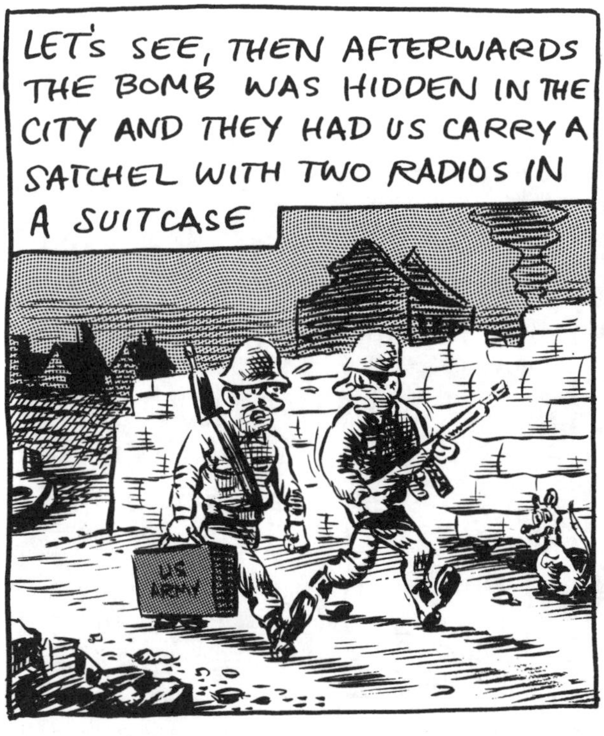
LET'S SEE, THEN AFTERWARDS THE BOMB WAS HIDDEN IN THE CITY AND THEY HAD US CARRY A SATCHEL WITH TWO RADIOS IN A SUITCASE
US ARMY

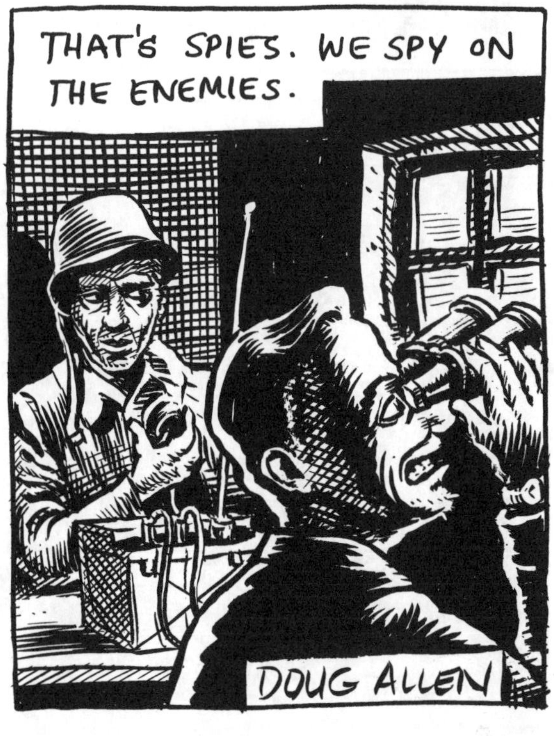
THAT'S SPIES. WE SPY ON THE ENEMIES.
DOUG ALLEN

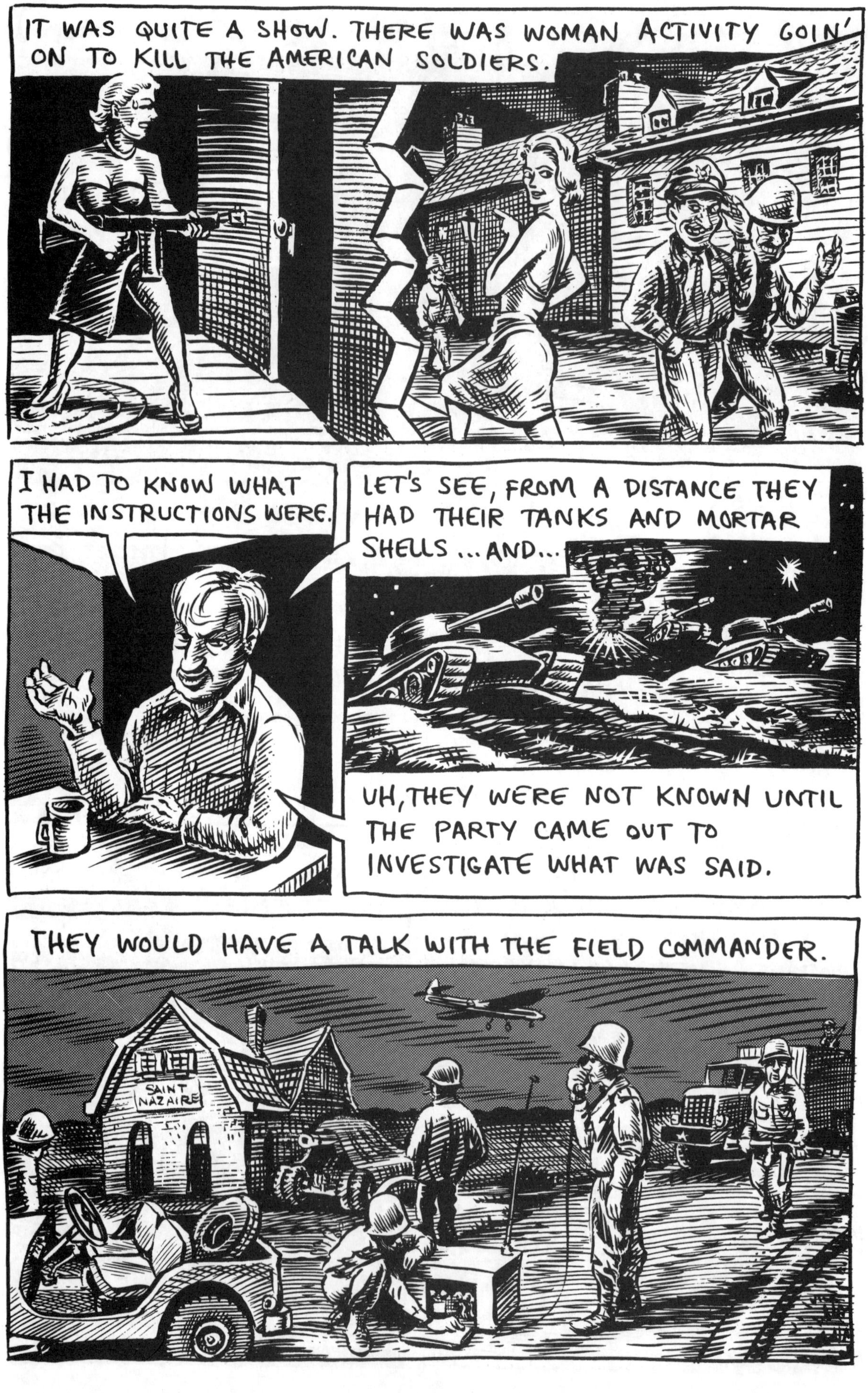
IT WAS QUITE A SHOW. THERE WAS WOMAN ACTIVITY GOIN' ON TO KILL THE AMERICAN SOLDIERS.
I HAD TO KNOW WHAT THE INSTRUCTIONS WERE.
LET'S SEE, FROM A DISTANCE THEY HAD THEIR TANKS AND MORTAR SHELLS ...AND...
UH, THEY WERE NOT KNOWN UNTIL THE PARTY CAME OUT TO INVESTIGATE WHAT WAS SAID.
THEY WOULD HAVE A TALK WITH THE FIELD COMMANDER.
SAINT NAZAIRE

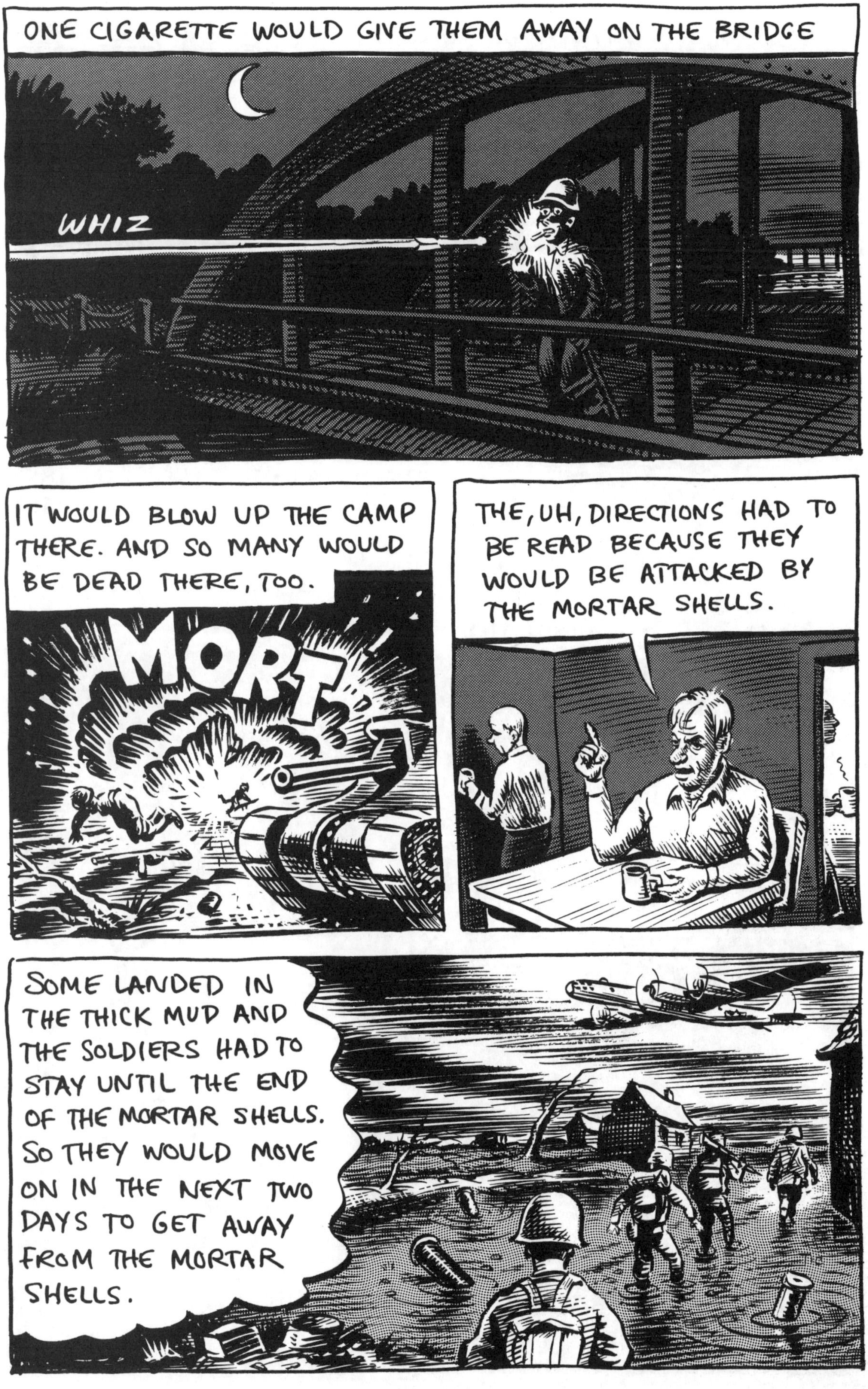
ONE CIGARETTE WOULD GIVE THEM AWAY ON THE BRIDGE
WHIZ
IT WOULD BLOW UP THE CAMP THERE. AND SO MANY WOULD BE DEAD THERE, TOO.
MORT
THE, UH, DIRECTIONS HAD TO BE READ BECAUSE THEY WOULD BE ATTACKED BY THE MORTAR SHELLS.
SOME LANDED IN THE THICK MUD AND THE SOLDIERS HAD TO STAY UNTIL THE END OF THE MORTAR SHELLS. SO THEY WOULD MOVE ON IN THE NEXT TWO DAYS TO GET AWAY FROM THE MORTAR SHELLS.

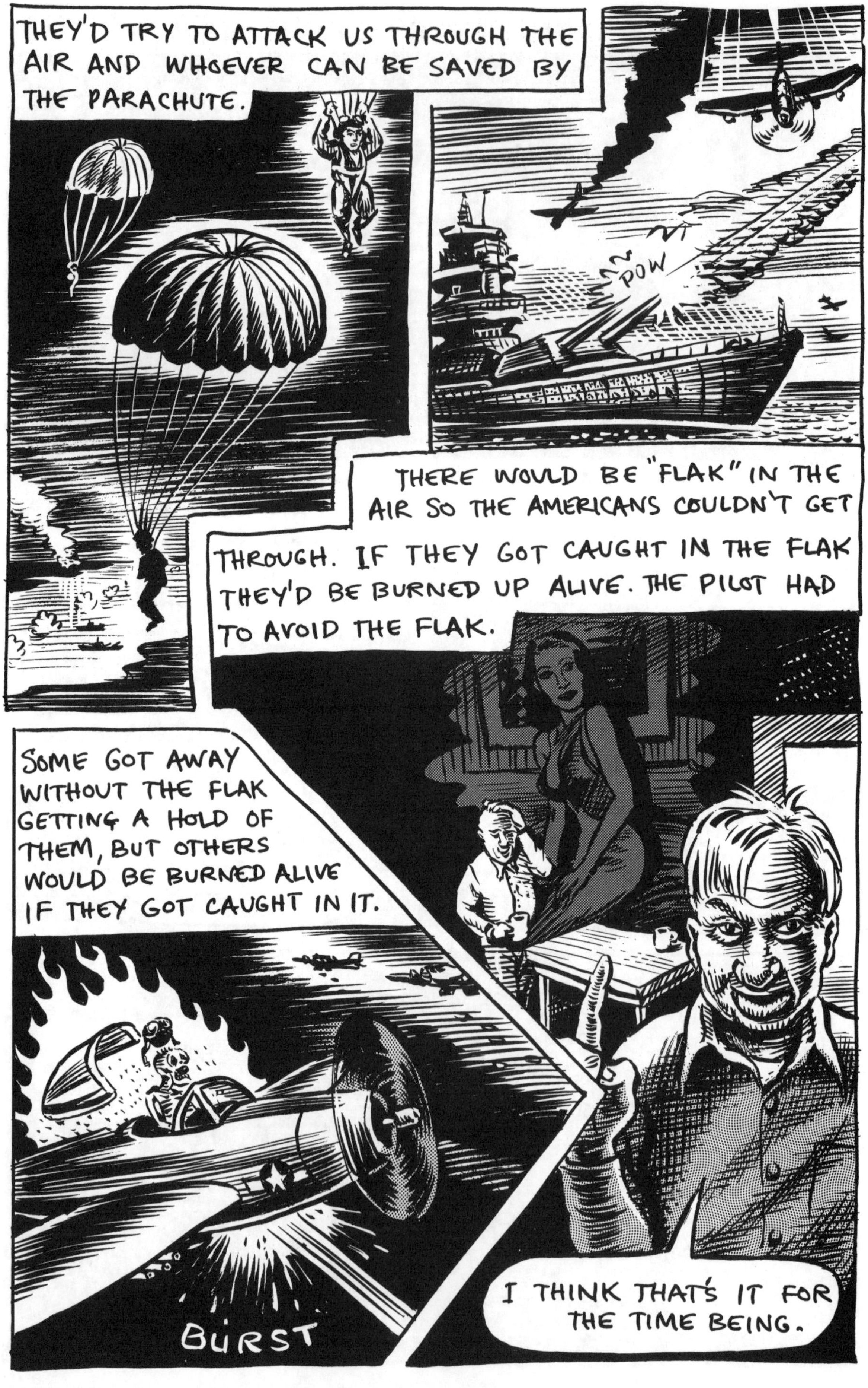
THEY'D TRY TO ATTACK US THROUGH THE AIR AND WHOEVER CAN BE SAVED BY THE PARACHUTE.
POW
THERE WOULD BE "FLAK" IN THE AIR SO THE AMERICANS COULDN'T GET THROUGH. IF THEY GOT CAUGHT IN THE FLAK THEY'D BE BURNED UP ALIVE. THE PILOT HAD TO AVOID THE FLAK.
SOME GOT AWAY WITHOUT THE FLAK GETTING A HOLD OF THEM, BUT OTHERS WOULD BE BURNED ALIVE IF THEY GOT CAUGHT IN IT.
BURST
I THINK THAT'S IT FOR THE TIME BEING.

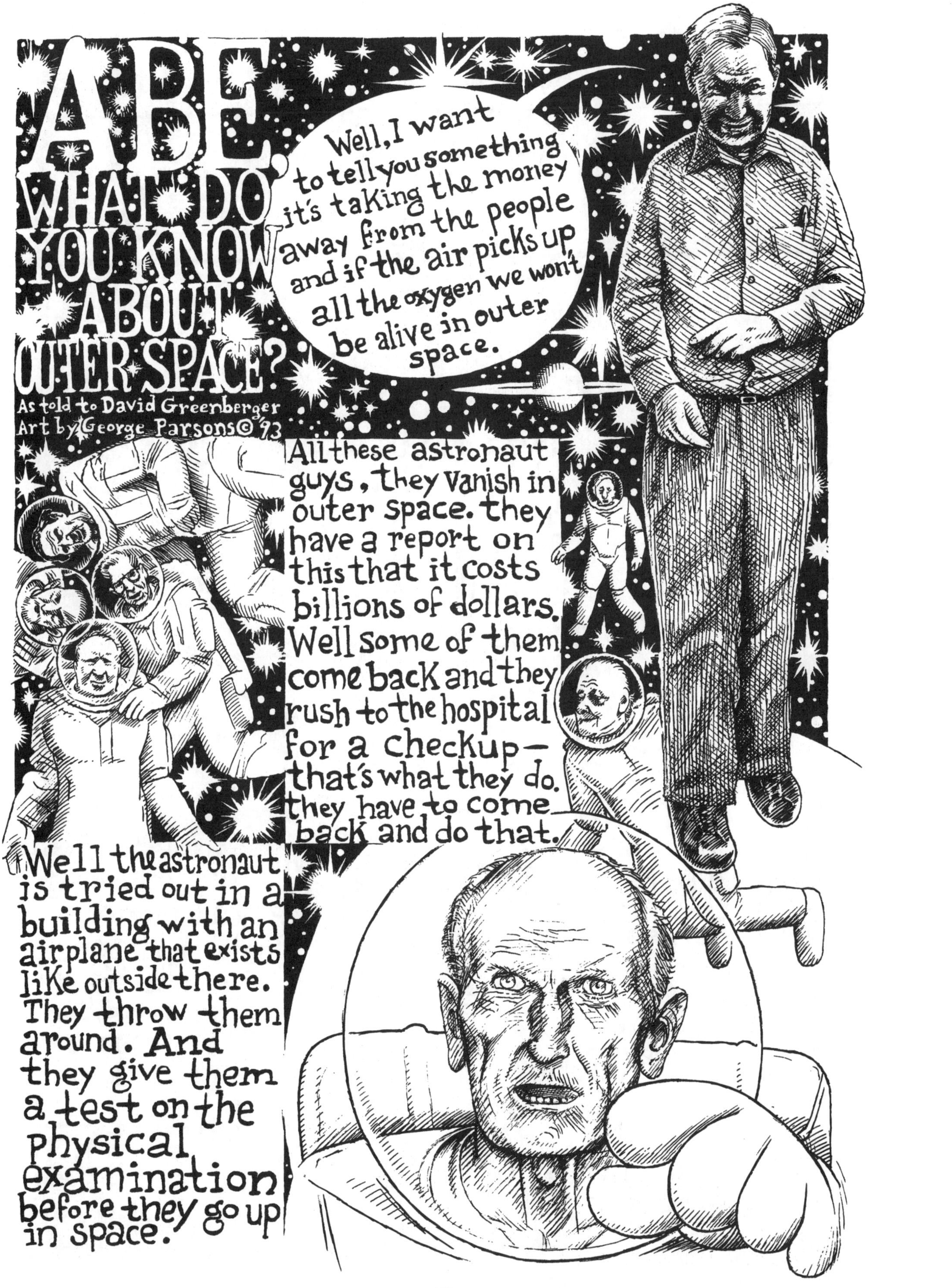

ABE, WHAT DO YOU KNOW ABOUT OUTER SPACE?
As told to David Greenberger
Art by George Parsons © '93
Well, I want to tell you something it's taking the money away from the people and if the air picks up all the oxygen we won't be alive in outer space.
All these astronaut guys, they vanish in outer space. they have a report on this that it costs billions of dollars. Well some of them come back and they rush to the hospital for a checkup— that's what they do. they have to come back and do that.
Well the astronaut is tried out in a building with an airplane that exists like outside there. They throw them around. And they give them a test on the physical examination before they go up in space.

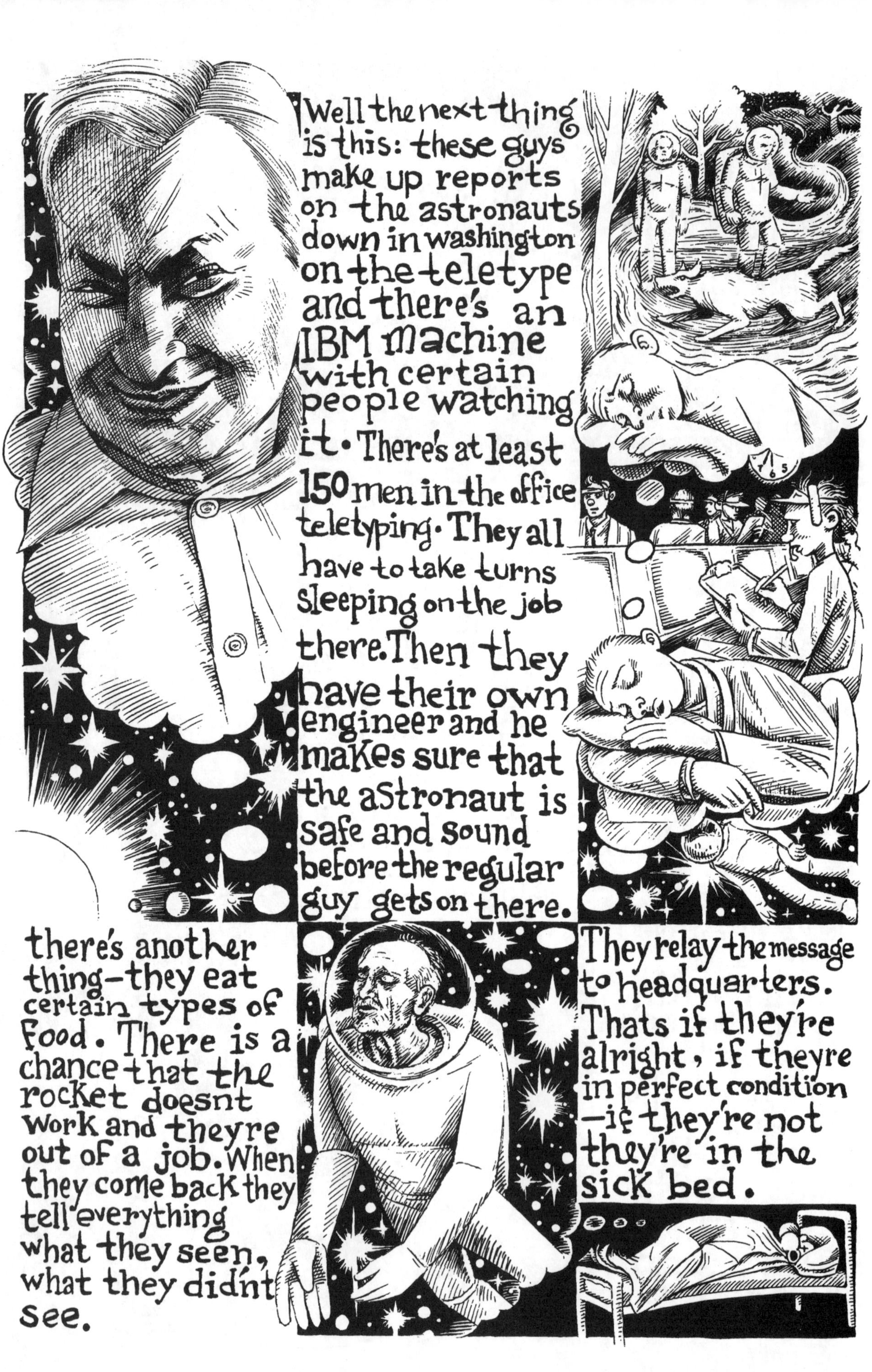
Well the next thing is this: these guys make up reports on the astronauts down in washington on the teletype and there's an IBM machine with certain people watching it. There's at least 150 men in the office teletyping. They all have to take turns sleeping on the job there. Then they have their own engineer and he makes sure that the astronaut is safe and sound before the regular guy gets on there.
there's another thing-they eat certain types of food. There is a chance that the rocket doesnt work and theyre out of a job. When they come back they tell everything what they seen, what they didn't see.
They relay the message to headquarters. Thats if they're alright, if theyre in perfect condition -if they're not they're in the sick bed.

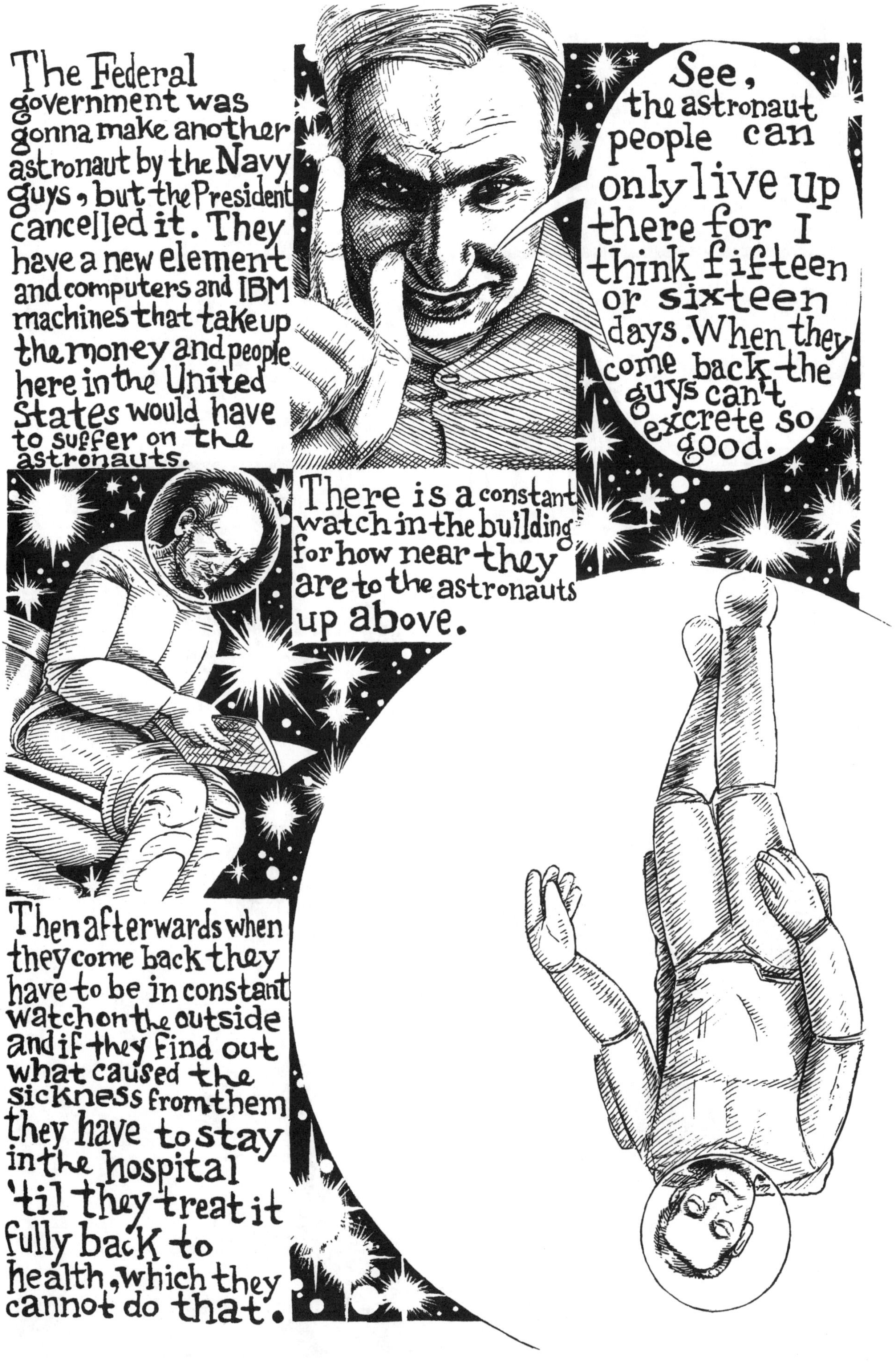
The Federal government was gonna make another astronaut by the Navy guys, but the President cancelled it. They have a new element and computers and IBM machines that take up the money and people here in the United States would have to suffer on the astronauts.
See, the astronaut people can only live up there for I think fifteen or sixteen days. When they come back the guys can't excrete so good.
There is a constant watch in the building for how near they are to the astronauts up above.
Then afterwards when they come back they have to be in constant watch on the outside and if they find out what caused the sickness from them they have to stay in the hospital 'til they treat it fully back to health, which they cannot do that.

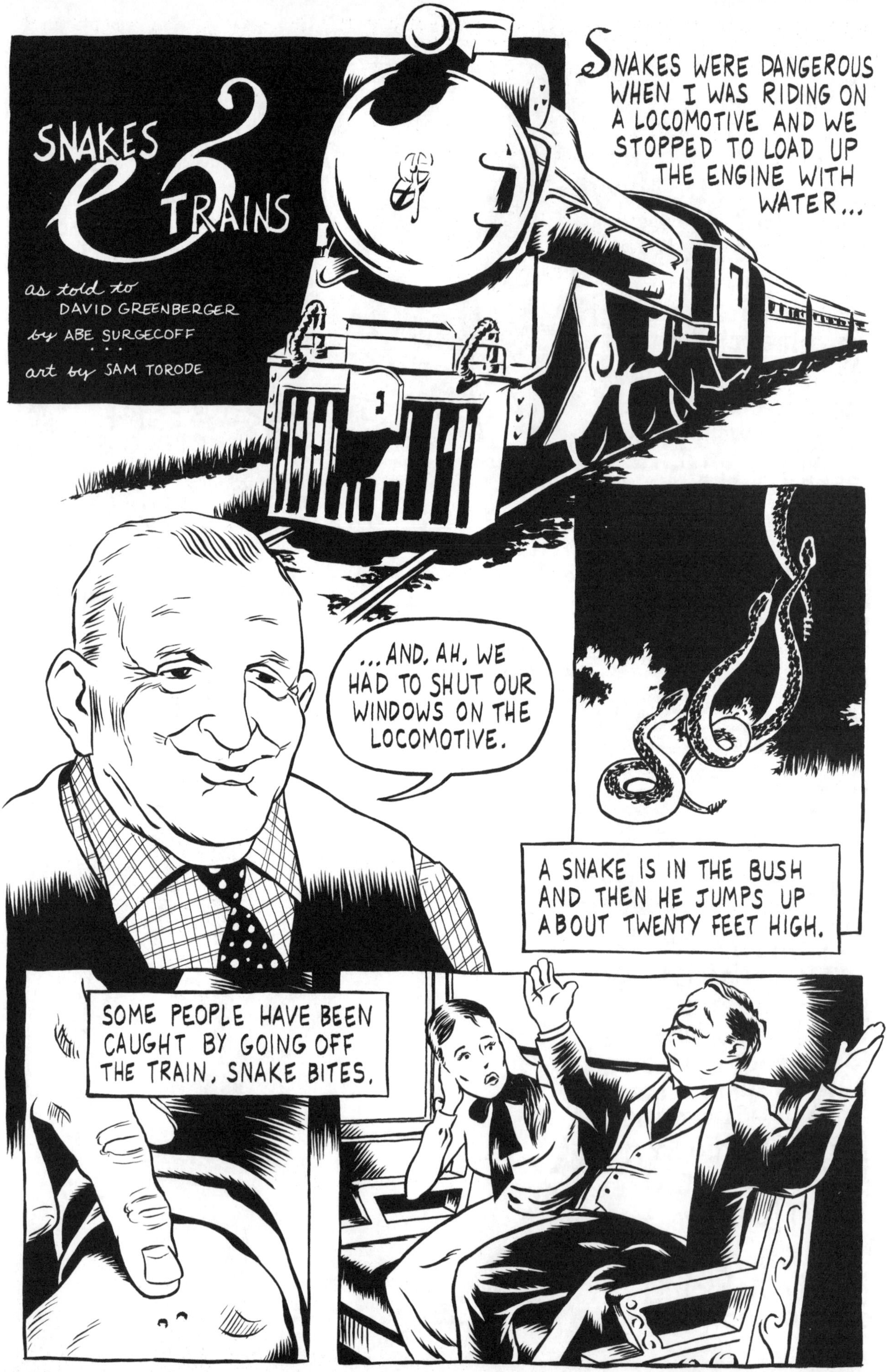
SNAKES & TRAINS
as told to DAVID GREENBERGER
by ABE SURGECOFF
art by SAM TORODE
SNAKES WERE DANGEROUS WHEN I WAS RIDING ON A LOCOMOTIVE AND WE STOPPED TO LOAD UP THE ENGINE WITH WATER...
...AND, AH, WE HAD TO SHUT OUR WINDOWS ON THE LOCOMOTIVE.
A SNAKE IS IN THE BUSH AND THEN HE JUMPS UP ABOUT TWENTY FEET HIGH.
SOME PEOPLE HAVE BEEN CAUGHT BY GOING OFF THE TRAIN, SNAKE BITES.

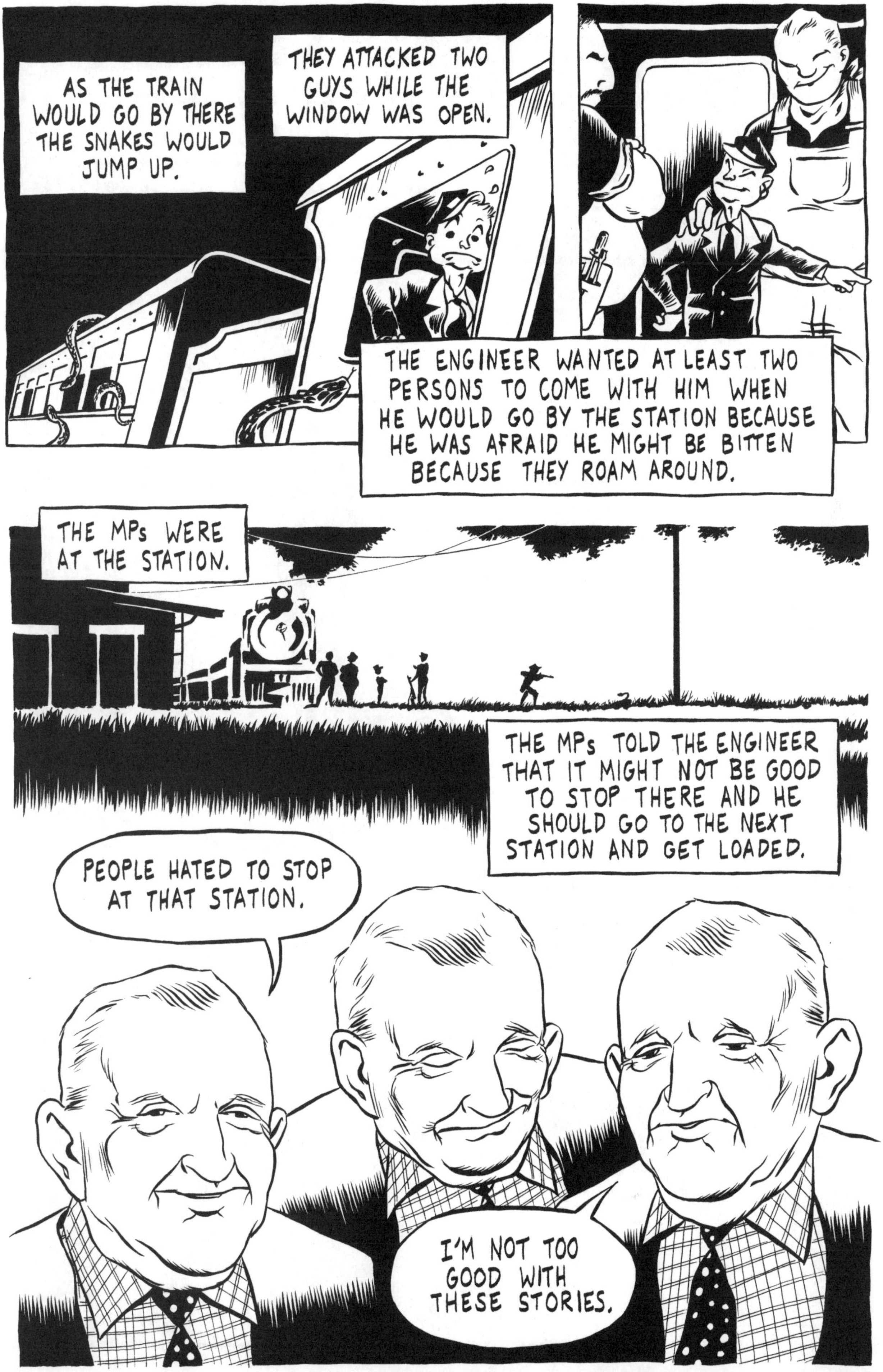
AS THE TRAIN WOULD GO BY THERE THE SNAKES WOULD JUMP UP.
THEY ATTACKED TWO GUYS WHILE THE WINDOW WAS OPEN.
THE ENGINEER WANTED AT LEAST TWO PERSONS TO COME WITH HIM WHEN HE WOULD GO BY THE STATION BECAUSE HE WAS AFRAID HE MIGHT BE BITTEN BECAUSE THEY ROAM AROUND.
THE MPs WERE AT THE STATION.
THE MPs TOLD THE ENGINEER THAT IT MIGHT NOT BE GOOD TO STOP THERE AND HE SHOULD GO TO THE NEXT STATION AND GET LOADED.
PEOPLE HATED TO STOP AT THAT STATION.
I'M NOT TOO GOOD WITH THESE STORIES.

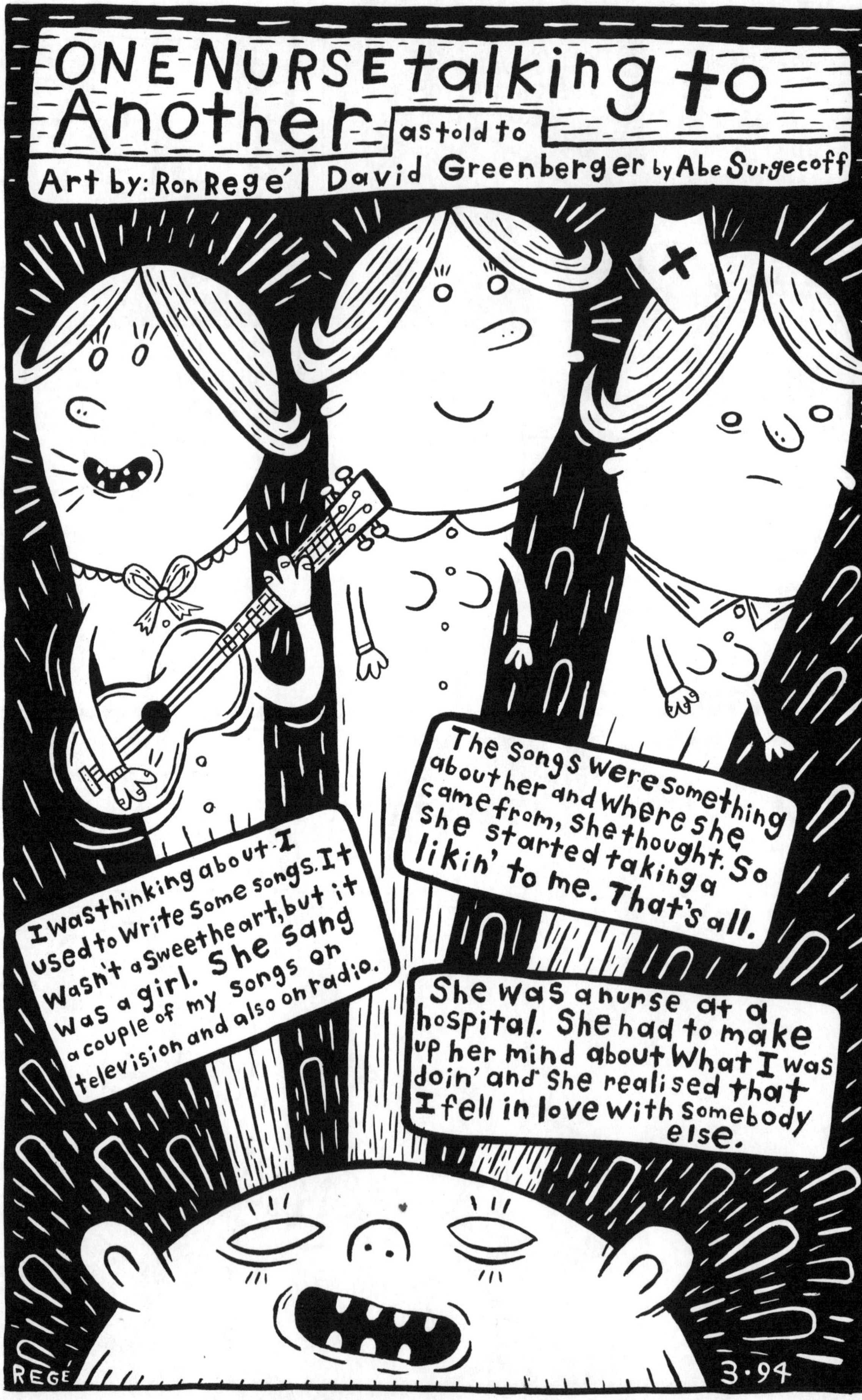
ONE NURSE talking to Another
as told to David Greenberger by Abe Surgecoff
Art by: Ron Regé
I was thinking about-I used to write some songs. It wasn't a sweetheart, but it was a girl. She sang a couple of my songs on television and also on radio.
The songs were something about her and where she came from, she thought. So she started taking a likin' to me. That's all.
She was a nurse at a hospital. She had to make up her mind about what I was doin' and she realised that I fell in love with somebody else.
REGÉ
3·94

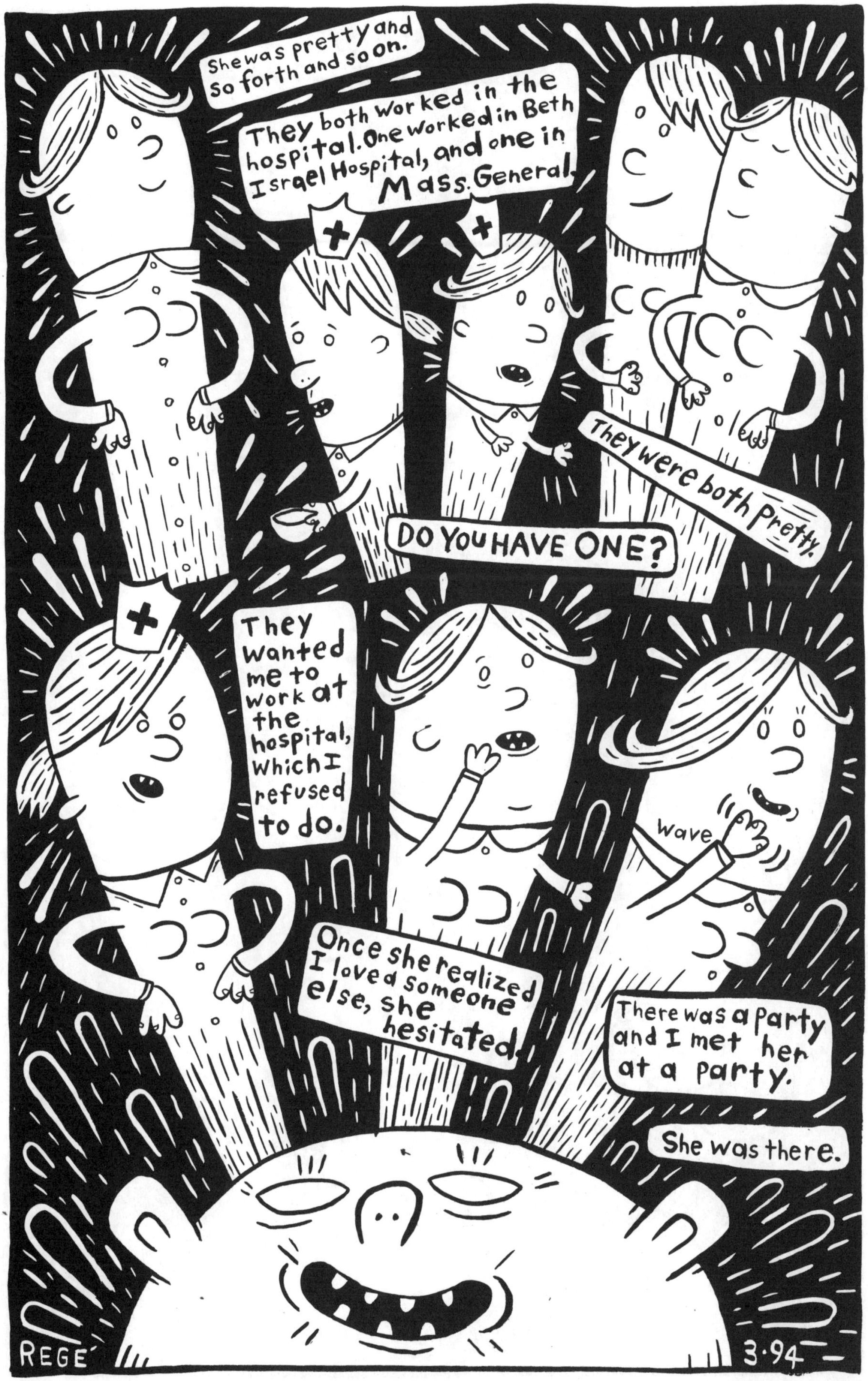
She was pretty and so forth and so on.
They both worked in the hospital. One worked in Beth Israel Hospital, and one in Mass. General.
DO YOU HAVE ONE?
They were both pretty.
They wanted me to work at the hospital, which I refused to do.
wave
Once she realized I loved someone else, she hesitated.
There was a party and I met her at a party.
She was there.
REGÉ
3·94

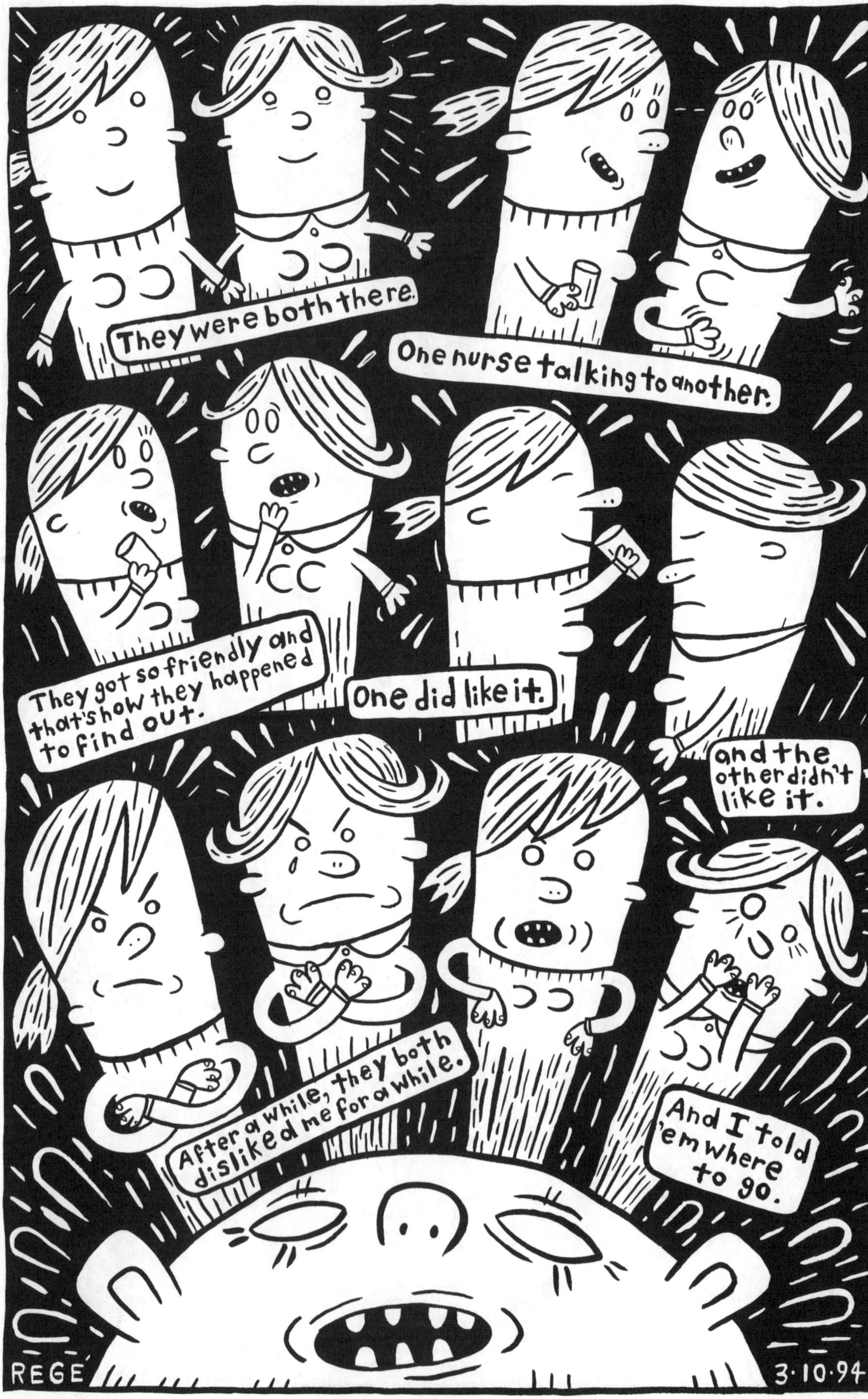
They were both there.
One nurse talking to another.
They got so friendly and that's how they happened to find out.
One did like it.
and the other didn't like it.
After a while, they both disliked me for a while.
And I told 'em where to go.
REGE
3·10·94

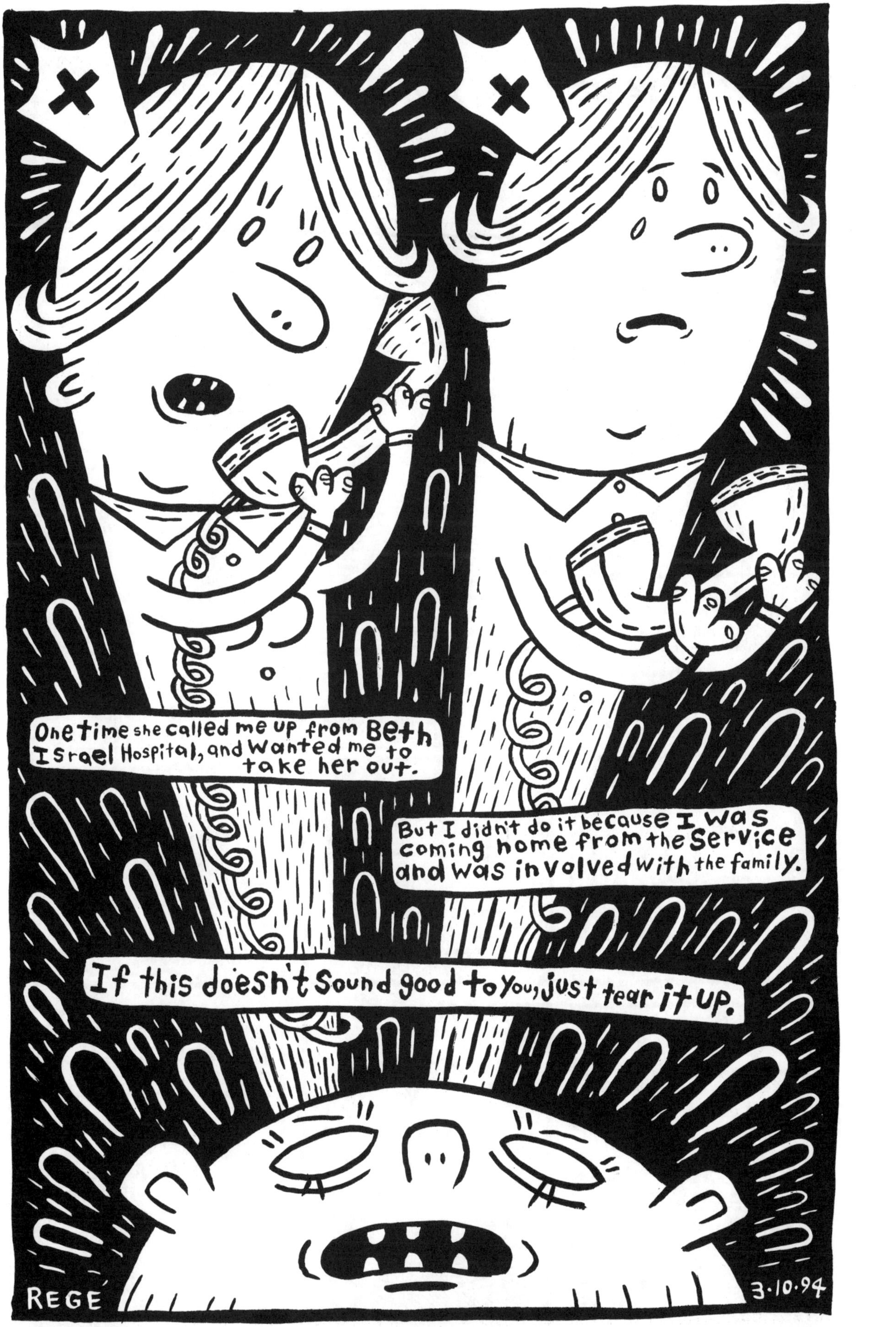
One time she called me up from Beth Israel Hospital, and wanted me to take her out.
But I didn't do it because I was coming home from the Service and was involved with the family.
If this doesn't sound good to you, just tear it up.
REGE
3.10.94

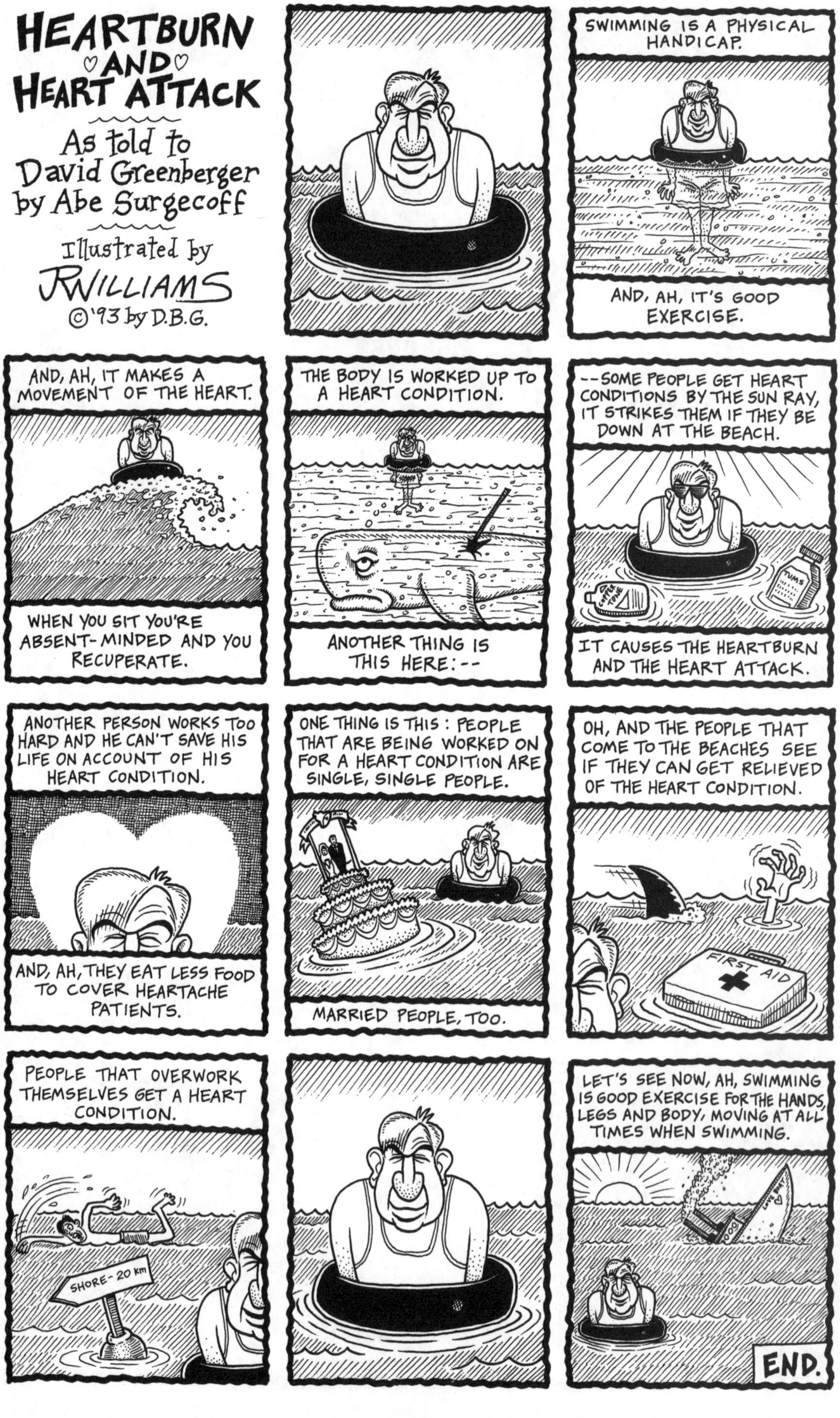
HEARTBURN AND HEART ATTACK
As told to David Greenberger by Abe Surgecoff
Illustrated by J.R. WILLIAMS
©'93 by D.B.G.
SWIMMING IS A PHYSICAL HANDICAP.
AND, AH, IT'S GOOD EXERCISE.
AND, AH, IT MAKES A MOVEMENT OF THE HEART.
WHEN YOU SIT YOU'RE ABSENT-MINDED AND YOU RECUPERATE.
THE BODY IS WORKED UP TO A HEART CONDITION.
ANOTHER THING IS THIS HERE: --
--SOME PEOPLE GET HEART CONDITIONS BY THE SUN RAY, IT STRIKES THEM IF THEY BE DOWN AT THE BEACH.
TUMS
IT CAUSES THE HEARTBURN AND THE HEART ATTACK.
ANOTHER PERSON WORKS TOO HARD AND HE CAN'T SAVE HIS LIFE ON ACCOUNT OF HIS HEART CONDITION.
AND, AH, THEY EAT LESS FOOD TO COVER HEARTACHE PATIENTS.
ONE THING IS THIS: PEOPLE THAT ARE BEING WORKED ON FOR A HEART CONDITION ARE SINGLE, SINGLE PEOPLE.
MARRIED PEOPLE, TOO.
OH, AND THE PEOPLE THAT COME TO THE BEACHES SEE IF THEY CAN GET RELIEVED OF THE HEART CONDITION.
FIRST AID
PEOPLE THAT OVERWORK THEMSELVES GET A HEART CONDITION.
SHORE - 20 km
LET'S SEE NOW, AH, SWIMMING IS GOOD EXERCISE FOR THE HANDS, LEGS AND BODY, MOVING AT ALL TIMES WHEN SWIMMING.
LOVE BOAT
END.

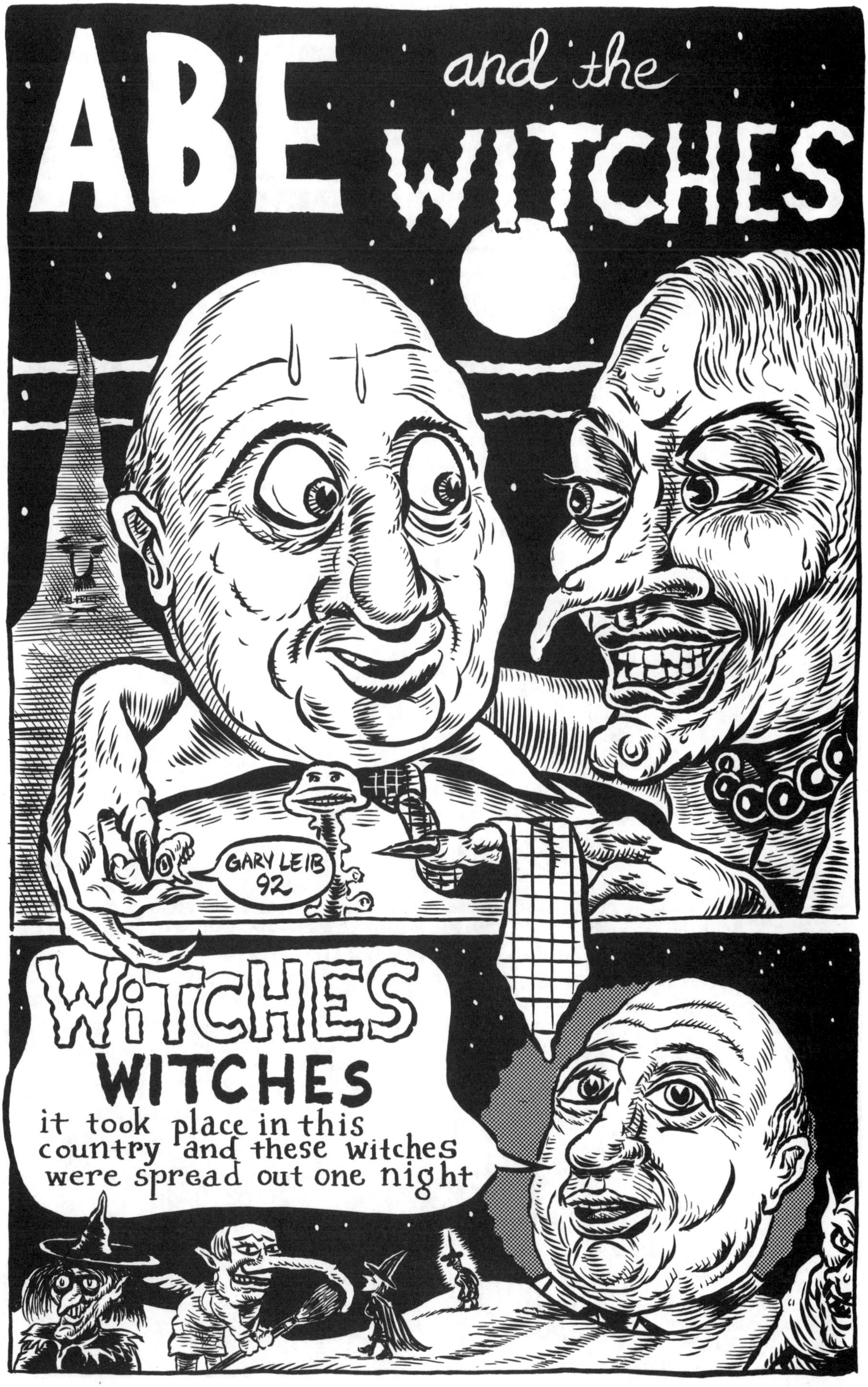
ABE and the WITCHES
GARY LEIB 92
WITCHES
WITCHES
WITCHES
it took place in this country and these witches were spread out one night

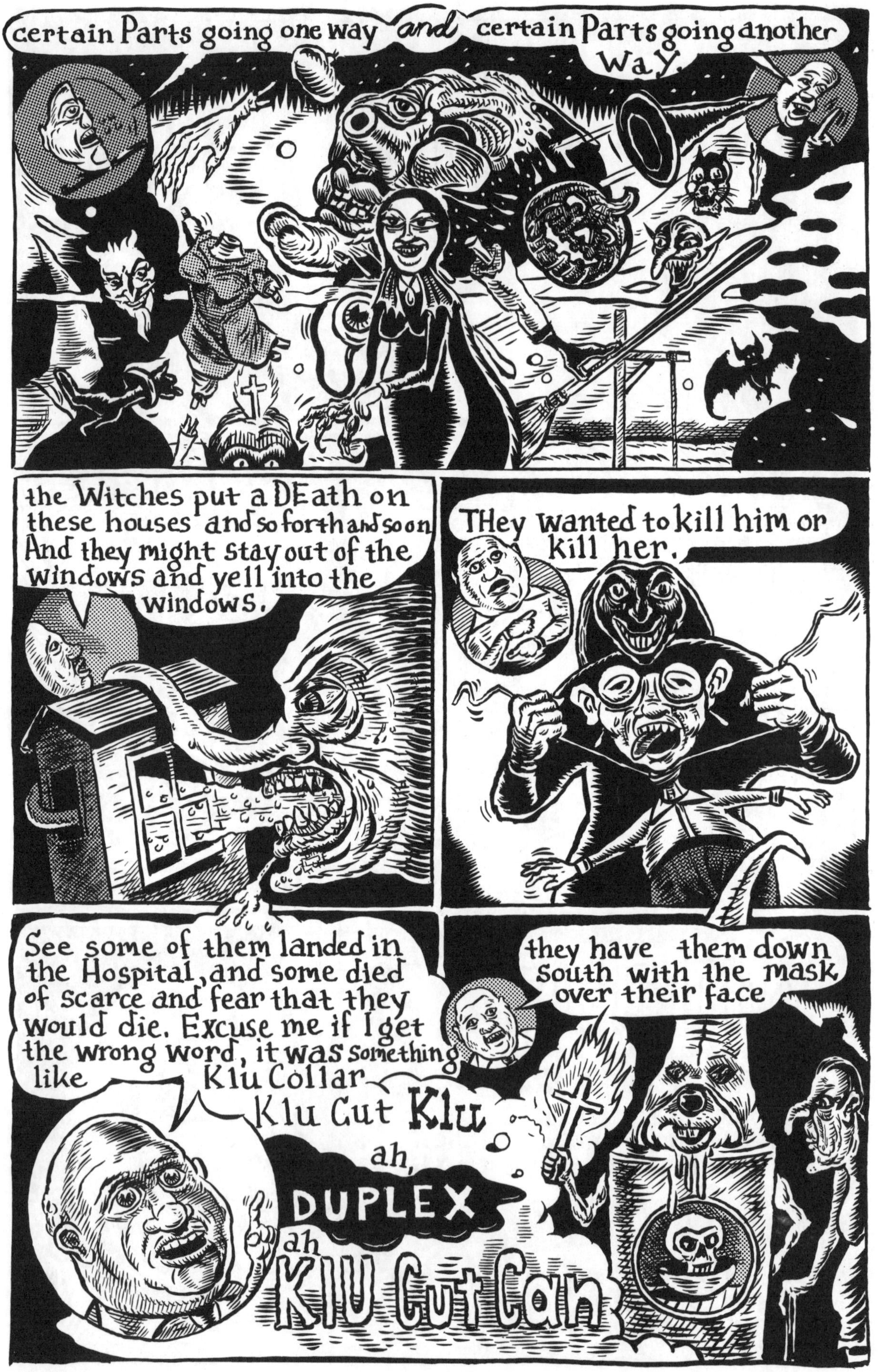

certain Parts going one way and certain Parts going another Way.
the Witches put a DEath on these houses and so forth and so on And they might stay out of the windows and yell into the windows.
THey wanted to kill him or kill her.
See some of them landed in the Hospital, and some died of scarce and fear that they would die. Excuse me if I get the wrong word, it was something like Klu Collar
Klu Cut Klu
ah,
DUPLEX
ah
KlU Cut Can
they have them down South with the mask over their face

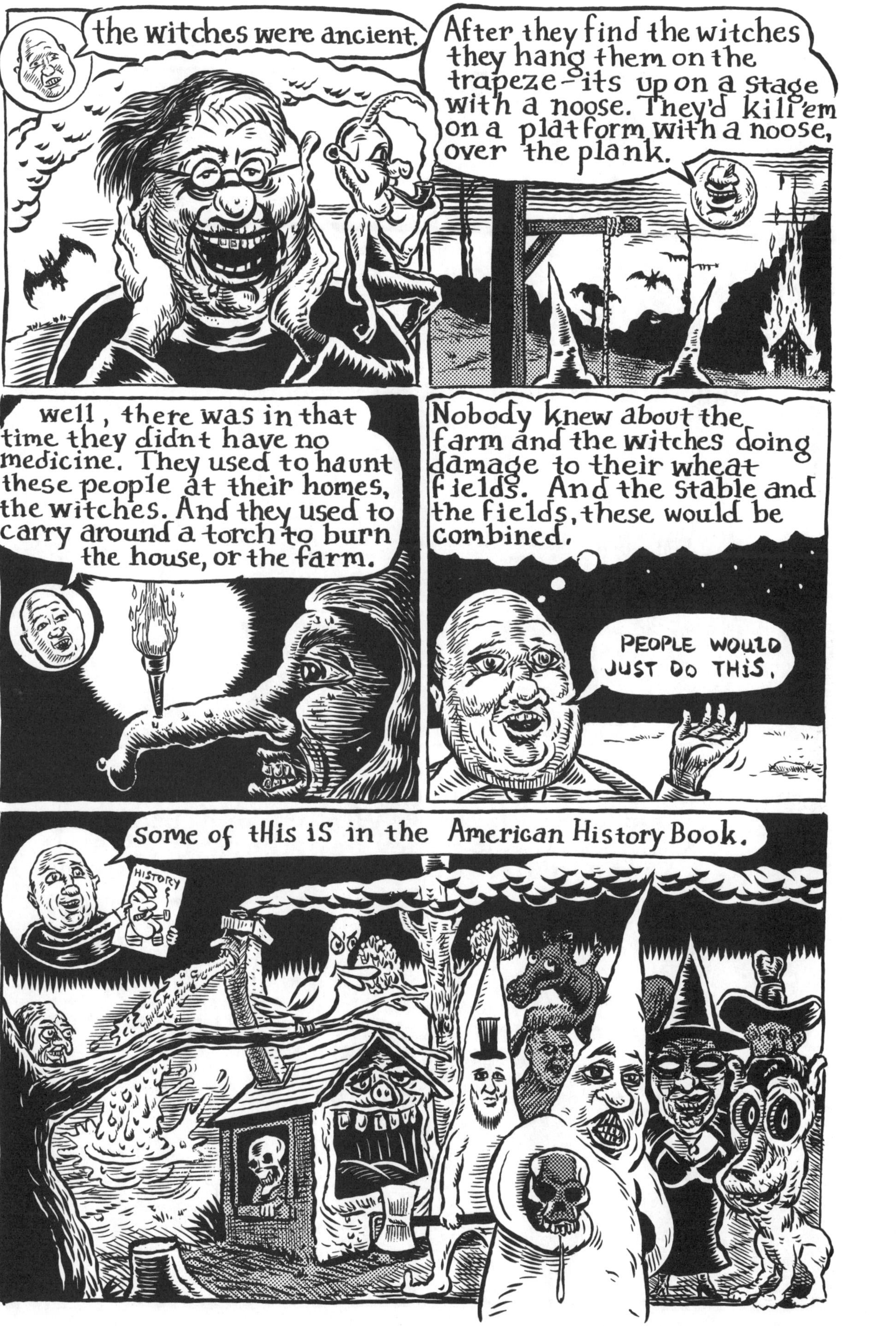
the witches were ancient.
After they find the witches they hang them on the trapeze - its up on a stage with a noose. They'd kill'em on a platform with a noose, over the plank.
well, there was in that time they didnt have no medicine. They used to haunt these people at their homes, the witches. And they used to carry around a torch to burn the house, or the farm.
Nobody knew about the farm and the witches doing damage to their wheat fields. And the stable and the fields, these would be combined.
PEOPLE WOULD JUST DO THIS.
Some of tHis iS in the American History Book.
HISTORY

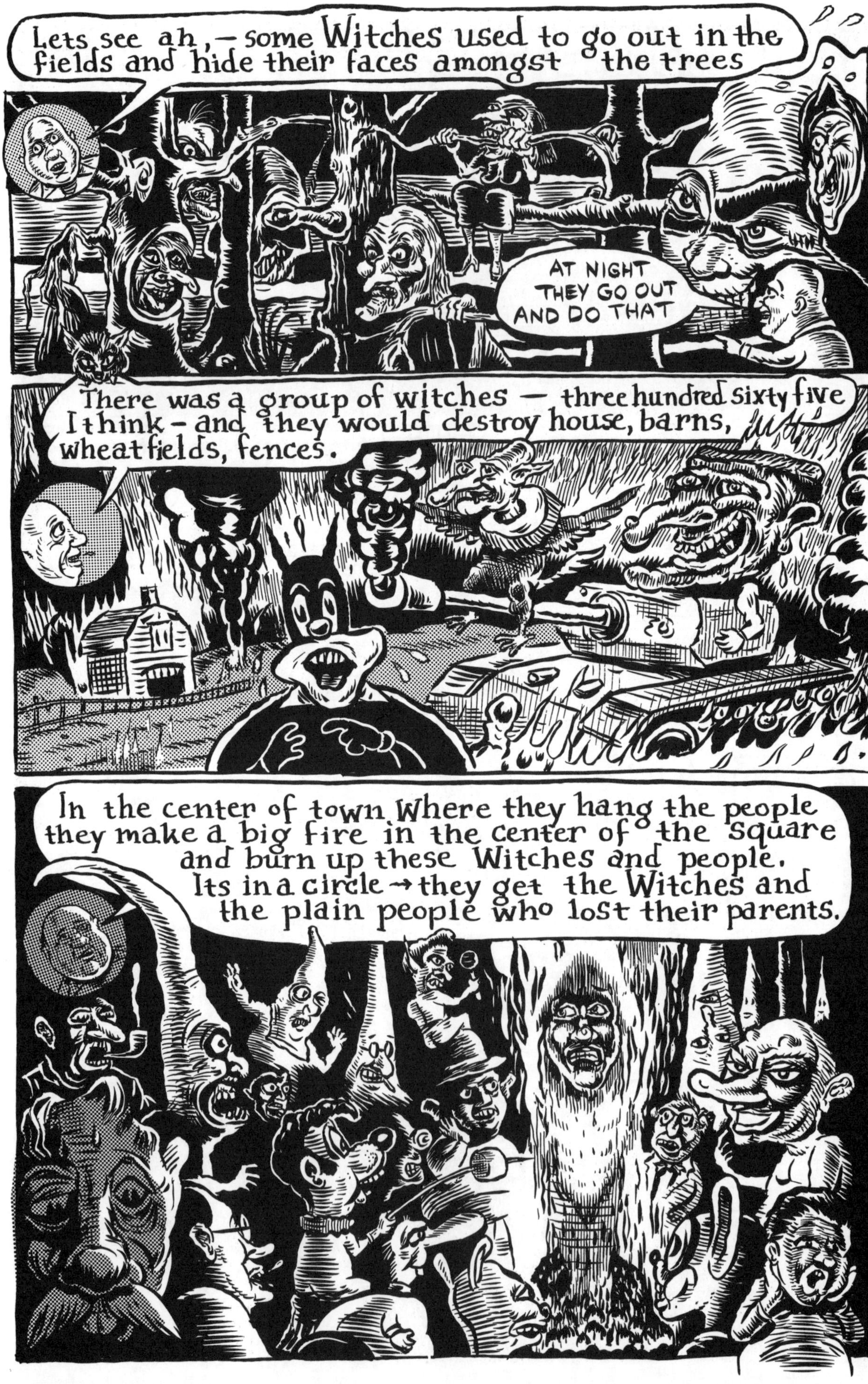

Lets see ah, — some Witches used to go out in the fields and hide their faces amongst the trees
AT NIGHT THEY GO OUT AND DO THAT
There was a group of witches — three hundred sixty five I think — and they would destroy house, barns, wheatfields, fences.
In the center of town where they hang the people they make a big fire in the center of the square and burn up these Witches and people. Its in a circle → they get the Witches and the plain people who lost their parents.

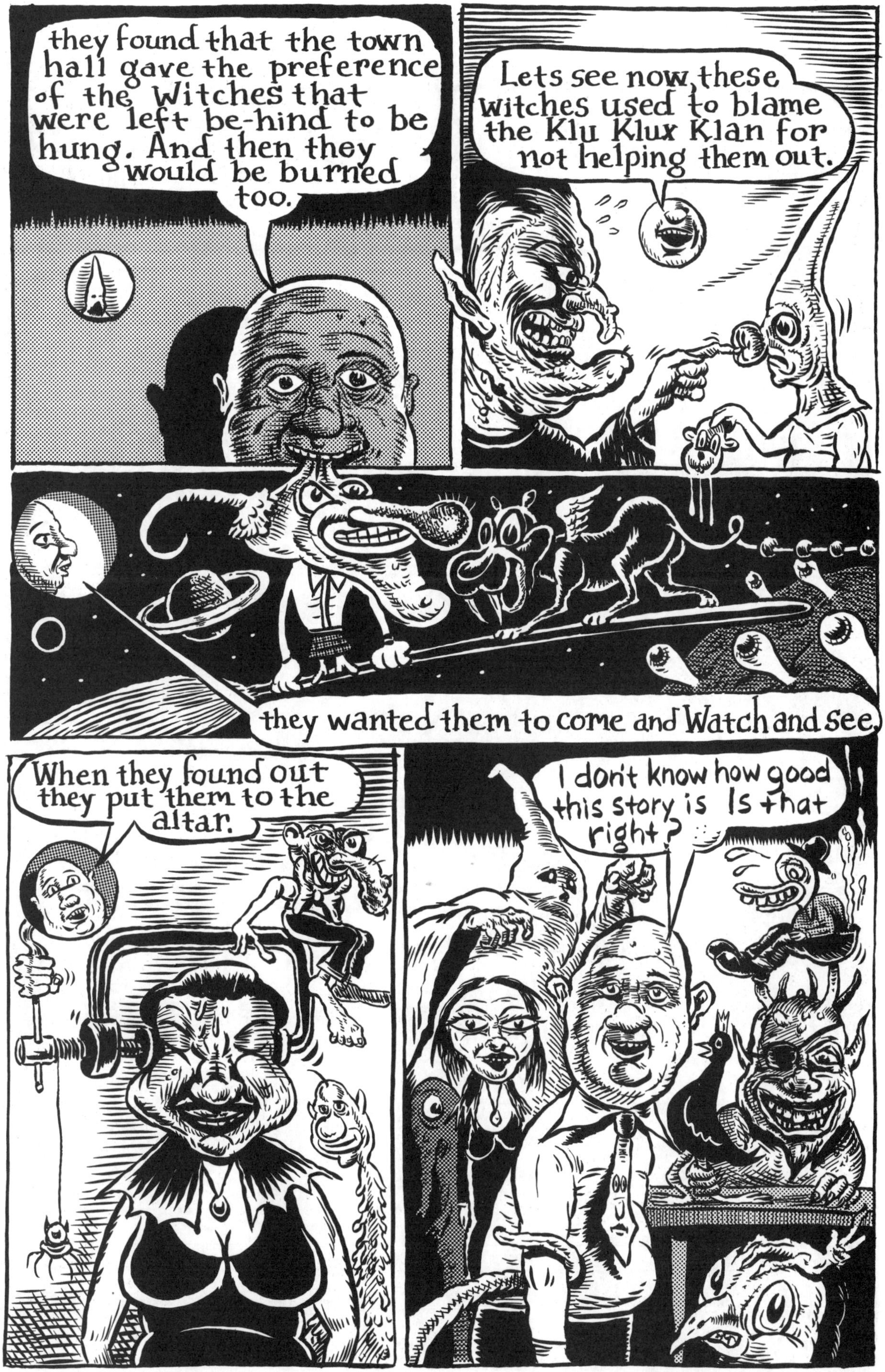
they found that the town hall gave the preference of the Witches that were left be-hind to be hung. And then they would be burned too.
Lets see now, these witches used to blame the Klu Klux Klan for not helping them out.
they wanted them to come and Watch and see.
When they found out they put them to the altar.
I don't know how good this story is Is that right?

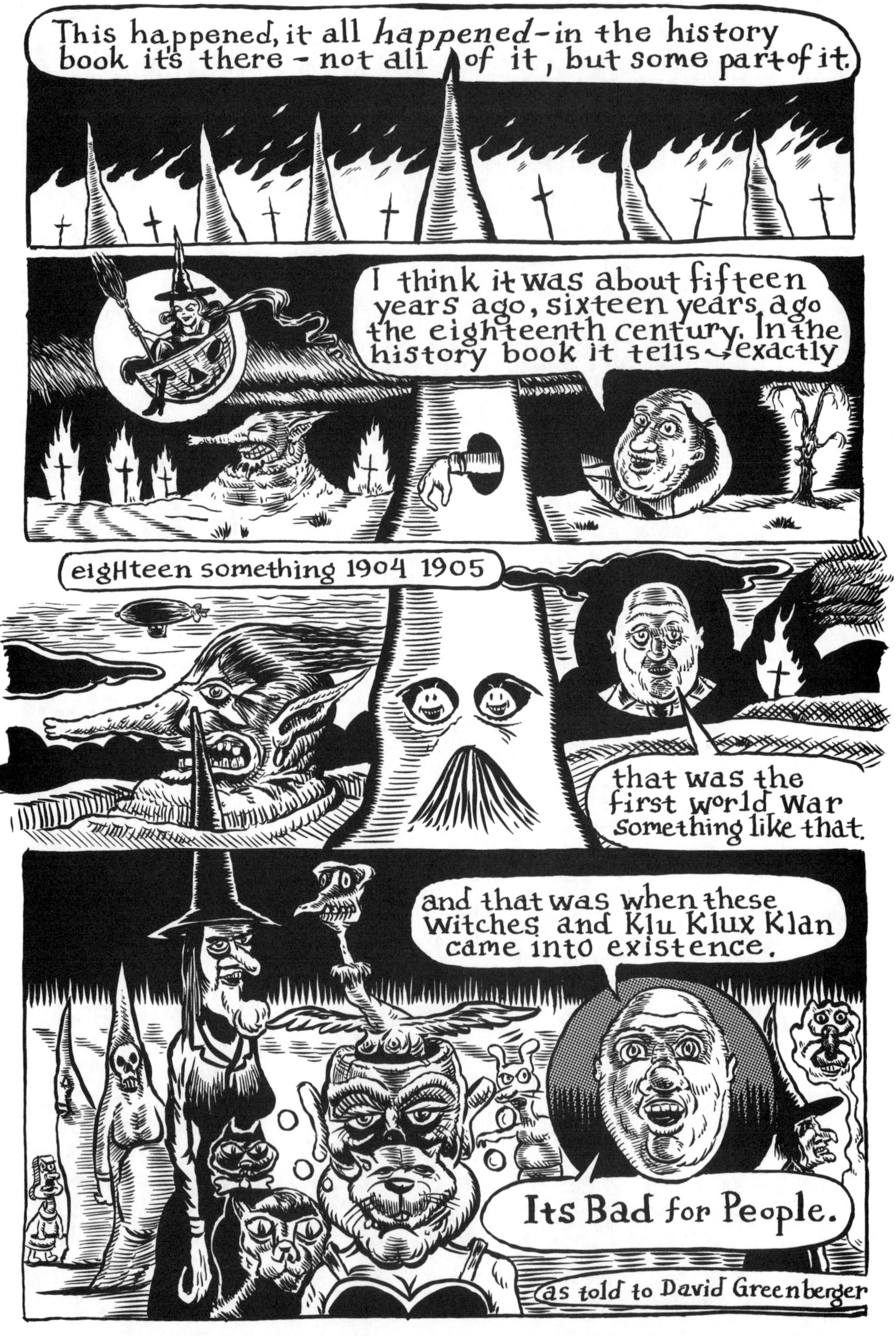
This happened, it all *happened* - in the history book it's there - not all of it, but some part of it.
I think it was about fifteen years ago, sixteen years ago the eighteenth century. In the history book it tells exactly
eighteen something 1904 1905
that was the first world war something like that.
and that was when these Witches and Klu Klux Klan came into existence.
Its Bad for People.
as told to David Greenberger

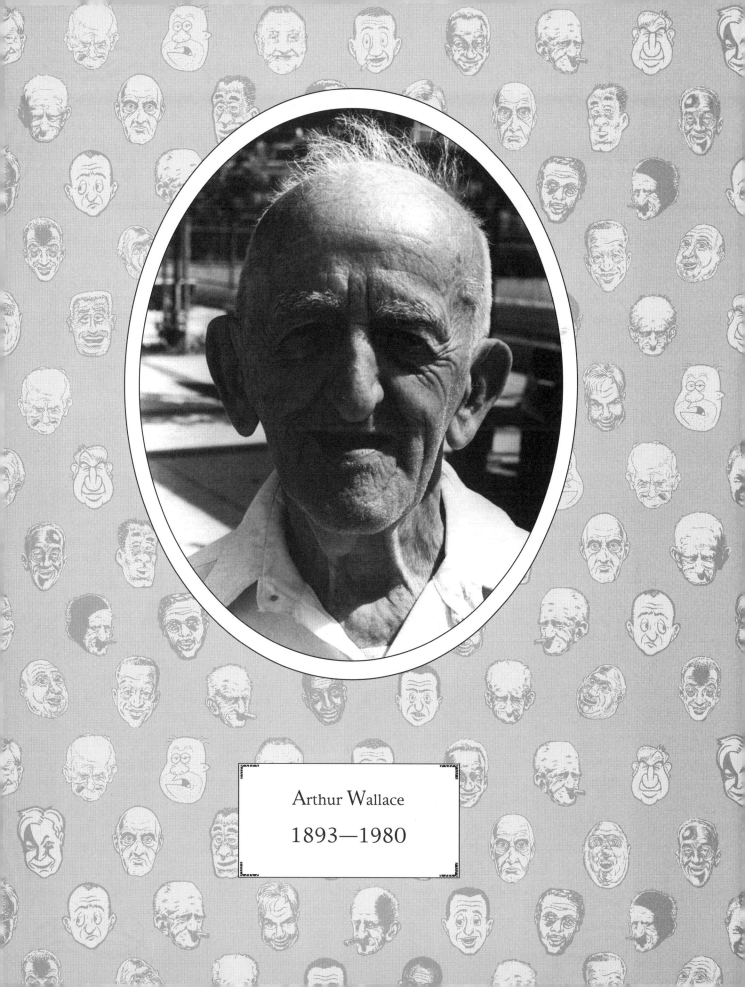

Arthur Wallace

1893—1980

Hey! Hey! Don't be worryin' about goddamn international politics! Go down and tell Mary I want some whiskey!

◆

The idea is, when it's too hot, get the hell out of the sun!

◆

They was sayin' prayers for me when I was ten or eleven on account of someone circulated a goddamn rumor that I was dyin'. I was an altar boy — an altar boy *and* a choir boy. The goddamn church had me on the run way back then. Yesterday I passed my 86th year, and that crazy Rosie who used to work here, when people would call up, she'd say, "Don't bother to call no more, he's dead and buried!" (*laughs*)

◆

There's no use runnin' around and gettin' all mixed up — you've got to consult the calendar.

◆

Khrushchev had one big problem — drinkin' too much booze. But he done alright. He was a strong man. His weakness was takin' gifts of wine and drinkin' 'em, see? He was a wino, see? That was his weak point, see? Stalin was a whiskey drinker, he bought his whiskey in South Boston, and he used to buy seven different brands of tobacco mixed together in Scully Square. Stalin was a heavy smoker, too, see? Stalin never drank vodka. That's the whiskey of Russia, but he never drank vodka, he drank whiskey, Mr. Boston Whiskey from South Boston. Joe Stalin's right name was Surge Surgovich — Joseph, son of Joseph, see? I followed them guys up you know. Lenin was never known to drink — he didn't drink at all, and he didn't fool around with women. He never married. Joe Stalin and Khrushchev were very able men as prime ministers, you know what I mean? They knew what the hell they were doing. They were strong men. That's why Russia grew strong, don't you understand?

◆

I'm kind of old you know. My age is against me. I'm 86 years and 86 days old today. that's kinda old, ain't it?

◆

I try not to be mixed up in troubles, see?

◆

Hey, Mary! Hurry up! Where's the whiskey? My blood's gettin' cold!

THE BUS RIDE

BY DAVID GREENBERGER ART BY DEAN ROHRER

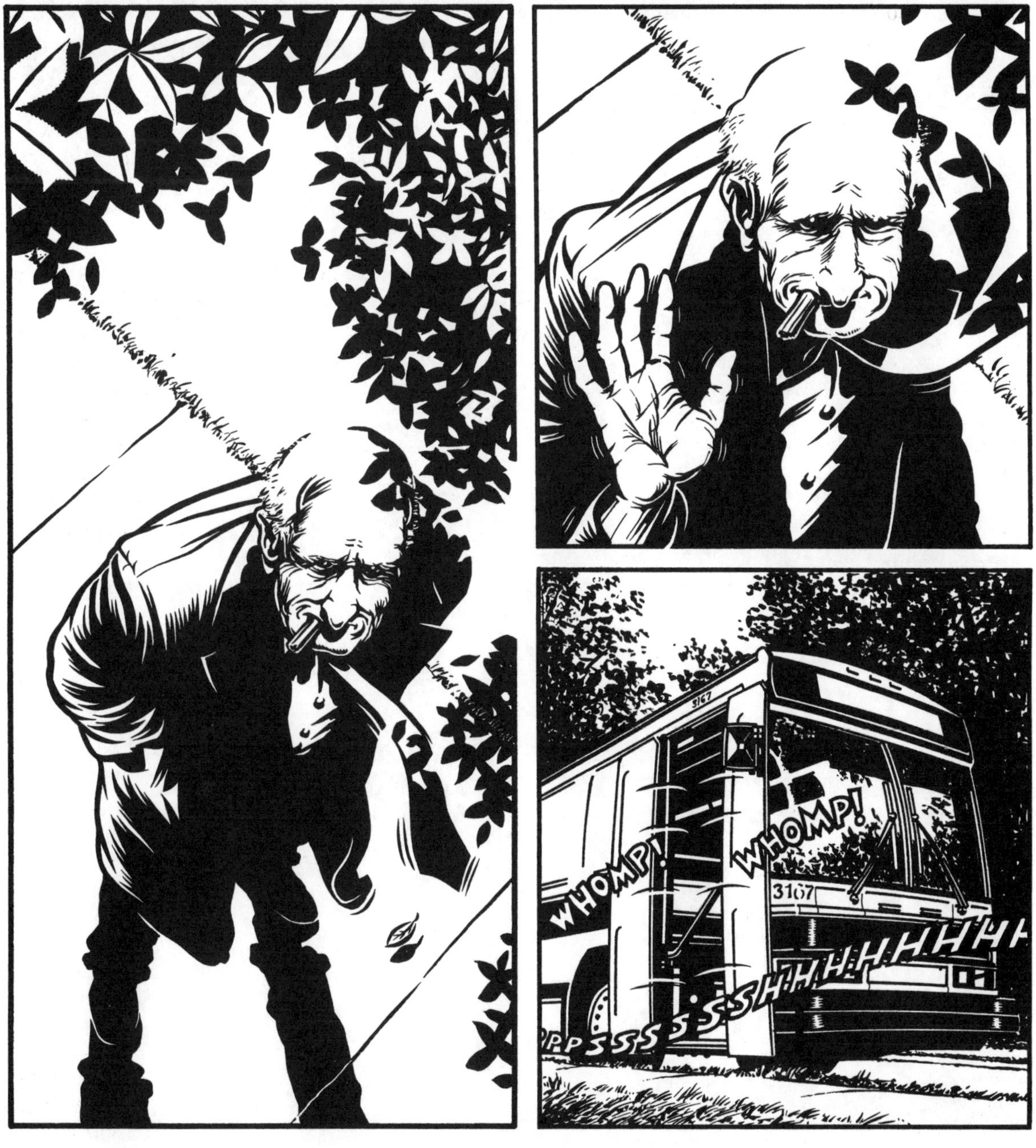

3167
3167
WHOMP!
WHOMP!
PPPSSSSSSSHHHHHHHHHHH

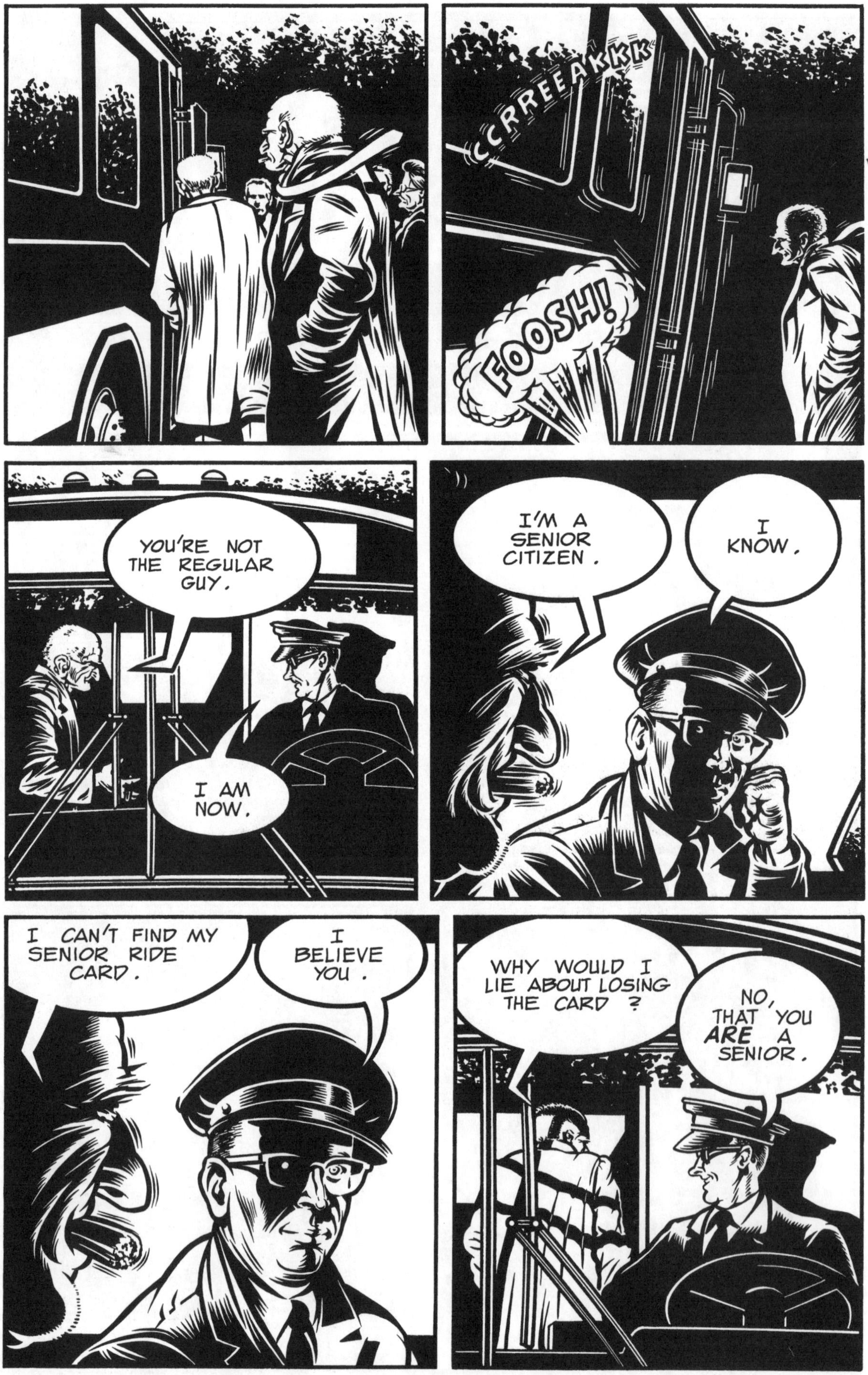
CCRREEEAKKK
FOOSH!
YOU'RE NOT THE REGULAR GUY.
I AM NOW.
I'M A SENIOR CITIZEN.
I KNOW.
I CAN'T FIND MY SENIOR RIDE CARD.
I BELIEVE YOU.
WHY WOULD I LIE ABOUT LOSING THE CARD ?
NO, THAT YOU *ARE* A SENIOR.

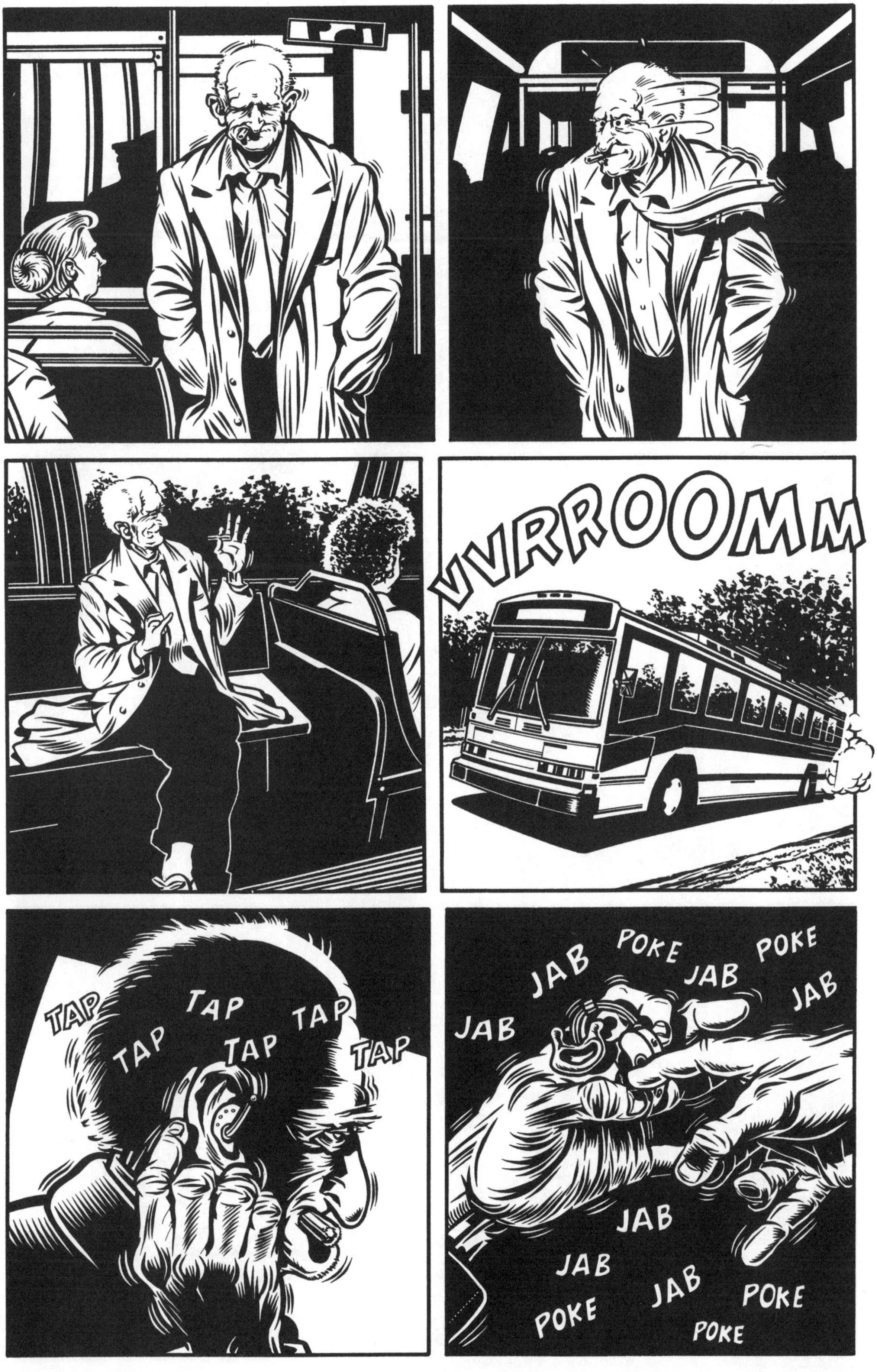
VVRROOMM
TAP
TAP
TAP
TAP
TAP
TAP
JAB
JAB
POKE
JAB
POKE
JAB
JAB
JAB
JAB
POKE
POKE
POKE

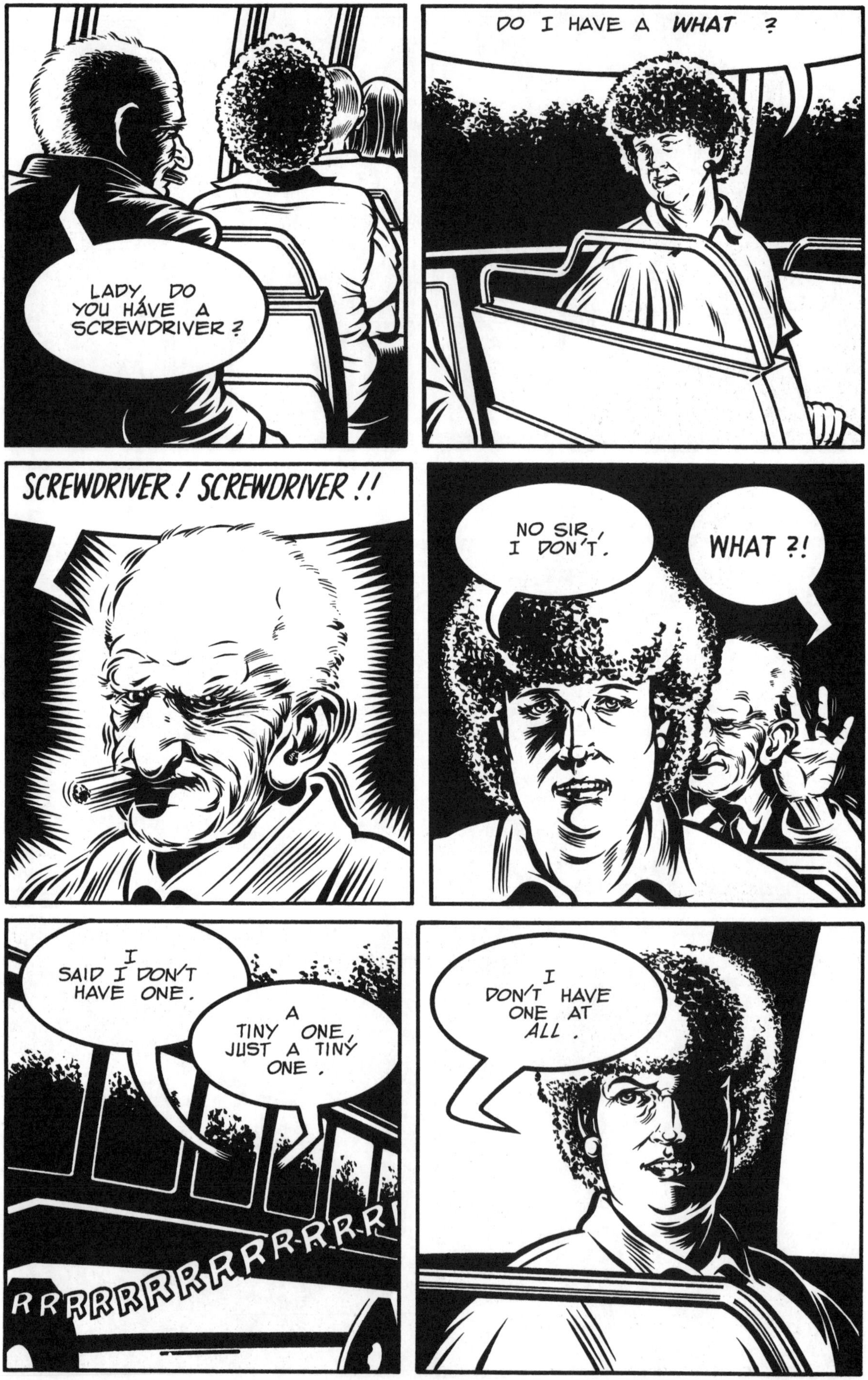
LADY, DO YOU HAVE A SCREWDRIVER ?
DO I HAVE A WHAT ?
SCREWDRIVER ! SCREWDRIVER !!
NO SIR, I DON'T.
WHAT ?!
I SAID I DON'T HAVE ONE.
A TINY ONE, JUST A TINY ONE.
RRRRRRRRRRR-R-R-R-R
I DON'T HAVE ONE AT ALL.

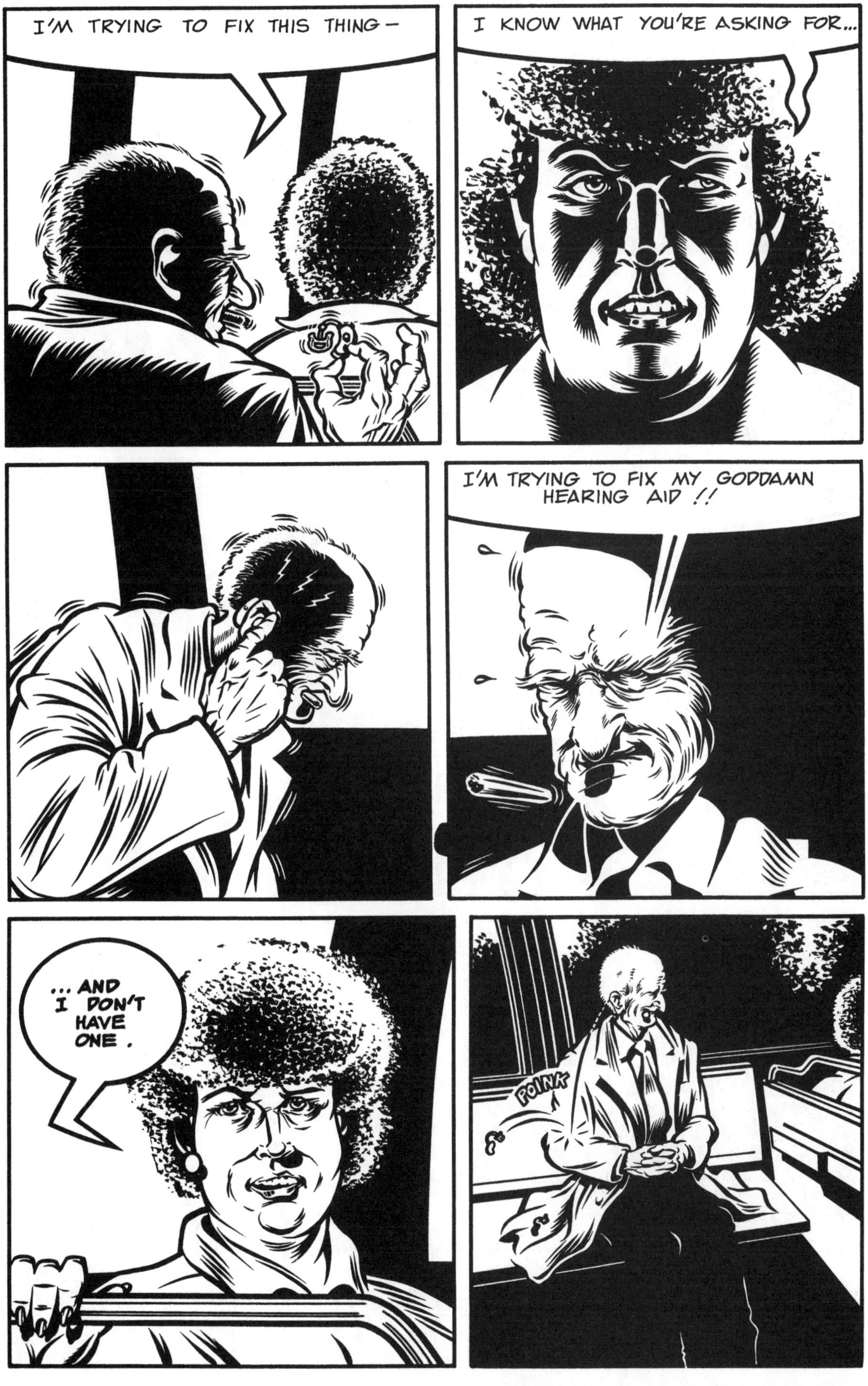
I'M TRYING TO FIX THIS THING—
I KNOW WHAT YOU'RE ASKING FOR...
I'M TRYING TO FIX MY GODDAMN HEARING AID !!
... AND I DON'T HAVE ONE .
POINK

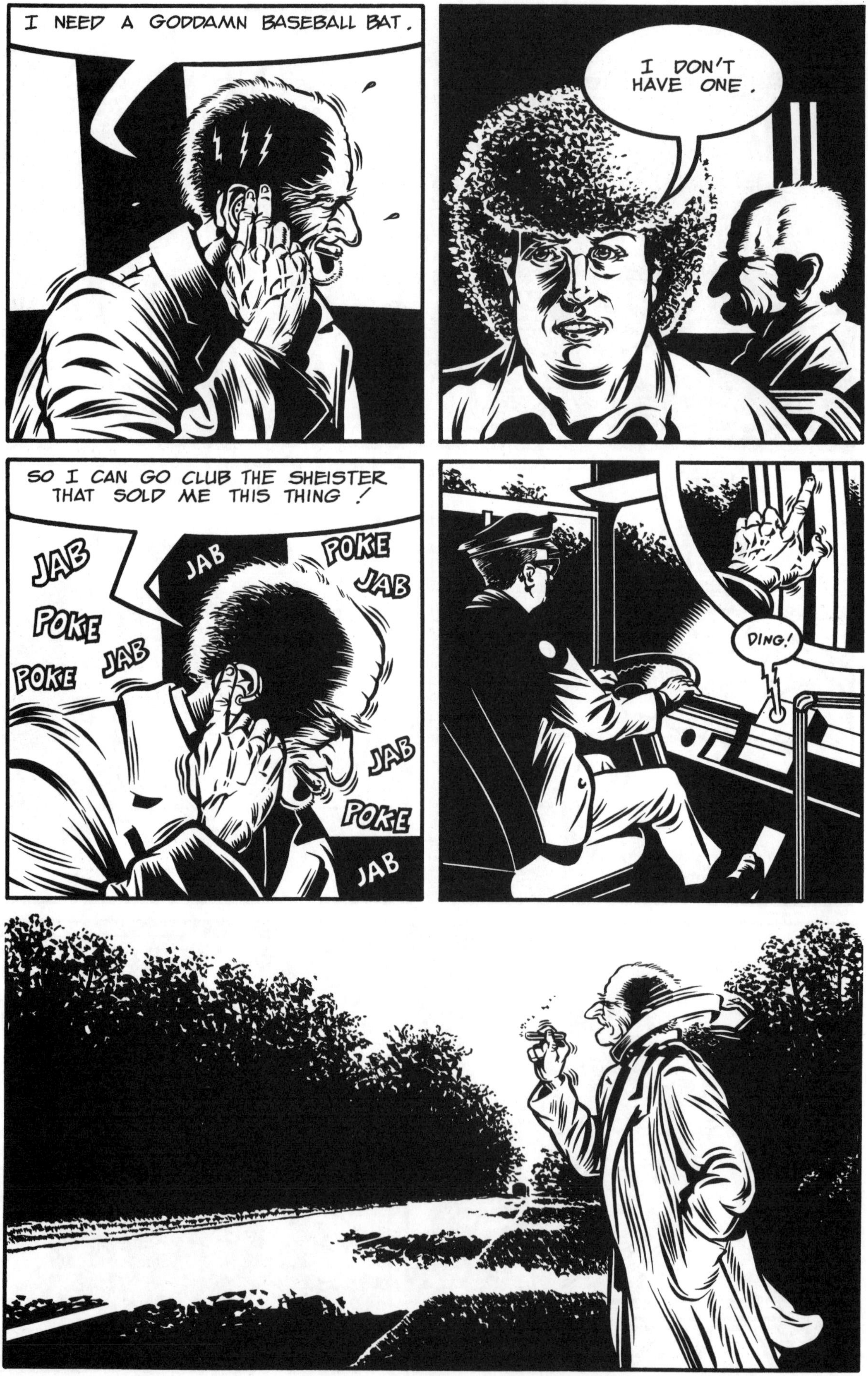
I NEED A GODDAMN BASEBALL BAT.
I DON'T HAVE ONE.
SO I CAN GO CLUB THE SHEISTER THAT SOLD ME THIS THING!
JAB
JAB
POKE
JAB
POKE
JAB
POKE
JAB
POKE
JAB
DING!

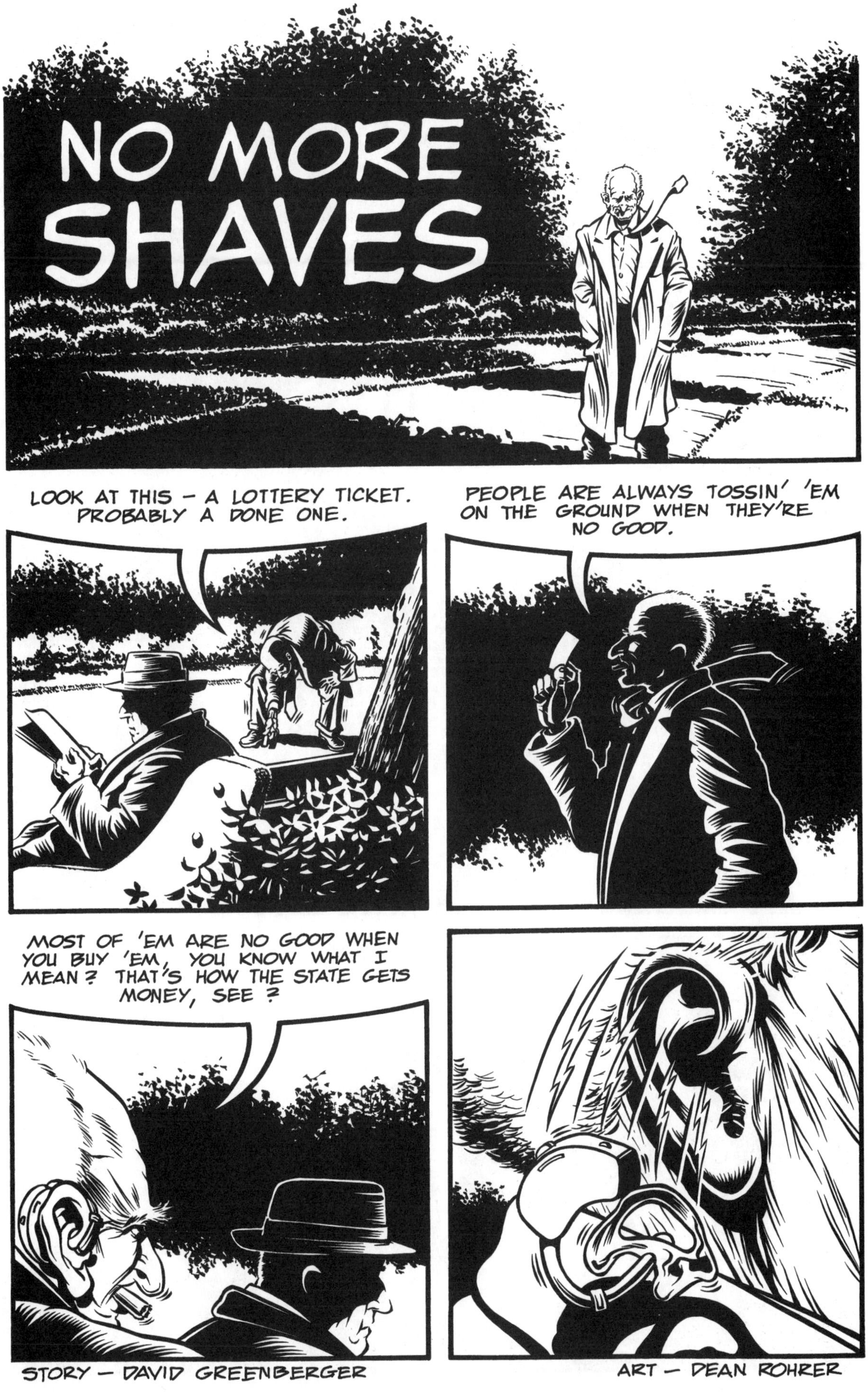
NO MORE SHAVES
LOOK AT THIS – A LOTTERY TICKET. PROBABLY A DONE ONE.
PEOPLE ARE ALWAYS TOSSIN' 'EM ON THE GROUND WHEN THEY'RE NO GOOD.
MOST OF 'EM ARE NO GOOD WHEN YOU BUY 'EM, YOU KNOW WHAT I MEAN? THAT'S HOW THE STATE GETS MONEY, SEE?
STORY – DAVID GREENBERGER
ART – DEAN ROHRER

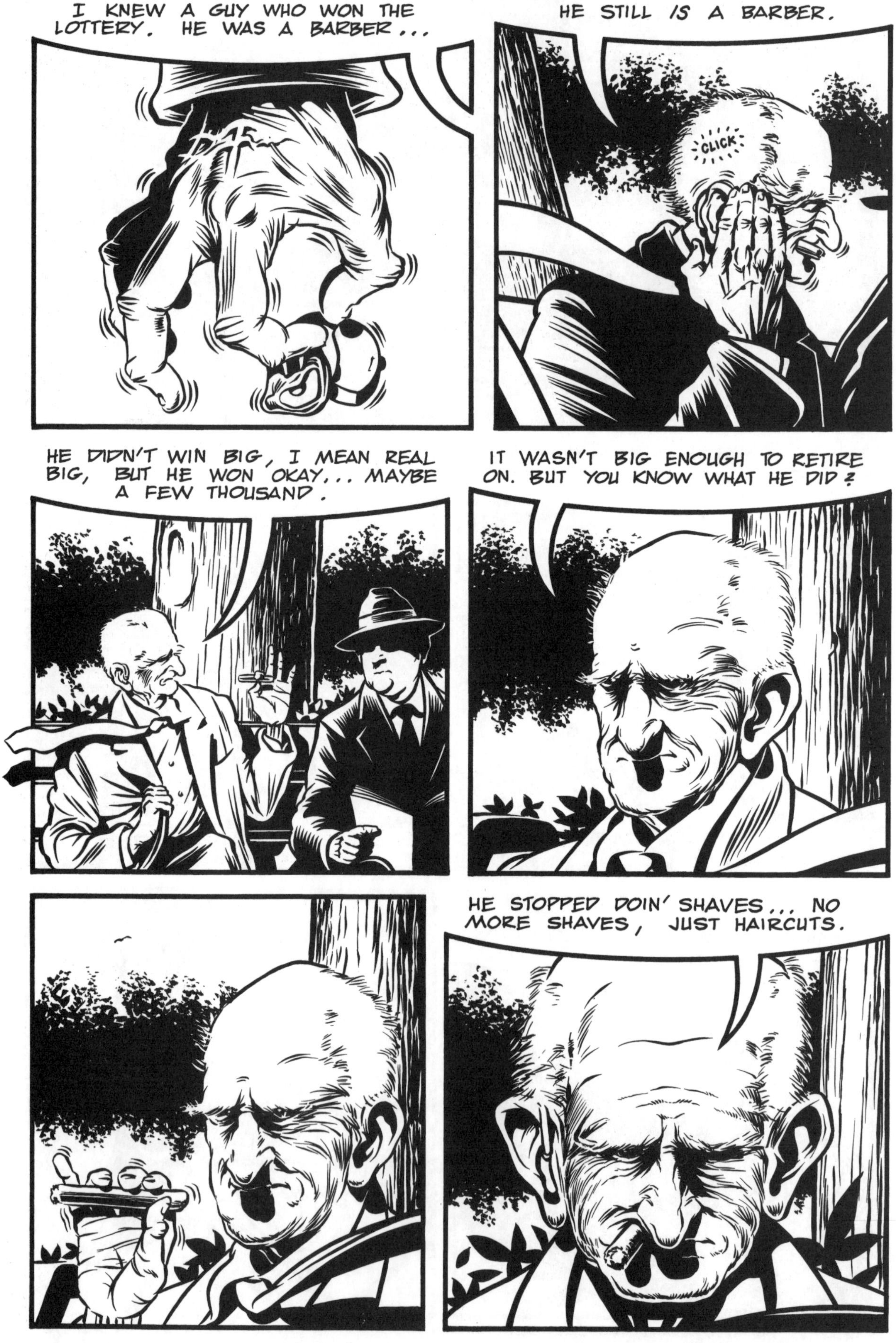
I KNEW A GUY WHO WON THE LOTTERY. HE WAS A BARBER...
HE STILL IS A BARBER.
CLICK
HE DIDN'T WIN BIG, I MEAN REAL BIG, BUT HE WON OKAY... MAYBE A FEW THOUSAND.
IT WASN'T BIG ENOUGH TO RETIRE ON. BUT YOU KNOW WHAT HE DID?
HE STOPPED DOIN' SHAVES... NO MORE SHAVES, JUST HAIRCUTS.

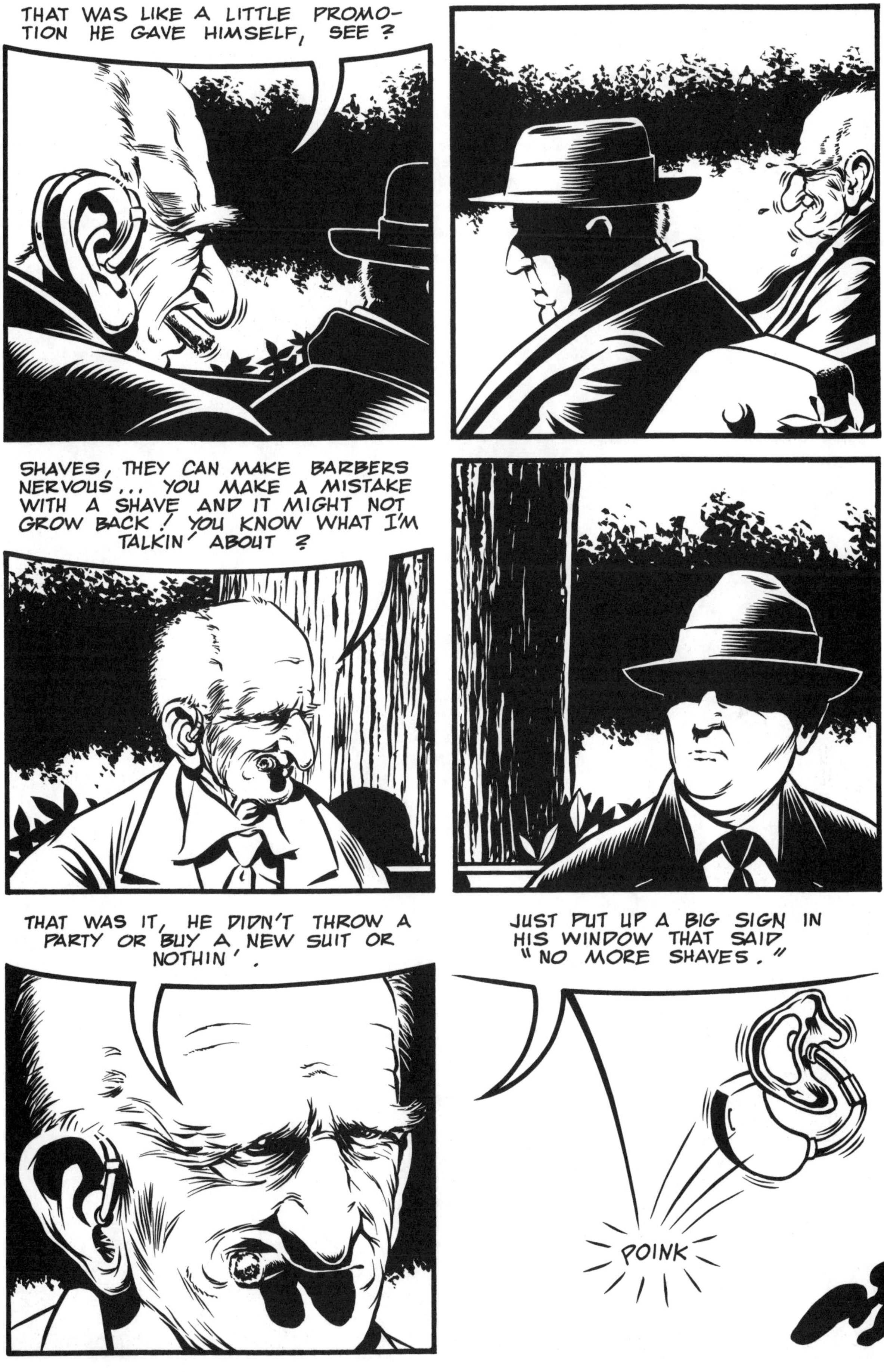
THAT WAS LIKE A LITTLE PROMOTION HE GAVE HIMSELF, SEE ?
SHAVES, THEY CAN MAKE BARBERS NERVOUS... YOU MAKE A MISTAKE WITH A SHAVE AND IT MIGHT NOT GROW BACK! YOU KNOW WHAT I'M TALKIN' ABOUT ?
THAT WAS IT, HE DIDN'T THROW A PARTY OR BUY A NEW SUIT OR NOTHIN'.
JUST PUT UP A BIG SIGN IN HIS WINDOW THAT SAID "NO MORE SHAVES."
POINK

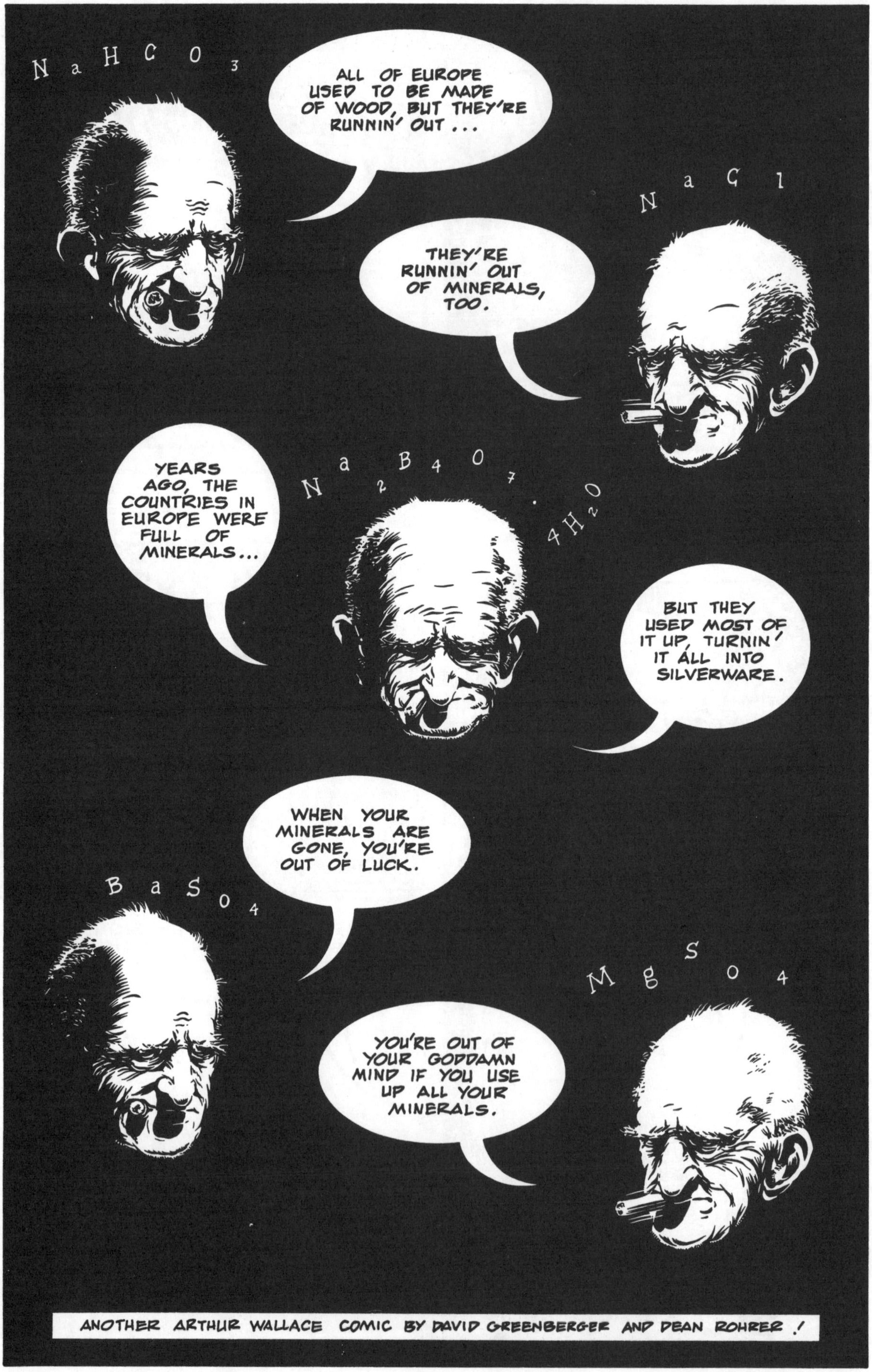

NaHCO3
ALL OF EUROPE USED TO BE MADE OF WOOD, BUT THEY'RE RUNNIN' OUT ...
NaCl
THEY'RE RUNNIN' OUT OF MINERALS, TOO.
YEARS AGO, THE COUNTRIES IN EUROPE WERE FULL OF MINERALS...
Na2B4O7 . 4H2O
BUT THEY USED MOST OF IT UP, TURNIN' IT ALL INTO SILVERWARE.
WHEN YOUR MINERALS ARE GONE, YOU'RE OUT OF LUCK.
BaSO4
MgSO4
YOU'RE OUT OF YOUR GODDAMN MIND IF YOU USE UP ALL YOUR MINERALS.
ANOTHER ARTHUR WALLACE COMIC BY DAVID GREENBERGER AND DEAN ROHRER !

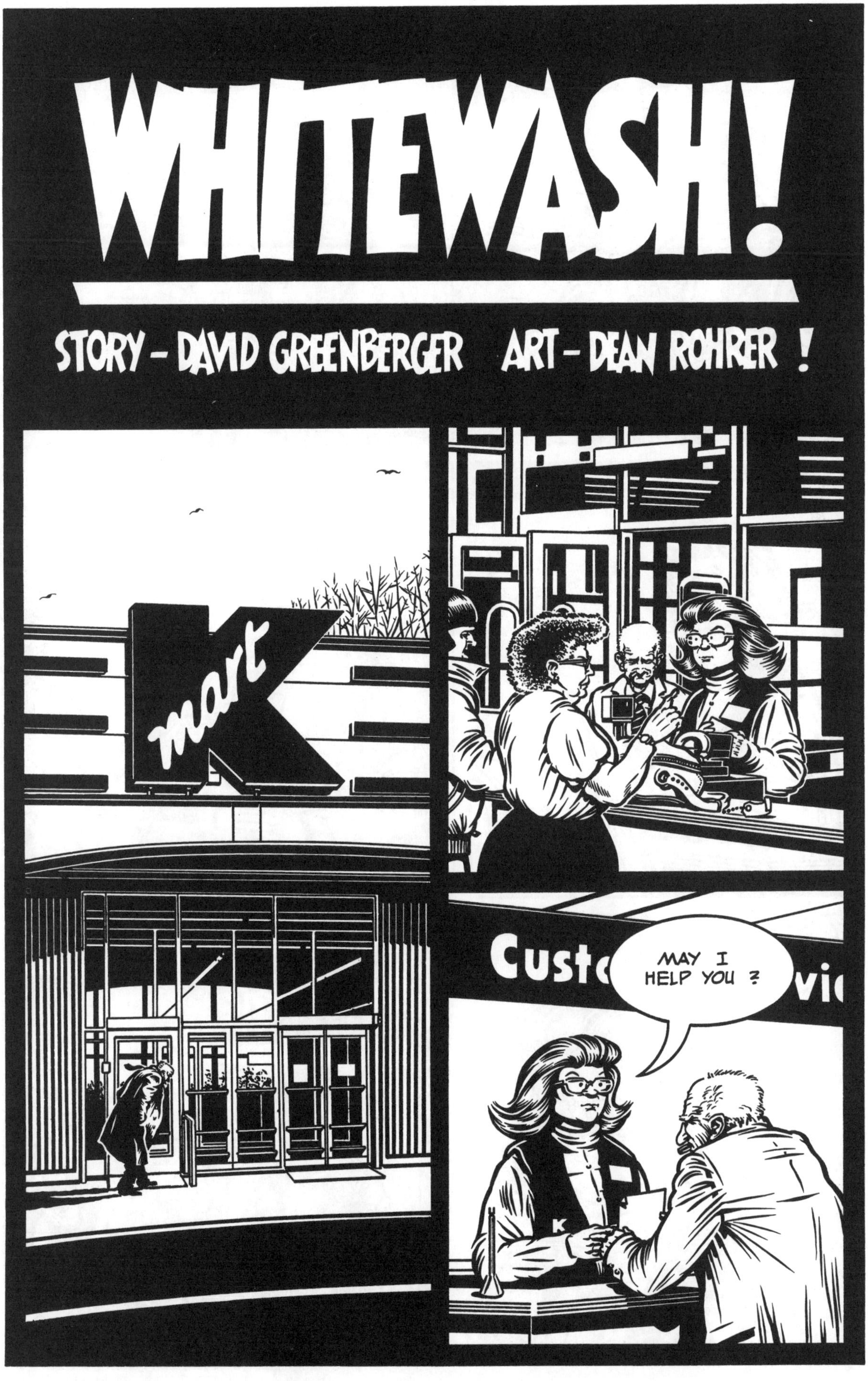
WHITEWASH!
STORY - DAVID GREENBERGER ART - DEAN ROHRER !
K mart
MAY I HELP YOU ?

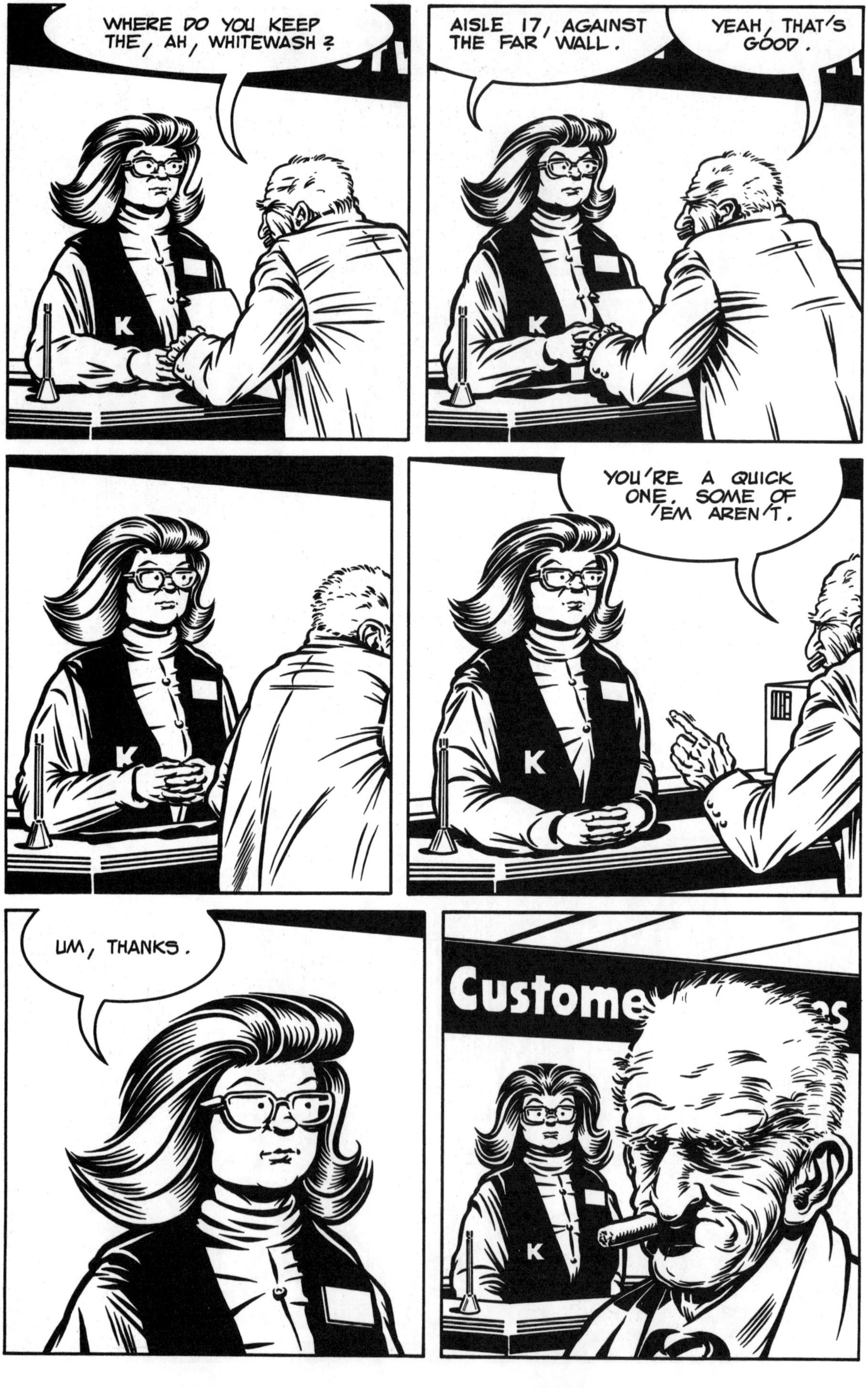
WHERE DO YOU KEEP THE, AH, WHITEWASH?
AISLE 17, AGAINST THE FAR WALL.
YEAH, THAT'S GOOD.
K
YOU'RE A QUICK ONE. SOME OF 'EM AREN'T.
UM, THANKS.
Custome
K

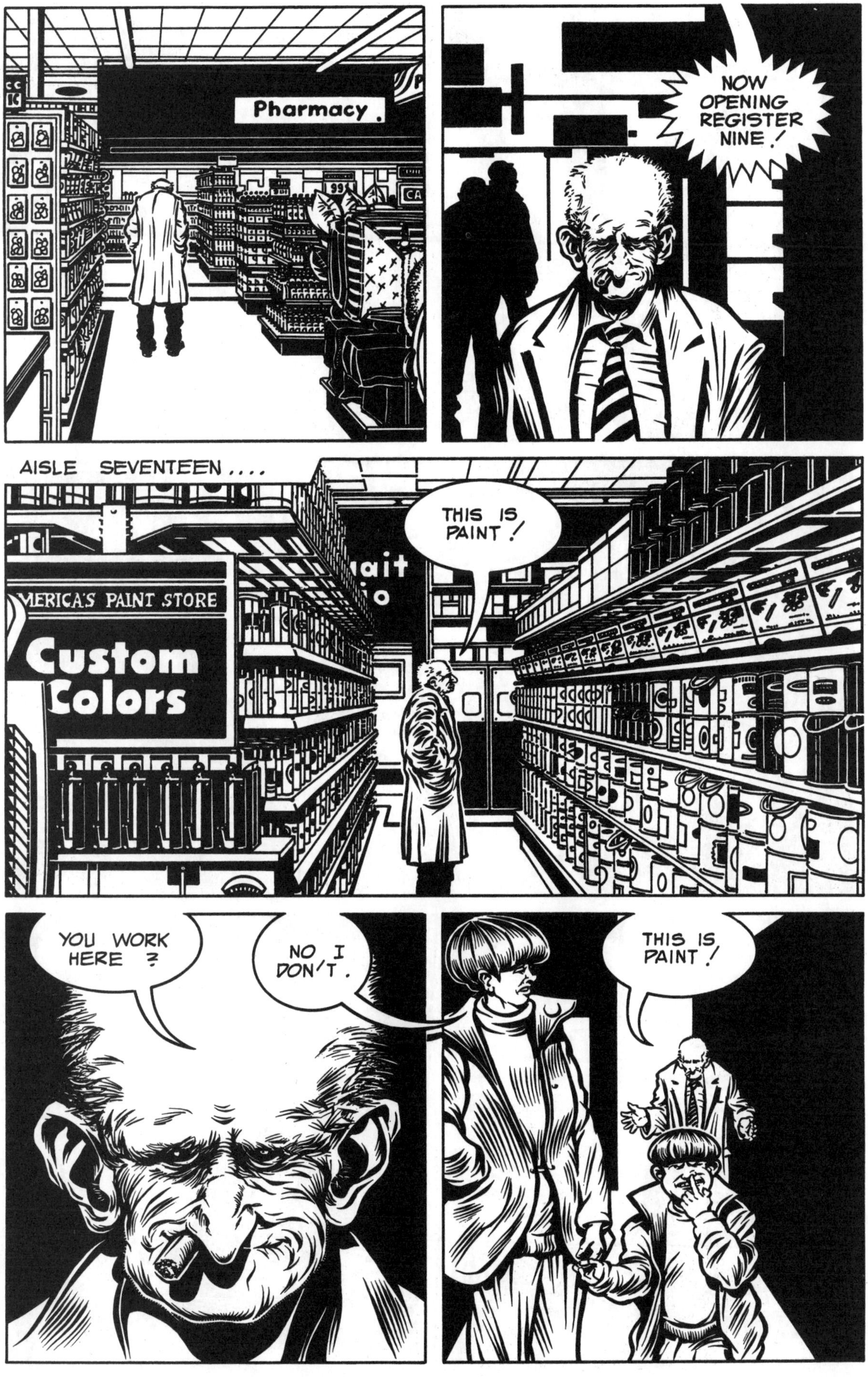
Pharmacy
NOW OPENING REGISTER NINE!
AISLE SEVENTEEN....
AMERICA'S PAINT STORE
Custom Colors
THIS IS PAINT!
YOU WORK HERE?
NO I DON'T.
THIS IS PAINT!

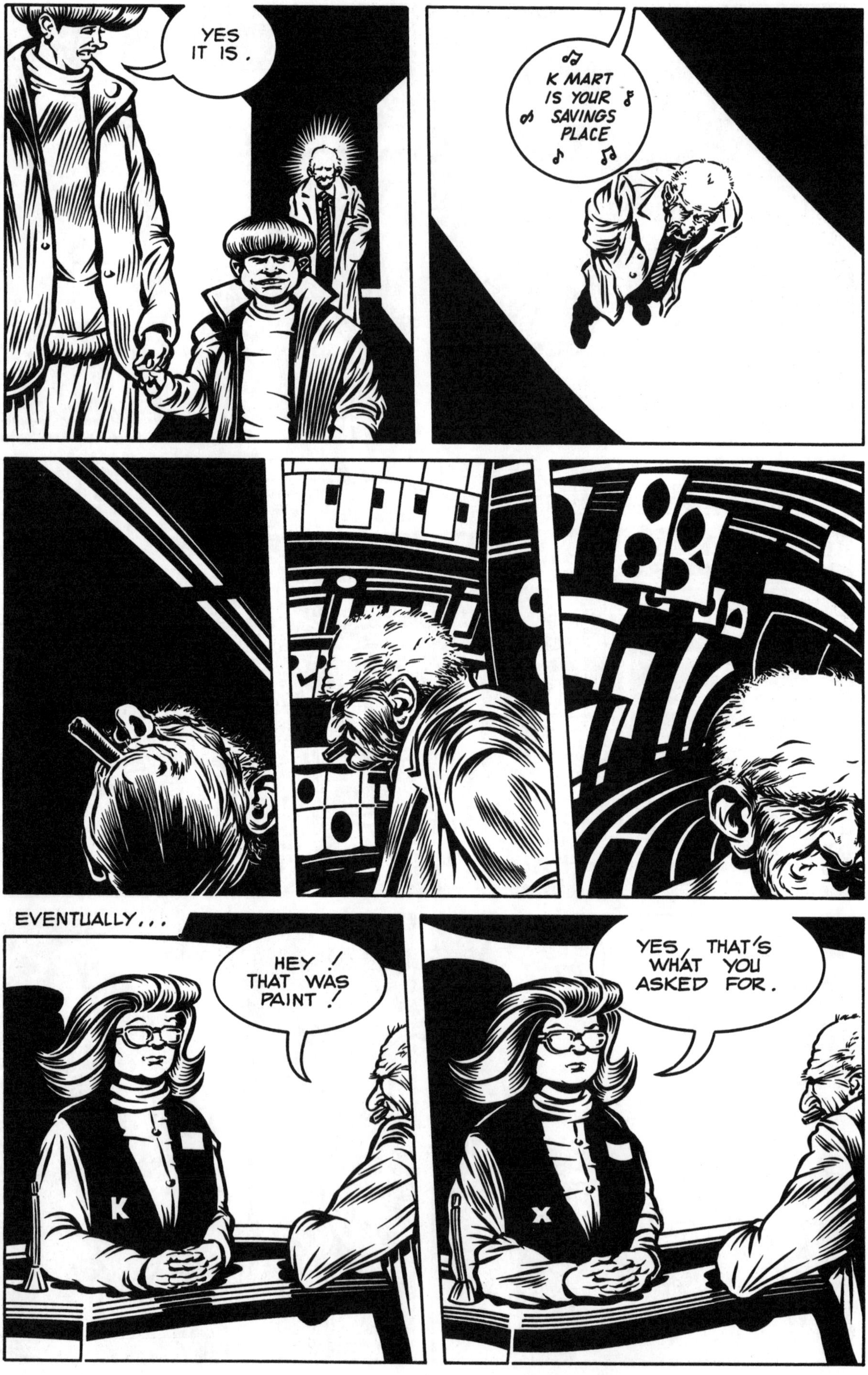
YES IT IS.
K MART IS YOUR SAVINGS PLACE
EVENTUALLY...
HEY! THAT WAS PAINT!
YES, THAT'S WHAT YOU ASKED FOR.

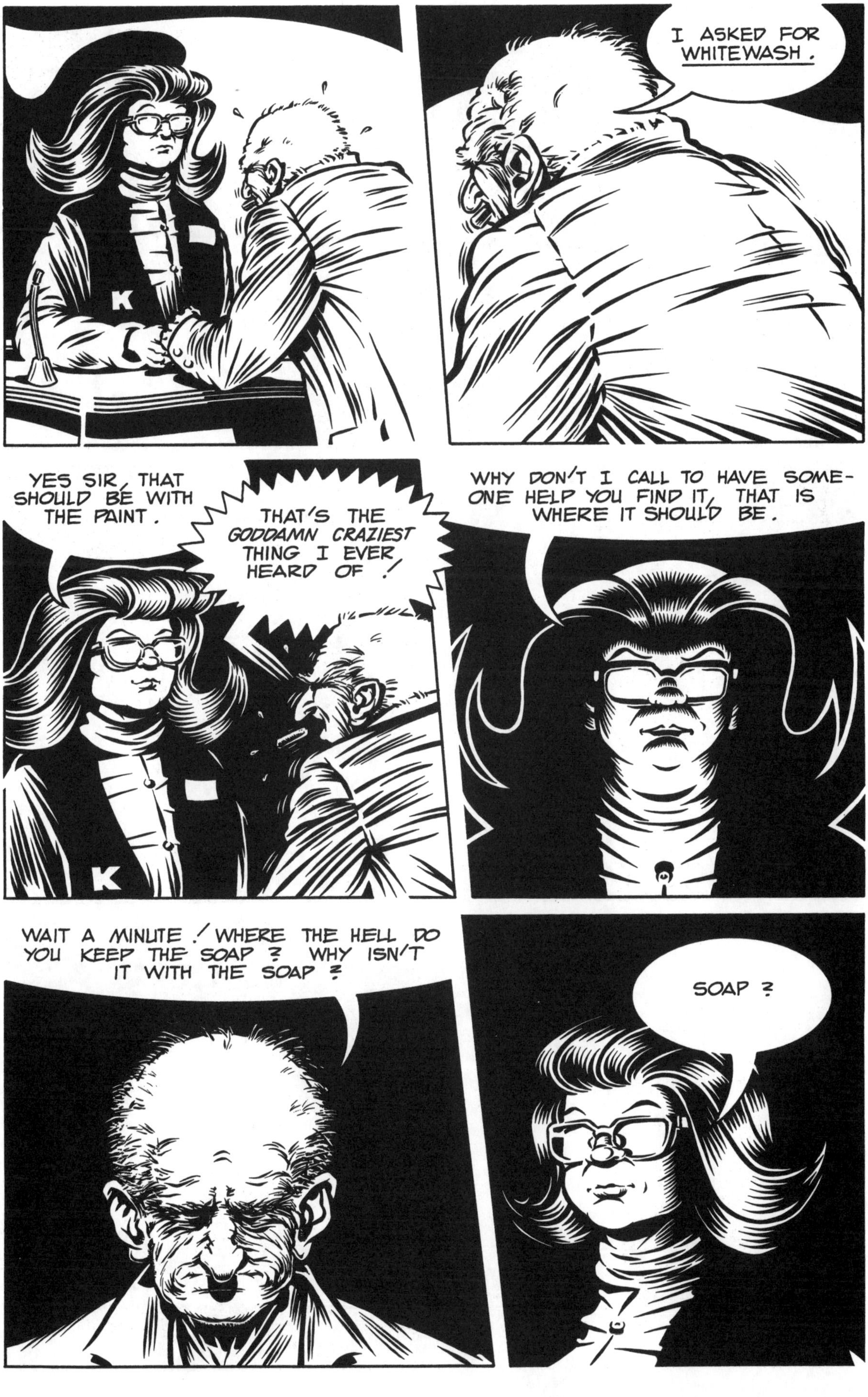
I ASKED FOR WHITEWASH.
YES SIR, THAT SHOULD BE WITH THE PAINT.
THAT'S THE GODDAMN CRAZIEST THING I EVER HEARD OF!
WHY DON'T I CALL TO HAVE SOME-ONE HELP YOU FIND IT, THAT IS WHERE IT SHOULD BE.
WAIT A MINUTE! WHERE THE HELL DO YOU KEEP THE SOAP? WHY ISN'T IT WITH THE SOAP?
SOAP?

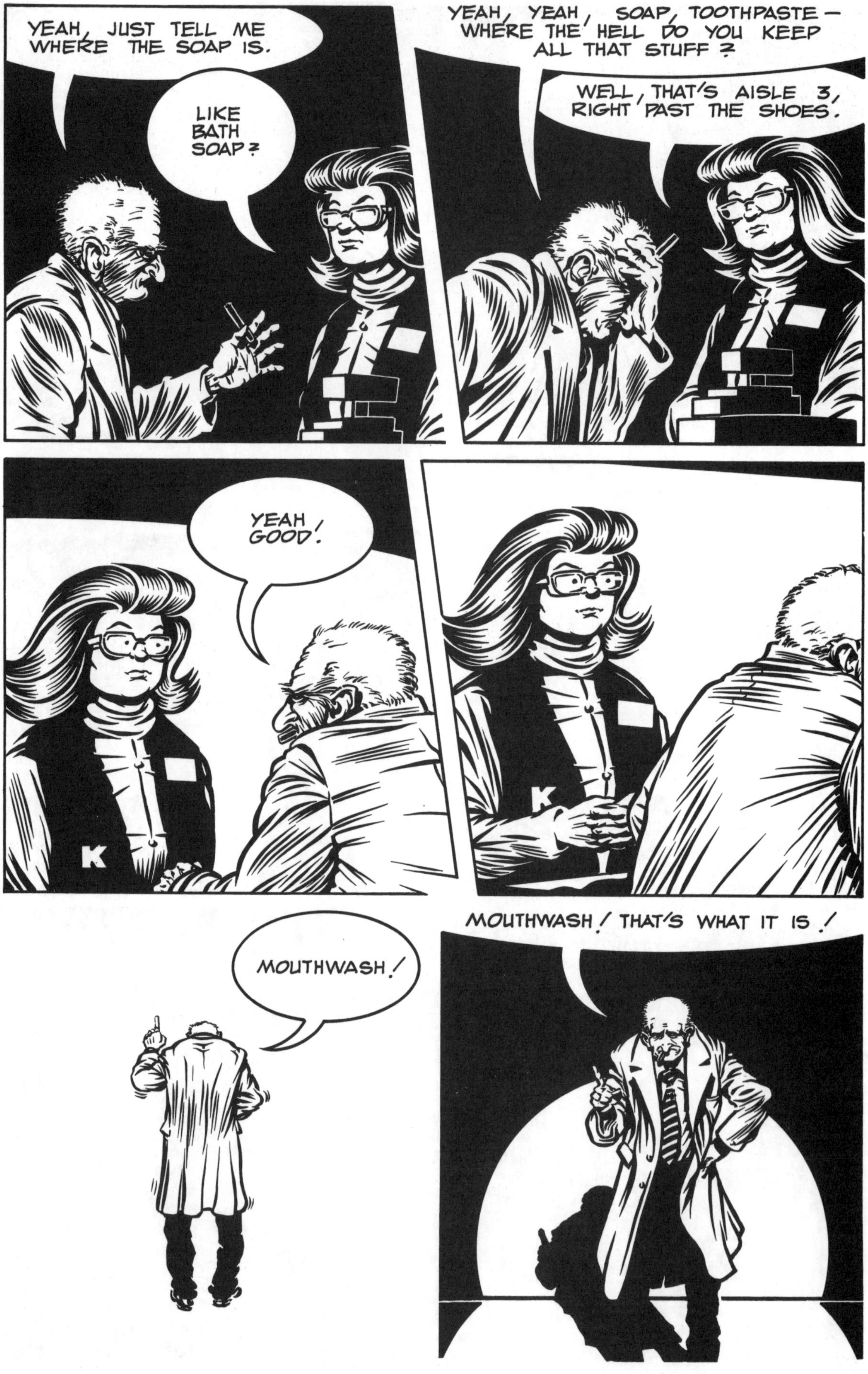
YEAH, JUST TELL ME WHERE THE SOAP IS.
LIKE BATH SOAP?
YEAH, YEAH, SOAP, TOOTHPASTE— WHERE THE HELL DO YOU KEEP ALL THAT STUFF?
WELL, THAT'S AISLE 3, RIGHT PAST THE SHOES.
YEAH! GOOD!
MOUTHWASH!
MOUTHWASH! THAT'S WHAT IT IS!

MY FIRST FUNERAL

BY DAVID GREENBERGER   ART BY DEAN ROHRER

THE FIRST FUNERAL I EVER WENT TO WAS IN 1979. ARTHUR BROWN, WHO LIVED AT THE DUPLEX NURSING HOME AND WAS 96, DIED.

I ASKED AROUND AT THE HOME TO SEE IF ANYONE WANTED TO GO TO THE FUNERAL.

ONLY ONE DID, ARTHUR WALLACE.

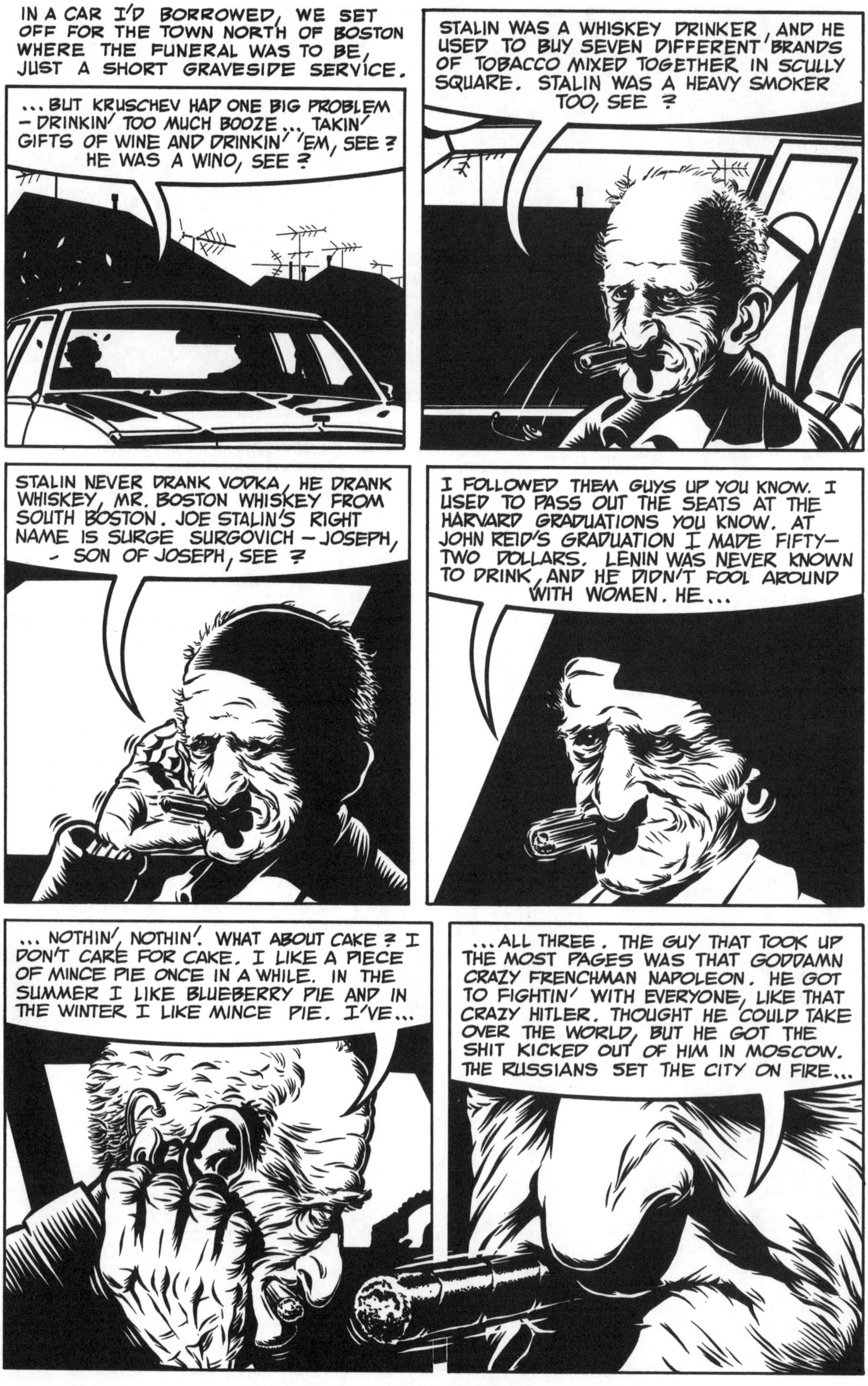
IN A CAR I'D BORROWED, WE SET OFF FOR THE TOWN NORTH OF BOSTON WHERE THE FUNERAL WAS TO BE, JUST A SHORT GRAVESIDE SERVICE.
... BUT KRUSCHEV HAD ONE BIG PROBLEM – DRINKIN' TOO MUCH BOOZE ... TAKIN' GIFTS OF WINE AND DRINKIN' 'EM, SEE? HE WAS A WINO, SEE?
STALIN WAS A WHISKEY DRINKER, AND HE USED TO BUY SEVEN DIFFERENT BRANDS OF TOBACCO MIXED TOGETHER IN SCULLY SQUARE. STALIN WAS A HEAVY SMOKER TOO, SEE?
STALIN NEVER DRANK VODKA, HE DRANK WHISKEY, MR. BOSTON WHISKEY FROM SOUTH BOSTON. JOE STALIN'S RIGHT NAME IS SURGE SURGOVICH – JOSEPH, - SON OF JOSEPH, SEE?
I FOLLOWED THEM GUYS UP YOU KNOW. I USED TO PASS OUT THE SEATS AT THE HARVARD GRADUATIONS YOU KNOW. AT JOHN REID'S GRADUATION I MADE FIFTY-TWO DOLLARS. LENIN WAS NEVER KNOWN TO DRINK, AND HE DIDN'T FOOL AROUND WITH WOMEN. HE...
... NOTHIN', NOTHIN'. WHAT ABOUT CAKE? I DON'T CARE FOR CAKE. I LIKE A PIECE OF MINCE PIE ONCE IN A WHILE. IN THE SUMMER I LIKE BLUEBERRY PIE AND IN THE WINTER I LIKE MINCE PIE. I'VE...
... ALL THREE. THE GUY THAT TOOK UP THE MOST PAGES WAS THAT GODDAMN CRAZY FRENCHMAN NAPOLEON. HE GOT TO FIGHTIN' WITH EVERYONE, LIKE THAT CRAZY HITLER. THOUGHT HE COULD TAKE OVER THE WORLD, BUT HE GOT THE SHIT KICKED OUT OF HIM IN MOSCOW. THE RUSSIANS SET THE CITY ON FIRE...

AFTER GETTING MILDLY LOST — TO ARTHUR'S DISGRUNTLEMENT — AND GETTING DIRECTIONS FROM A SERVICE STATION,

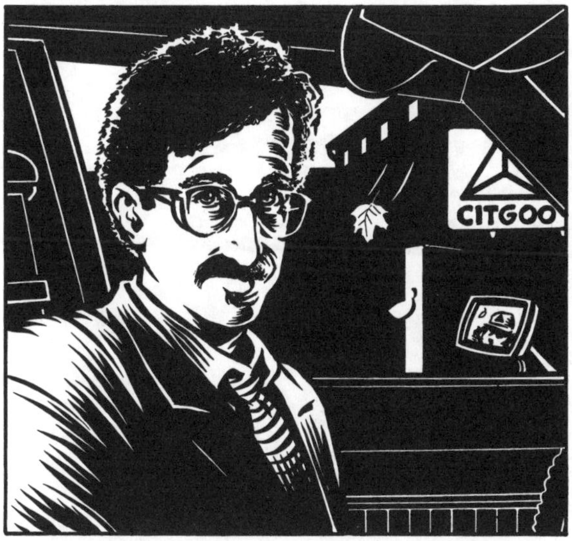
CITGOO

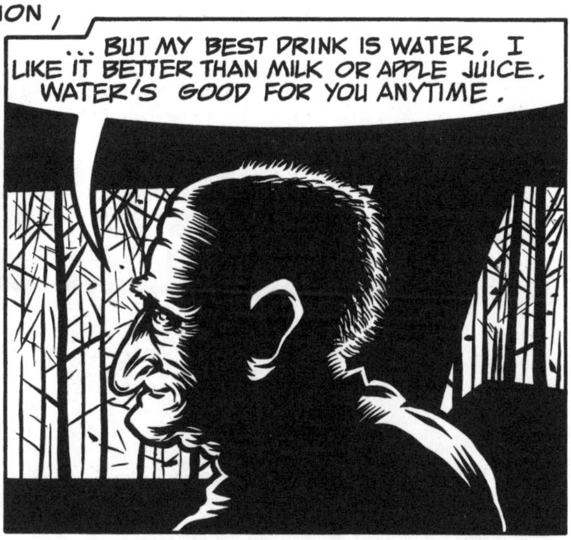
... BUT MY BEST DRINK IS WATER. I LIKE IT BETTER THAN MILK OR APPLE JUICE. WATER'S GOOD FOR YOU ANYTIME.

I FINALLY FOUND THE CEMETARY.

IT WAS MID-NOVEMBER : THE TREES WERE BARE, LEAVES THAT WERE STILL ON THE GROUND WERE COVERED WITH A LIGHT SNOW.

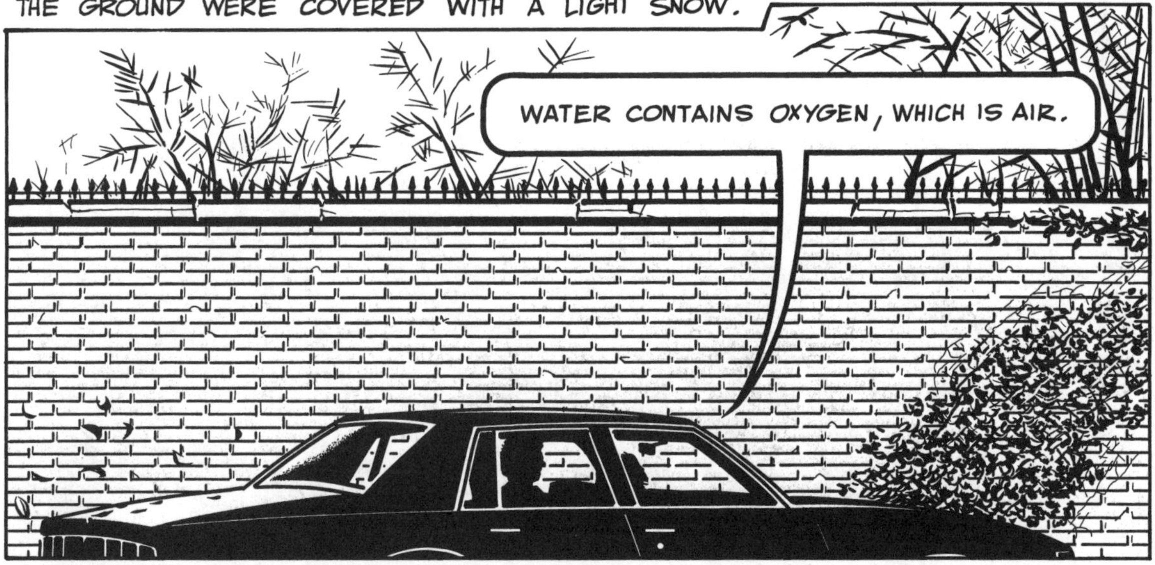
WATER CONTAINS OXYGEN, WHICH IS AIR.

I PARKED THE CAR, HELPED ARTHUR OUT AND WALKED WITH HIM ACROSS THE FROZEN GROUND.

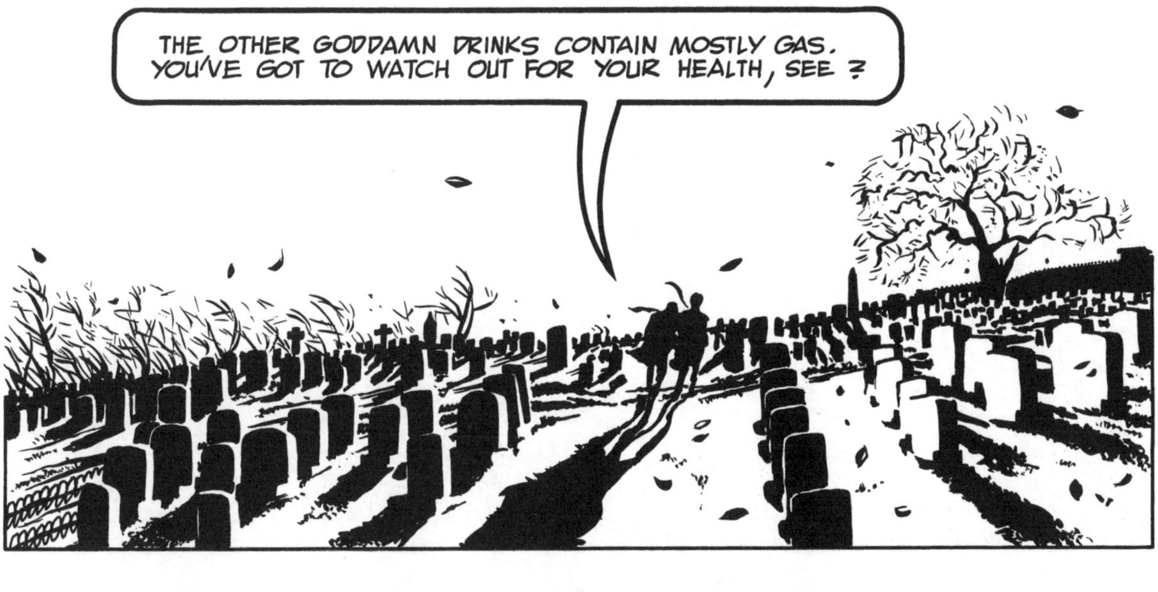
THE OTHER GODDAMN DRINKS CONTAIN MOSTLY GAS. YOU'VE GOT TO WATCH OUT FOR YOUR HEALTH, SEE ?

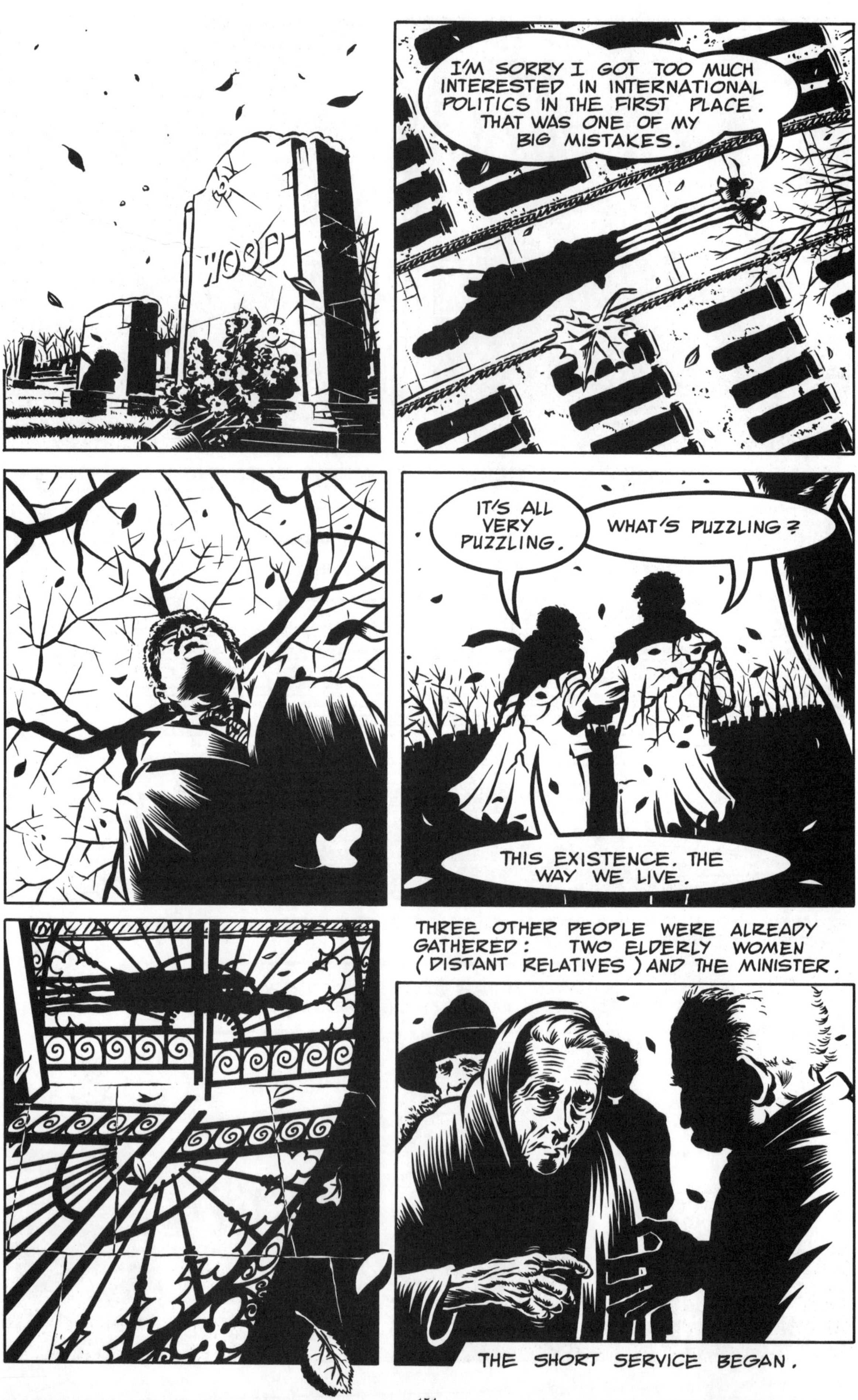
I'M SORRY I GOT TOO MUCH INTERESTED IN INTERNATIONAL POLITICS IN THE FIRST PLACE. THAT WAS ONE OF MY BIG MISTAKES.
IT'S ALL VERY PUZZLING.
WHAT'S PUZZLING?
THIS EXISTENCE. THE WAY WE LIVE.
THREE OTHER PEOPLE WERE ALREADY GATHERED: TWO ELDERLY WOMEN (DISTANT RELATIVES) AND THE MINISTER.
THE SHORT SERVICE BEGAN.

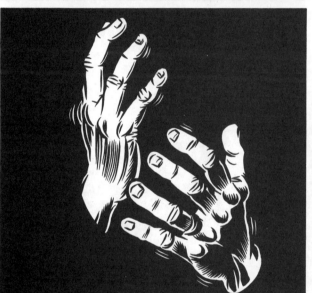

WHEN THE MINISTER WAS THROUGH HE ASKED IF ANYONE ELSE WANTED TO SAY ANYTHING.

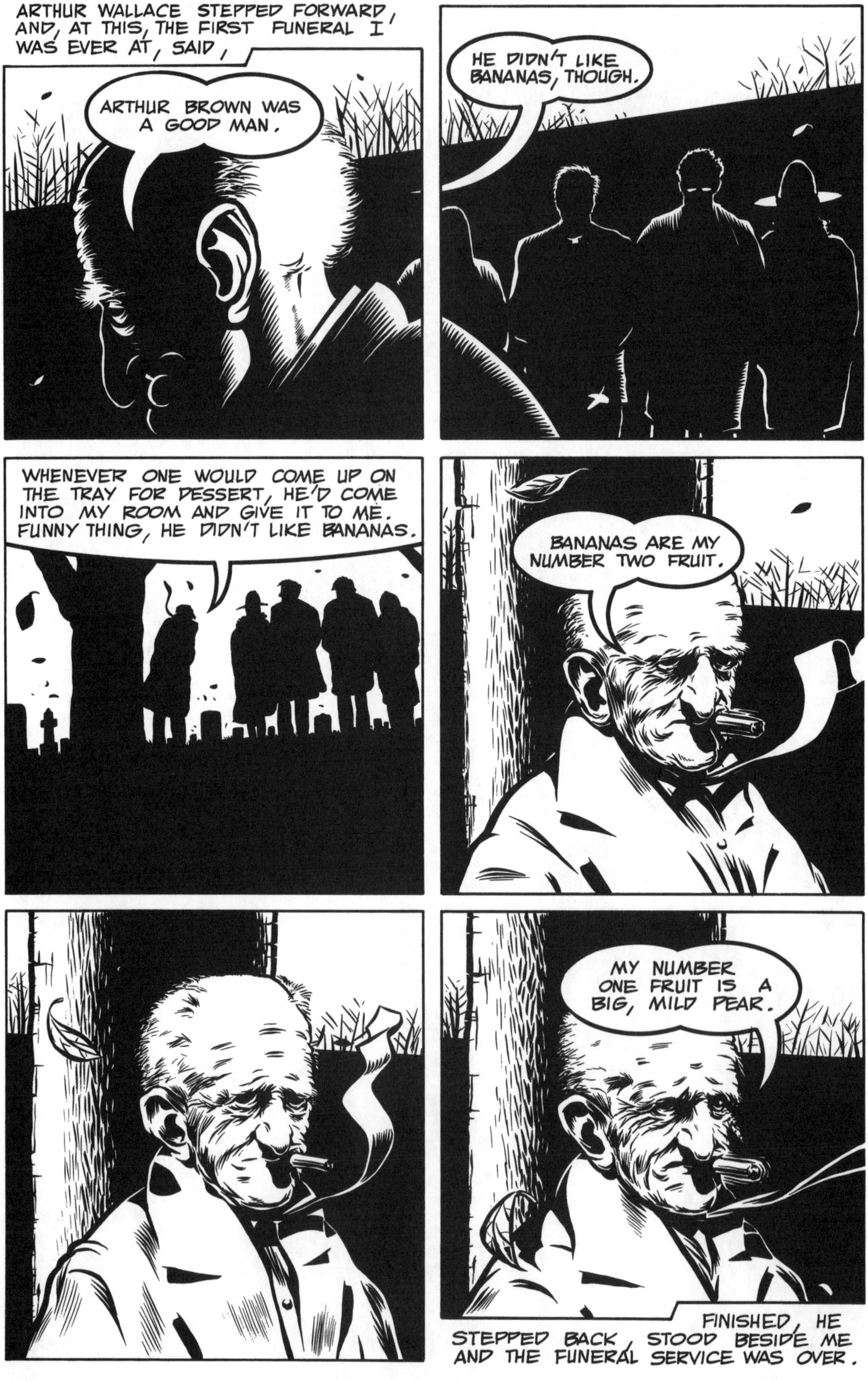
ARTHUR WALLACE STEPPED FORWARD, AND, AT THIS, THE FIRST FUNERAL I WAS EVER AT, SAID,
ARTHUR BROWN WAS A GOOD MAN.
HE DIDN'T LIKE BANANAS, THOUGH.
WHENEVER ONE WOULD COME UP ON THE TRAY FOR DESSERT, HE'D COME INTO MY ROOM AND GIVE IT TO ME. FUNNY THING, HE DIDN'T LIKE BANANAS.
BANANAS ARE MY NUMBER TWO FRUIT.
MY NUMBER ONE FRUIT IS A BIG, MILD PEAR.
FINISHED, HE STEPPED BACK, STOOD BESIDE ME AND THE FUNERAL SERVICE WAS OVER.

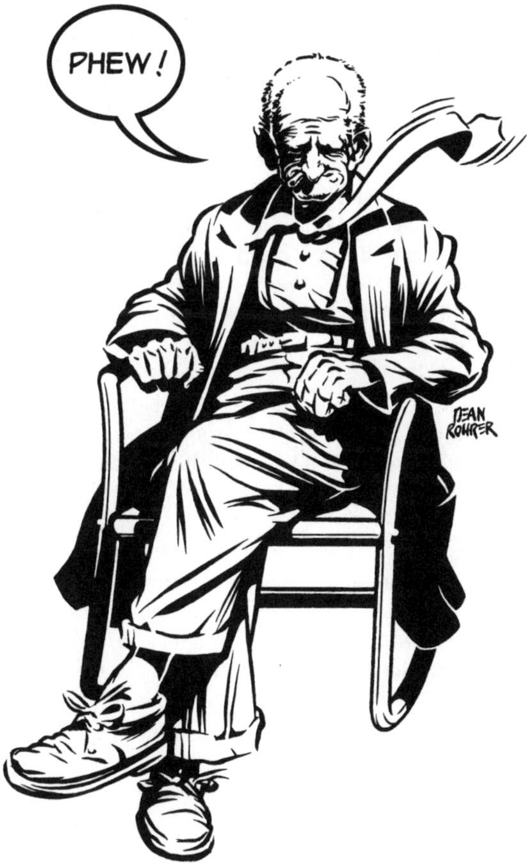
PHEW!
DEAN ROHRER

David Greenberger has been exploring issues of aging and decline (as well as our culture's avoidance of the subject) since he started publishing *The Duplex Planet* in 1979. Since then, the ruminations, conversations and interviews which fill its pages have been collected into books (*Tell Me If I've Stopped, Duplex Planet: Everybody's Asking Who I Was, Trees Breathe Out People Breathe In*) and CDs (his most recent CD is *The Duplex Planet Radio Hour* with music by Terry Adams of NRBQ), performed in monologues, been the source of two documentary films and adapted into comic books and a play. David lives in New York state with his wife Barbara, and daughter, Norabelle. More information about the Duplex Planet is available at the website: duplexplanet.com.

Doug Allen is the creator of *Steven*, America's favorite alcoholic child. His work appears regularly in the *NY Press* and he is an ongoing contributor to *Blab!*. He is also half of the creative braintrust behind the nonsensical *Idiotland*. Check out www.dougallencomics.com for further grisly details.

Rick Altergott is the creator of *Doofus*, which has earned tremendous accolades. ("The unsung genius of American comedy," says Dan Clowes. "I want to direct the film version," comments Terry Zwigoff, director of Crumb.) 2002 saw the release of the *Doofus Omnibus*, a dense and crazed collection of almost all of Rick's work, and the first issue of *Raisin Pie*, a collaboration with his wife Ariel Bordeaux that features new adventures of Doofus (both from Fantagraphics). He has also contributed to *Dirty Stories*, from Fantagraphics/Eros. Rick and Ariel live in Providence, RI, and you can check out his website: www.rickaltergott.com.

Dan Clowes is the creator of the award-winning comic book, *Eightball*. His graphic novel collections include *Like a Velvet Glove Cast in Iron, #$@&!: The Official Lloyd Llewellyn Collection, Pussey!, David Boring,* and *Ghost World*, which was turned into an Oscar- and Golden Globe-nominated film by Terry Zwigoff in 2001; his most recent release was the collection *20th Century Eightball*. Dan's comics have appeared in *Details, The New Yorker, Blab!, Cracked, World Art, Village Voice, Esquire*, and elsewhere. Dan lives in Berkeley, California with his wife, Erika, where he is working in the next issue of *Eightball* and his second screenplay, *Art School Confidential*.

Dave Cooper exploded into the first rank of contemporary cartoonists with his series *Weasel*. Cooper's work has also appeared in *Bizarro, Dark Horse Presents* and *Dirty Stories,* and his other graphic novels include *Suckle: The Status of Basil, Crumple, Dan and Larry,* and *Completely Pip and Norton*. 2003 will see the release of *Weasel #6* (a full-color edition devoted to his paintings, tied in with a gallery show) and *Ripple*, from the pages of *Weasel*, both from Fantagraphics. Visit his website: www.davegraphics.com!

Dame Darcy has drawn and written *Meat Cake* comics for a dozen years now. She's collaborated with Alan Moore on "The Cobweb" for ABC Comics, as well as working as a freelance illustrator and cartoonist for several international publications. Her current books include a graphic novel entitled *Frightful Fairytales* (Ten Speed Press), the upcoming *Meatcake Compilation* (Fantagraphics), and a French collection of her work. She is also a musician, actress, animator, doll crafter, and fine artist. She currently resides in Los Angeles where she performs cabaret on a regular basis with her current band Aye Aye Captain. Her website is www.damedarcy.com.

Andy Hartzell won a Xeric grant for his comic book *Bread & Circuses*. He draws a weekly comic strip called *Fool's Paradise*.

Tim Hensley, besides being a great cartoonist, is also a very talented musician. He is perhaps best known amongst comic fans for his band Victor Banana, which created the soundtrack to Dan Clowes' *Like A Velvet Glove Cast In Iron*. He currently makes music under the name Neil Smythe, and contributes sporadically to comics anthologies such as *Dirty Stories* and *The Comics Journal Special Edition*.

Jeff Johnson is now living as Jessica Johnson in Atlanta, GA, where she works as IT Director for an advertising agency. She is also the art director of a quarterly magazine serving the transgender community. In her larval incarnation as a depressive cartoonist, she concocted the poisonous *Nurture the Devil* (Fantagraphics) and a supplementary host of noxious substances; a contaminating mess of dark mixtures, all distilled from the inky outpourings of an overactive guilt gland. She's all better now. Visitors welcome at www.solipstick.com.

Gary Leib, along with Doug Allen, created *Idiotland*. His work has regularly appeared in *Blab!*, and his animation has been seen in films, on MTV and elsewhere.

Jason Lutes stormed the comics world with his Xeric Grant-funded *Jar of Fools* graphic novel, and is now in the midst of the epic comic book series *Berlin*, both published by Drawn and Quarterly. He is a former art director who has worked for Fantagraphics and Seattle's weekly paper, *The Stranger* (where *Jar of Fools* was initially serialized). He currently resides in Asheville, NC.

Pat Moriarity's crazy illustrations and cartoons have appeared in such publications as *Experience Hendrix magazine*, *ACHE*, *Nickelodeon*, *National Geographic World*, *Zero Zero*, *Seattle Weekly* and *Washington Law & Politics*. He also has done numerous CD covers, reigned as art director of *The Comics Journal* for several years, and created Fantagraphics' *Big Mouth* series. If you enjoyed *No More Shaves* be sure and get Top Shelf's collection, *Bern & Edwina* (featuring the only fictional characters in the *Duplex Planet Illustrated* series), created by Greenberger and Moriarity. Pat, who works from Port Orchard, Washington, teaches cartooning every summer with Shary Flenniken at the Seattle City Center Academy and is a recent Artist Trust grant winner. Moriarity's website is www.cartoondepot.net by Pat.

Paul Nitsche came to Chicago to receive his BFA at the School of the Art Institute of Chicago. His comic work has been published by Fantagraphics, Caliber and Dark Horse. His work has also appeared on many CDs and records, as well as a theatrical set and program. Continuing to live in Chicago, he has been focusing on his constructions of wood, stained glass, lithography and porcelain dolls.

George Parsons was born in Nevada City, California in 1953. His favorite planet is Saturn. His artwork and/or writing has appeared in *Pictopia*, *Real Stuff*, *Pulse*, *Op*, *Goldmine*, *Creem*, *The Stranger*, *Rip-Off*, *Monkeywrench*, *Option*, *Seattle Laughs*, and other publications. He's been active as a D.J. for the last 21 years.

Ron Regé Jr., a small press staple for years, is the creator of the great graphic novel *Skibber Bee-Bye* (Highwater Books). His work has also appeared recently in *Drawn & Quarterly*, *Rosetta*, *Legal Action Comics*, *The Ganzfeld*, *Non*, Chicago's *New City*, Canada's *National Post*, and *The New York Times magazine*. He is currently artist in residence at Naragansett Grange Hall #1, in South County Rhode Island.

Dean Rohrer is a nationally syndicated newspaper op-ed artist. His illustrations have also appeared in *The New Yorker*, *Harper's*, *Men's Health*, *Details*, *Spin*, Simon & Schuster Books, Oxford U Press, etc. His work in the field of comics has been published by Dark Horse, Mirage, Kitchen Sink, Cosmic Comics and Fantagraphics.

Greg Ruth recently wrote and drew *Suddenly Gravity*, the first installment of his ongoing obsession with the rather large and spooky Bentham Hospital. He is currently working on two books, M.A.R.S. and *Failure*, and living in Brooklyn, New York.

Oscar Stern publishes *Wu Wei* and considers New York to be the "greatest city in the world." Stern's comic work has appeared in *Duplex Planet Illustrated*, *Buzzard*, *Porn Free* and *POPsmear*. As a fine artist, Oscar has had his work shown in galleries in NYC as well as other parts in the US and Europe. He also works as a graphic designer in NYC, with work appearing in magazines, newspapers, and on TV and the worldwideweb.

Eric Theriault is the creator of the self-published comic book *Veena*, stories about the adventuress of kitsch, with some nostalgia and time-travel added to the mix. In addition to appearing in many comics in Quebec (Canada) since the early '80s, he has been published in the American releases *Real Stuff*, *Melody*, *The Jam*, *Flock of Dreamers* and *9-11: Emergency Relief*. He also worked ion the award-winning animated show *Arthur*. His latest project is an adaptation of the classic radio detective show *Yours Truly, Johnny Dollar* from Moonstone comics. Discover more on his web site at: http://www.cam.org/~veena

Sam Torode is a freelance writer and artist living in rural Wisconsin with his wife, Bethany, and son, Gideon. He is the author of a collection of comics, *The School of the Pathetic*. His website is www.torodedesign.com.

Wayno created *Beer Nutz* for the ill-fated Tundra Publishing Company in the early 1990s. Today, he works primarily as an illustrator for such diverse clients as *Nickelodeon Magazine*, *Entertainment Weekly*, *The London Guardian*, *Bizarre*, *National Geographic World*, *Cool & Strange Music Magazine*, and American Greetings Company. For an ongoing project with Rhino records, Wayno produced black and white portraits of over 125 recording artists. He lives in Pittsburgh PA, and on the web at www.wayno.com.

J.R. Williams now works primarily in the animation field. In the world of comics, he is the creator of *The Completely Bad Boys*, *Crap*, *Damnation*, *Bummer* (all published by Fantagraphics), and dozens of other strips, and has contributed to *Weirdo*, *Heavy Metal*, *Snake Eyes*, *Zero Zero*, *Real Stuff*, and *Dark Horse Maverick*.

Holly Jane Zachary studied at the School of the Art Institute of Chicago and graduated from the Savannah College of Art and Design, where she focused on illustration. She also makes hand-sewn dolls and painted furniture and is currently teaching art in grades one through eight.

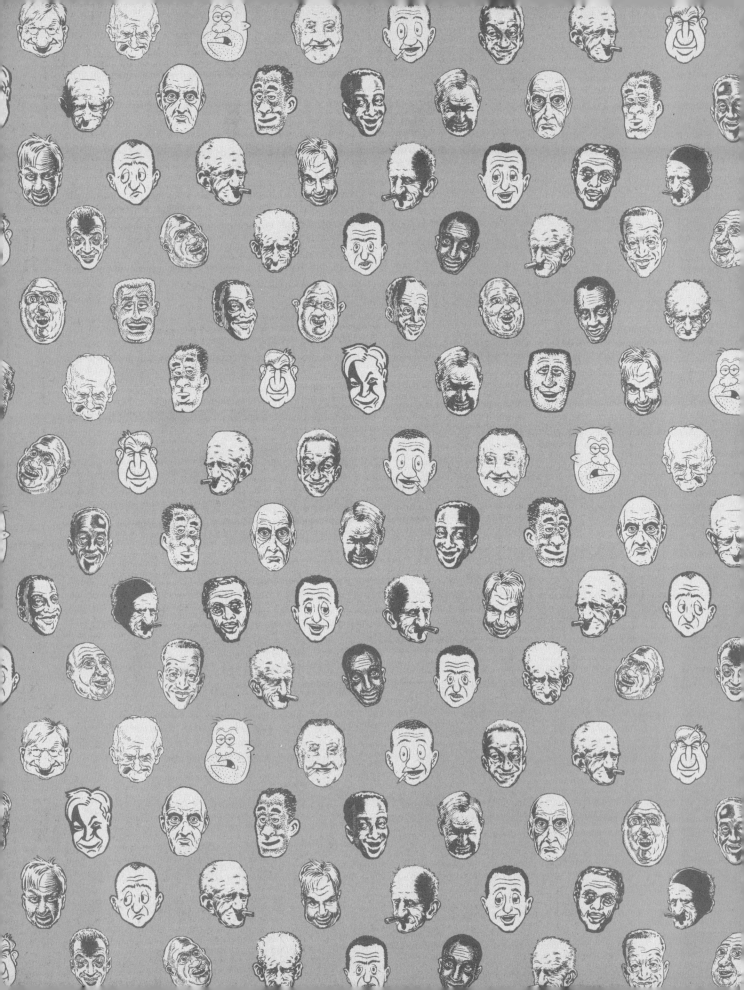